**HIRSCHBERGER, Johannes. A short history of Western philosophy, tr.
from the German by Jeremy Moiser. Westview, 1977 (c1976). 218p
index 76-25125. 12.75 ISBN 0-89158-642-3. C.I.P.**

CHOICE   *JAN. '78*
Philosophy

Hirschberger is a longtime professor at the University of Frankfurt and
the author of a two-volume *History of philosophy* (1958–59). This brief
work is a narrative history of Western philosophy that places an emphasis on the genesis of its various stages. Summaries of the teachings
of major figures are given. Considerable space is devoted to German
philosophers from Meister Eckhart and Nicholas of Cusa through Kant
to the many post-Kantian German writers. Kant receives the longest
and most sympathetic treatment, and Hirschberger has a tendency to
criticize earlier philosophers from a post-Kantian viewpoint. Some of
the interpretations of ancient and medieval thinkers are open to question. The translation flows well. Indexes of names and subjects. No
bibliography. S. E. Stumpf's *Socrates to Sartre* (2d ed., 1975; 1st ed.,
CHOICE, Jul.-Aug. 1966) is twice as long and puts more emphasis on
British and American philosophers. N. P. Stallknecht and R. S.
Brumbaugh's *The spirit of Western philosophy* (1950) is more of a textbook introduction to philosophy problems. The nearest equivalent to

HIRSCHBERGER

CHOICE   *JAN. '78*
Philosophy

Hirschberger seems to be Francis H. Parker's *The story of Western
philosophy* (1967), which goes only through Hegel but is a more intellectually perceptive and stimulating work.

a
short history of
WESTERN PHILOSOPHY

Johannes Hirschberger, one of
Germany's most eminent teachers
and writers on the history of
philosophy, was educated at the
Catholic Seminary and Teachers'
College of Eichstätt and received his
Ph.D. from the University of
Munich in 1930. In 1939 he returned
to Eichstätt to teach, and since 1953
he has been a professor at the University of Frankfurt.

A
Short History of
WESTERN PHILOSOPHY

by

JOHANNES HIRSCHBERGER

Translated from the German by Jeremy Moiser

WESTVIEW PRESS : BOULDER, COLORADO

9TH EDITION © 1971 HERDER VERLAG, FREIBURG IM B.

ENGLISH TRANSLATION © 1976 LUTTERWORTH PRESS

First published in Great Britain 1976

Published in 1977 in the United States of America by
Westview Press, Inc.
1898 Flatiron Court
Boulder, Colorado 80301
Frederick A. Praeger, Publisher and Editorial Director

Library of Congress Cataloging in Publication Data
Hirschberger, Johannes.
A short history of Western philosophy.
Translation of Kleine Philosophiegeschichte.
Includes index.
1. Philosophy-History. I. Title.
B82.H5613   1976b   190   76-25125
ISBN 0-89158-642-3

Text set in 11/13 pt Monotype Baskerville, printed by
letterpress, and bound in Great Britain at
The Pitman Press, Bath

CONTENTS

PART FOUR – THE PHILOSOPHY OF THE NINETEENTH AND TWENTIETH CENTURIES

CHAPTER ONE: FROM THE NINETEENTH TO THE TWENTIETH CENTURY

CHAPTER TWO: TWENTIETH CENTURY PHILOSOPHY

Index of Names
Index of Subjects

FOREWORD

It is a bold man who sets out to fit into one small volume the entire history of philosophy. I feel, however, that despite inevitable shortcomings, the attempt is worthwhile in that it helps to give us a bird's-eye view. Having grasped the outline of the whole, we are in a better position to understand the parts that make it up. To put this another way, essential features and the significance of philosophy as a whole emerge much more clearly in a condensed treatment than in a detailed one. May I therefore warn the reader beforehand: if he is looking for a reference-book of individual philosophers and details of philosophical themes, this work is not for him. It offers no more than an introduction to the spirit of philosophy. The reader of German who wishes to have a more detailed account is referred to my two-volume *History of Philosophy* (8th German edition, Herder 1965).

JOHANNES HIRSCHBERGER

INTRODUCTION

A study of the historical development of philosophy both requires and stimulates intellectual detachment. The person who limits himself to the present can easily fall a prey to passing fashions; he becomes a slave of the latest -ism. Intellectually rootless and inexperienced, he succombs to something that may exercise considerable attraction at this particular moment, but that soon withers and passes. For example, Ernst Haeckel's theories once exercised an enormous fascination on all sorts of people; they were even hailed as the definitive word in philosophy. Nowadays they are more likely to cause amusement than anything else. The same may be said of Nietzsche's philosophy, or materialism, or vitalism, or idealism.

Before we can come to a balanced judgement in our search for truth, we have to take a broad view. We need opportunities for comparison; we need to see things not just from one angle but from many; in short, we need to see the wood, not just the trees. And above all we need a deeper understanding of our own ideas, which means tracing them back to their roots. All intellectual life is the result of a growth reaching back into the distant past and there adopting the lines of development which fix our thoughts in set patterns. This is not, of course, to advocate a return to the past for the sake of it. We want to free ourselves from the past. But we also want to free ourselves from slavery to the present, and the only way we can do that is to give ourselves an idea of the relativity of much that passes for novelty. Only a thorough study of history can reveal the present as it really is.

We may usefully divide the history of philosophy into four periods: Antiquity, the Fathers and the Middle Ages, Modern Times, and the Present.

PART ONE

THE PHILOSOPHY OF ANTIQUITY

Ancient philosophy is the spiritual heritage of the west. Ultimately it explains how modern philosophy came to be what it is. It is not out of date, it is not a matter that requires no further study. One has only to look at the works of the great philosophers to appreciate how much ancient philosophy has occupied men's minds in every century since.

Its basic divisions are: the Pre-Socratics, the Attic philosophy of Socrates, Plato and Aristotle, and the great schools of the Hellenistic period, particularly Stoicism, Epicureanism and Neo-Platonism.

CHAPTER ONE: THE PRE-SOCRATICS

The cradle of Greek philosophy was Ionia, on the coast of Asia Minor. The philosophers of the Pre-Socratic period lived at Miletus, Ephesus, Klazomenai, Kolophon, Samos. Pre-Socratic philosophy is therefore sometimes called Ionian philosophy, although strictly speaking this is not correct inasmuch as there were famous names in southern Italy and Sicily. It is also strictly speaking incorrect to call the philosophy of the Pre-Socratics simply natural philosophy (or Ionian natural philosophy), as is sometimes done, because although their reflexion started from the nature around them, what really interested them was the essence and laws of *being*. It was therefore a metaphysics and even a theology, because it inquired into the ultimate reasons or causes of being and becoming. But as Aristotle said, their method differed from that of Homer and Hesiod, who had also, in their own way, 'theologized', because while Homer and Hesiod still resorted to mythical

I

images and ideas in their language and thinking, the Pre-Socratics adopted an 'inferential' or 'demonstrative' style of thought which was not content with stories but set out to understand and so prove something through its own critical observation and reflexion. This emergence of conceptual thought in the Pre-Socratics was at the same time, we may say without exaggeration, the emergence of western philosophy.

1. The problems of the Pre-Socratics

A whole series of concepts which we still use today, for example principle, element, atom, matter, spirit, substance, form, were forged by the Pre-Socratics. These thinkers created a mental currency the validity of which has lasted two thousand years. Their attempts at coining an effective philosophical language were admittedly defective and to our way of thinking somewhat rudimentary, but in my view they are not to be dismissed as cumbersome relics from the past distorting our thought and cramping our mental style. However that may be, the decisive feature of this period was not the words and ideas so much as the *method of questioning*. The problems the Pre-Socratics set out to answer and the approach they adopted are more important than their concepts and terminology.

The main problem which engaged their attention was the question of the *arche* or principle of things. *Arche* means origin or beginning, but for the Pre-Socratics this was taken less in a temporal than in an essential sense. The real question, in other words, was: what constitutes the inmost being of the things which look so varied and so different to our senses? Is what we see any more than an appearance, an outer skin, a surface? Is the inner core of things quite different? Does this inner core 'appear' to the senses, or is it accessible only to thought? Do the data of sense-experience yield the truth?

This distinction between externals and internals, between an appearance accessible to the senses and a proper being accessible only to thought, between the incidentals and the essentials of a thing, led to another distinction. Outwardly everything was particular and individual, but in essence things

2

were alike: being was universal. And this universal element now came to be thought more important (and therefore also more essential) than individual things.

And then a third distinction seemed to follow naturally from this: the inner essence, which is the same in everything, is the permanent, enduring, calculable, knowable factor in the universe as opposed to the transient, accidental, uncertain and shadowy factor, which cannot be the object of knowledge but at most the object of imagination and opinion. When *Thales of Miletus* (*c* 624–546 B.C.), the first of these thinkers, said that the principle of everything was water: water was the source, the element, from which everything arose and to which everything could be reduced, he was talking not about the individual entities which are the objects of sense-experience and the special sciences, but about being in general, which he made the object of knowledge. He created what Aristotle was later to call the science of being as being, 'first philosophy', wisdom or theology, and what later thinkers, following Aristotle's lead, were to call metaphysics. The answers of western philosophy to this question are innumerable. Reflexion on being, beings, essences, phenomena (appearances), universals, the basis of things, will never now come to an end.

The Pre-Socratics adopted a number of different directions in their search for answers. A first attempt to solve the question of the primary element in being was the dual concept of *matter and form*. According to the three Milesian philosophers, the primary element was matter: water for Thales, as we have mentioned, *apeiron* for Anaximander, and air for Anaximenes. That water and air are material is clear. *Apeiron* was equally material. Literally it meant the unlimited, the infinite, but it was pictured as a sort of limitless store of substance from which everything that is ultimately draws whatever materiality it possesses (not directly, only after a great many transformations). We should not see in this prime element of the Milesians the merely material – they were no materialists; we have to notice equally importantly that their 'stuff' of the universe had something prepotent, basic, eternal, divine about it. This is particularly evident in *Anaximander* (*c* 610–545). Aristotle informs

3

us that his *apeiron* 'embraces everything, controls everything', is 'immortal, incorruptible and divine'. In the solemn hymnodic style in which Anaximander speaks of his *apeiron*, the reader glimpses something of his veneration for it and begins to understand the respect in which this theological inquirer among the early Greek thinkers has been held.

Despite the many advantages, however, in talking about infinite matter or living matter (hylozoism), the concept of a basic matter was not enough to explain the world's reality. It was to the merit of the *Pythagoreans* (after Pythagoras, who was born on Samos in 570 B.C.) to have seen this. They referred to the idea at the opposite pole to that of matter, namely form. They did not deny the validity of the idea of matter, but they understood its limitations better than the Milesians. Matter was always shaped or formed, it was water or air or fire or whatever, never just pure matter. The Pythagoreans set about reflecting on this phenomenon. Like Anaximander they called matter the unlimited element at the basis of the world's reality (*a-peiron*), and to their mind there immediately emerged 'determination' or 'limit' (*peras*) as a necessary complement. Determination set limits to what was in itself unlimited and turned it into this or that concrete thing. The difference between things therefore depended on their form or, as the Pythagoreans said, on their number. This is the significance of their famous dictum that 'everything is number'. It did not mean that everything was only number or form or limit without also being matter. As well as the numbering limiting factor, there was also what was numbered: matter, which was in itself without number. Even today modern natural science working with numbers has to accept something apart from mathematical means of thought which is grasped by numbers, remains outside them and continues to defy analysis.

As well as the idea of number, the Pythagoreans developed another important concept: harmony. The forms which give order to being do not emerge arbitrarily; they follow a system, they form a meaningful whole, a cosmic harmony. 'The whole heaven is harmony and number.' 'The sages teach that heaven and earth, gods and men foster community and friendship

4

and order and measure and justice, and they therefore call it all the cosmos.' It has rightly been said that the Pythagoreans' discovery has had the very greatest influence on science.

One thing had not yet been examined: the changes undergone by matter and form, the phenomenon of transition, or, in a word, *becoming*. According to *Heraclitus* (*c* 544–484), becoming was more of a principle than matter and form. Things are what they are only because there exists the eternal restlessness of becoming. He thought of fire as the symbol of this becoming: 'No god or man created this world, it always was and will ever be an eternally living fire measures of which light up and measures of which die down.' Becoming was therefore not without its rules. It was controlled by measure, by the logos (meaning, law). Even opposition and dialectic came under this law. Heraclitus did not, like modern vitalism which frequently appealed to him, relativize everything. He did not maintain that every age and every person, and so ultimately every situation and moment, was no more than itself, and that there was no overlapping truth or law since everything was subject to time. It was not until the Heraclitans that the phrase 'Everything is in motion', attributed by Aristotle to Heraclitus himself, took on this radical sense. Heraclitus rejected the relativizing tendencies of individual and collective subjectivity: 'All laws', he said, 'feed on the divine.' One may not act as if each of them had its own meaning: the universal logos with its truth and law is decisive. This is properly the origin of all reflexion on the natural law.

The opposite pole of Heraclitism was Eleatism. Its father, *Parmenides*, from Elea in southern Italy (*c* 540–470), denied becoming and placed being at the centre of his philosophy. Only being is. Becoming can be no more than a flux, and so cannot be, it does not remain, it is impermanent. It is only our senses that register the appearance of change and with it the Many. Only if there are the Many can there be transition, becoming, and vice versa. If, however, the philosopher rejects this illusory path of 'common sense', that is, of sense-experience, and treads the path of truth by relying on thought, he will

5

discover true and real being, which is one: Being, not beings. 'Thought and being are the same.' Did Parmenides anticipate the later idea that the people who submerge themselves in the Many, even the Many of the natural sciences, are in danger of losing the One: being, truth, the real world, because they allow what is not specifically human, namely material existence which animals share, to absorb their energies? *Thought* is peculiarly human, and only thought raises us above the world of experience and enables us to grasp the One, truth and being. As Bertrand Russell was to say two thousand years after Parmenides: 'Men fear thought as they fear nothing else on earth – more than ruin, more even than death. Thought is subversive and revolutionary, destructive and terrible; thought is merciless to privilege, established institutions and comfortable habits; thought is anarchic and lawless, indifferent to authority, careless of the well-tried wisdom of the ages. Thought looks into the pit of hell and is not afraid. It sees man, a feeble speck, surrounded by unfathomable depths of silence; yet it bears itself proudly, as unmoved as if it were lord of the universe. Thought is great and swift and free, the light of the world, and the chief glory of man' (*Principles of Social Reconstruction* 5). Parmenides must be numbered among the great metaphysicians who would like to offer more than mere erudition. His theme was wisdom, because he sought the Whole and the One. This programme has persisted in philosophy from his time.

What in Parmenides himself was still a sort of mystical gaze of higher reason bringing opposites together his direct disciples, the Eleatics (Zeno, Melissus and others), tried to support with verbal and conceptual gymnastics. It was because of this that Aristotle saw in Zeno the inventor of a dialectic confined to words, or eristic (the art of controversy) as the ancients used to call it.

A completely different direction was taken by another group of Pre-Socratics called *Mechanists*. They seized on the concept of matter which the Milesians had used as a principle of being and developed it.

One of them was *Empedocles* (c 492–432) from Akragas

(modern day Agrigento in Sicily), who, in the words of Matthew Arnold,

> ... could stay swift diseases in old days,
> Chain madmen by the music of his lyre,
> Cleanse to sweet airs the breath of poisonous streams,
> And in the mountain chinks inter the winds.

He worked out the notion of an element. He was, as we now know, wrong in positing only four elements (which he called 'roots'), fire, water, air and earth, but he had the inspired idea, quite acceptable still to modern ears, that there must be ultimate material particles which make up the corporeal world. These particles were the principles of all the variety we see in nature and enabled that variety to be reduced to a few basic elements. Until well into modern times the four elements were accepted. (The fifth one, or *quinta essentia*, quintessence, was the matter of the eternal stars.) The specifically mechanistic slant was furnished by Empedocles when he maintained that these four roots, which were to some extent daemonic-divine, functioned according to a higher mechanical law: that of the alternating play of Love and Hate in the rotation of the four cosmic periods.

Anthropomorphism, which was still accepted by Empedocles, was completely absent and replaced by a pure mechanism, which was also pure materialism, in *Democritus of Abdera* (*c* 460–370). There were no gods for Democritus and no ideas apart from man's. His *archai* were atoms: tiny indivisible (a-tomos) ultimate particles exactly alike in quality and differing only in shape and size. Subsidiary concepts invoked by Democritus were empty space (the Void) and eternal motion. The atoms had been falling in empty space from eternity, and everything which now existed was composed of them. As far as our senses were concerned, things varied in shape, form, colour etc., but in themselves (*physei* = according to their nature) they were all no more than agglomerations of atoms. Things contained nothing else. For Democritus, therefore, nature was nothing but 'atoms hurled about in empty space'. There was no god in charge, no providence, no meaning, no purpose, but no chance either: everything happened 'of itself' (automatically) according to laws built into the quantum of matter. The ability to foresee the workings of nature depended on a knowledge of these laws. This is also the ideal of modern natural science. Against Democritus Aristotle objected that his talk of the eternity of movement altogether evaded the question of movement's ultimate foundation; and that if similar shapes continue to appear in nature, it is because behind them lies a principle that cannot be explained on materialistic grounds: form.

Anaxagoras (*c* 500–420) referred to both matter and form, and introduced a new principle, mind (*nous*). It was mind, an external power, which caused movement and guided everything on a meaningful pattern. Aristotle was lavish in his praise of Anaxagoras: 'When he maintained that there was Reason in nature as in rational beings like ourselves, and that it was the origin of the cosmos and of all order, he distinguished himself from his predecessors like a wise man among fools.' Anaxagoras regarded *nous* as something divine. It was infinite and autonomous, existed for itself, was omniscient and omnipotent. Anaxagoras also considered the ultimate components of nature. They were not, as for Democritus, only quantitatively different from each other, they differed qualitatively, so that what a thing was as a whole it already was in each one of its parts (*homoiomerien*). Among Anaxagoras' followers, the idea of order and direction (teleology) became a philosophy with an enormous influence, especially in so-called natural theology, which concluded from the meaningfulness and purposefulness of the cosmos to an all-wise and divine Mind who created it all, and in the qualitative-eidetic rather than quantitative consideration of Nature, which as late as Leibniz was considered quasi-infinite.

2. The Pre-Socratic Method

The great ideas of Pre-Socratic philosophy depended on the quite simple natural speculations of common sense. The Pythagoreans were led to the concept of harmony by observing

8

the relationship of pitch to the length of the vibrating string. When Democritus, watching corn being sieved and waves splashing up on the seashore, noticed how like produced like, he concluded that the process by which our world and its myriad forms emerged from the primitive vortex was something similar. Anaxagoras thought about human nutrition and wondered how hair came from non-hair and flesh from non-flesh: surely it was because the matter from which a thing arose was already, in some hidden way, what it was to become? This led him to his concept of *homoiomerien*.

The way in which the Pre-Socratics conducted their thinking gives us a valuable insight into the nature of philosophical thought in general: philosophy is a basic human activity, and far from being the preserve of specialist sciences is something universally human and fundamentally accessible to common sense. Kant once said that the insights necessary to true humanity do not depend on the subtlety of learned syllogisms but properly belong to natural reason which, if not distorted by artifice, does not fail to lead us to the true and useful. The Pre-Socratics prove it.

3. Sophism – Words and Distorted Values

The Sophists in their turn proved how dangerous the mind could be as an instrument of inquiry. It was capable of a great deal that passed for brilliance but which was in reality so many empty words. To see through the sophism, mere mind was not enough: maturity of mind was needed.

Sophism arose at a time when Greece was preparing to enter the arena of high politics. Experts were needed. The Sophists offered their services. They promised to teach *arete*. If we translate this word literally as virtue and take virtue in the conventional sense, we have more or less the opposite of what was meant. On the lips of the Sophists, *arete* meant no more than dexterity (verbal and practical), and a dexterity that was not too fastidious. They propounded an omniscient expertise (*panurgia*), as Plato pertinently observed. For the Sophists the important thing was *rhetoric*, the art of speaking and writing

9

persuasively. Political leaders needed it. And they now had some dangerous maxims at their disposal: if you want to be somebody, you must learn how to be first, how to acquire and retain power, how to assert yourself, how to master life and enjoy it. Everything was justified in the service of this aim – hence the Sophist principle that the clever speaker must be able to make the weaker cause the stronger not by shedding the light of truth but simply by persuasion. Plato's constant reproof was that the Sophists were concerned not with reality or truth or justice, but only with power, and that at bottom they lacked all genuine insight into the truth and worth of man – they did not lead, they led astray.

The Sophists adopted the appropriate view of life, a universal *relativism*: there was no truth, and even if there were we could not know it, and even if we could know it, it would be incommunicable – this was a favourite theme of *Gorgias'* (*c* 483–375). Or as one of their best known members, *Protagoras* (*c* 481–411), held, everything was relative, subjective, dependent entirely on the personal opinions of the individual: 'What seems to me to be so, is so for me, and what seems to you to be so, is so for you.' It would follow that there was nothing over against man: no objective facts, no eternal laws, no gods. 'Man is the measure of all things', said Protagoras. The Sophists left no avenue unexplored in their attempts to show the relativity of the judgements of justice, morality and religion. There was no place for 'nature' (universal validity), everything depended on human decision and agreement. For their ideology of power too they cast around for a philosophical camouflage. They chose the law of nature according to which the strong prevail over the weak. For them this was 'natural law', a view which was to be resurrected, centuries later, by Hobbes and Nietzsche.

It did not occur to them that their much-vaunted relativity affected not moral values but only the human awareness of moral values, not objective validity but only its historical expression. They also overlooked the distinction between 'natural law' (in their sense) and natural greed, as Thomas Hobbes was much later rightly to call it. One man saw through their blindness – Plato. All his early writings were directed against the Sophists. His most cutting argument was that of the liar and the thief. The principle that the only matter of consequence was ability must, he said, be subjected to rigorous scrutiny. If it were really true, the liar would be 'better' than the person who speaks the truth, because he out-talks him; similarly the thief is 'better' than the watchman, because he 'does' more in that he outwits him. Ability alone, then, is nothing to the purpose.

The Sophists' arguments were not always seen through, however. The art of fine speech and writing, the humanistic ideal of *formal creation*, will always find adherents. Plato wrote for these people in vain, as they then simply turned on *him* with their sophistries. To his way of thinking they were no more than lovers of the word (*philologoi*), not lovers of thought and its wisdom (*philosophoi*); they lacked maturity of mind, feeling for the truth and appreciation of moral reason. There is always a sophism which takes more pleasure in appearances than in reality. People are always dazzled by expertise. If, however, man's ability, even in knowledge or will-power, is not subject to principles of moral value and derived from them, certain consequences inevitably follow. In a philosophy orientated uniquely to performance and power, egoism becomes a necessity. It can be masked, lies can be called propaganda and theft the common good, but under a regime of naked power falsehood will fester. The person who is out to make the most of his advantages will always rely on the smooth cunning of the experienced practitioner whose conscience jibs at nothing.

CHAPTER TWO: ATTIC PHILOSOPHY

With the great names in Greek philosophy, Socrates, Plato and Aristotle, Attica the motherland came to prominence. The Pre-Socratics had lived on the very edge of Greece. Not until the Sophists do we find important figures in Greece itself; but then they were concerned more with political ideology than with philosophical thought. It was through Socrates, Plato and Aristotle, that a truly great eternal philosophy first achieved verbal expression.

1. Socrates – Knowledge and Value

The most important thing about Socrates (c 470–399) was himself. He wrote nothing, but his life embodied everything he would have wished to say. What we know about him we learn from Plato and a few other sources. We realize that with Socrates philosophy was more practice than theory. The philosophical inquiry into the why and the wherefore of things, and especially moral value or virtue, shaped his very existence.

In his philosophical inquiry, two things were particularly characteristic: his maieutics and his irony. *Maieutics* was Socrates' 'art of midwifery'. It consisted in drawing out of his partners in dialogue – particularly the young people whom he involved in philosophical discussion – something which they were as yet unaware of knowing, but which they could know, as Socrates showed them with his skilful interrogation, as soon as they approached a problem from the right angle. Socrates' method created the finest philosophical school. He always made the young feel they should not be prematurely sure of their ideas and judgements. He did not overestimate the answers given; he preferred to remain dissatisfied until he had probed further and further into the question. He asked 'ironically' whether his listeners believed they had already understood things correctly, whether they had grasped the essential matter and not just incidentals, whether the characteristics of this or that were fully mastered, whether there were not contrary reasons against the advanced position, and so forth. Even of himself he was quite ready to admit that 'he knew he knew nothing'. His method was *irony*. It could annoy, but it aimed at stimulating. Socrates is one of the great teachers of mankind, not only in his methods in conversation with young people, but more so in his guidance into the observation and experience of moral goodness.

Like knowledge, value stood at the heart of his dialogue with men. The Sophists were constantly speaking about *arete* and taking it in the sense of an omnicompetent expertise. Socrates too centred his thought on *arete*, but by that he understood genuinely moral virtue, unequivocally directed to moral values in will and conviction. He caused great scandal, partly because to politicians his reference to conscience and feeling for value, to the 'daimon' within man, was uncomfortable, partly because his deeper ethical awareness seemed to contradict popular religion. So he was persecuted, imprisoned and finally forced to drain the cup of hemlock. He drank it in peace and with unswerving firmness of character. 'Fellow citizens,' he said, 'you are dear and worthy people, but I must obey God more than you. And as long as I breathe and have strength in me, I shall not cease to seek the truth and urge you and enlighten you and speak to your consciences as I have always done. My friend, are you, a citizen of the greatest city, so prominent for its culture, not ashamed to care about filling your purse and to scheme for fame and honour instead of being concerned for moral judgement, truth and the improvement of your soul?' Socrates is one of the greatest ethicists in the history of philosophy.

His ethical vocabulary and theory admittedly fell short of this existential reality of goodness: Socrates failed to give a clear-cut *theoretical* explanation of the true nature of morality. He drew on a whole series of ideas which properly belonged to the world of purpose and utility characteristic of purely technical thought and which, solely from the theoretical point of view, suggested a utilitarianism and eudaemonism, and therefore a morality of usefulness and well-being, which were in fact far from him. For example, moral good was explained on the lines of an efficient tool. Man, however, is no tool. When we call him morally good, by 'good' we mean something quite different. It often seems as if for Socrates the entire moral world exhausted itself in knowledge and expertise. This has been called Socratic intellectualism and has led to comparisons between Socrates and the Sophists; in reality, however, his morality was far from being mere intellectualism and technical virtue. It was will-power and strength of character. It depended on the ideas current in his time which were not really adapted to his intentions. It was precisely this lag of philosophical reflexion behind the existential reality which most stimulated his great disciple Plato to place genuine ethical reality at the centre of his philosophy and to look for the true and proper essence of moral good, of the ideal.

Although Socrates is important first and foremost for his contribution to the theory of value, he made another very significant contribution to purely theoretical philosophy with an achievement which almost ranks as an invention: his *method of arriving at concepts*. Aristotle said of him: 'Two things must be ascribed to Socrates: his search for universal concepts and his analysis of reality with their help.' Plato has given us many examples of Socrates' method in his early dialogues. For instance, Socrates is inquiring about *arete*. Someone says: 'We see *arete* when someone can rule in the State, serve his friends and damage his enemies; when he is brave, prudent, shrewd, and so on.' Socrates' reply is in each case the same: these are all examples of *arete*, they are individual virtues, but they are not themselves virtue; if you examine them closely, you will see that there is something underlying them all, a common form or *eidos* or essence, and that it is that which is important. This was Socrates' 'universal', and in his view it should shape our thought on all the particular virtues. Then we should have knowledge and wisdom, and not just an idea tied to the individual reality. Socrates distinguished the necessary from the accidental, and therein lies his importance for theoretical philosophy.

This is at once evident in his great disciple Plato, who based his entire philosophical system on this universal form, the *eidos* or essence of a thing.

2. Plato – The World of Ideas

Whereas the philosophizing of Socrates is, to some extent, characterized by his humble origin, that of Plato (427–347) is clearly the product of an aristocrat. However, Plato's philosophy also concerned daily life, because it was aimed at forming righteous men and a righteous State; but it set about this with a consciously sophisticated and ingenious theory, the famous doctrine of the Platonic ideas.

(a) The doctrine of ideas

Plato's philosophy began where Socrates had left off, at the question of what constitutes true and proper goodness or, in other words, moral value. Socrates had been the living exponent of moral value. What, however, was its essence? How could it be explained theoretically? Plato replied with his doctrine of 'ideas' or 'forms', one approach to which was the path of ethics.

For Plato, one thing stood out quite clearly from the moral experiences of Socrates' life: that values, for example the four cardinal virtues wisdom, justice, courage and moderation, as well as the other virtues, were absolute, incontrovertible, unalterable and eternal. Their knowledge and practice could be defective and full of mistakes, could fail to embody, or even distort, the values' real nature. There could even be people who knew nothing about them, who were blind to value and the awareness of value varied from age to age, race to race, culture to culture, individual to individual. The Sophists were right in holding that goodness and justice were everywhere different. Despite all this, however, the Sophists were wrong when it came to the essence, the inner objective nature, of values. Value was independent of human willing, desire, needs, inclinations and subjective intentions, it was *absolute*. There were, of course, values which depended on supply and demand, market or material values as one might say, whose worth was geared to their usefulness to the individual. Apart from these, however, one could see in man's moral activity, which concerns what is specifically human (character, sentiment, respect and so forth), values quite different from material and subjective usefulness, in other words ideal objective and universally binding realities. Plato called them simply virtue (*arete*). Socrates had repeatedly emphasized, against the Sophists, the universal element in virtue. For Plato this was enough to prove his case, as if in Socrates he had seen the essence of virtue with his own eyes. His vision he has passed on to us in his writings.

What precisely was meant by goodness or virtue, asked Plato. Dialogue with the Sophists had revealed time and again that it was not simply knowledge and ability, not simply perfection in the sense of accomplished technique. The concept of perfection did not in itself imply any univocal moral value. After all, a thief and a liar could be perfect. Nor was the concept of purpose enough. The moral quality of a person could not be established on the presence of aims and intentions in his life, because the same could be said of intention as of knowledge, ability and perfection: there were bad aims as well as good ones, just as there was bad knowledge and bad perfection. Intentionality could not in itself be a principle of ethics. Moral conduct demanded *proper* knowledge, ability, perfection, and purpose. But what did 'proper' mean in the context of man's life? The specific feature of Plato's philosophy emerges here. It used the concept of being. Plato postulated a *realm of ideal essences* or ideal being. There was such a thing as man in himself, justice, goodness, beauty. On earth, in space and time, there was no perfect justice or perfect goodness. And yet men did not cease striving to improve their laws and to prevent the merely relative, mere privilege perhaps or power, from passing itself off for justice. They wanted absolute right. Hence men judged human lives on their rectitude and value. Such absolutes did not, of course, lie to hand like set squares: otherwise all life and history would come to an end because there would be no struggle for the infinite; but men knew about them none the less. There was a knowledge which was equally knowledge and non-knowledge, a different kind of knowledge from history and quantity. As one strove for it one possessed it, it led one as one looked for it. The being of these values-in-themselves, however, was quite unlike the being of the things we see about us in space and time. It could not be grasped, it was not material and time-conditioned; it was not just privilege or power or pleasure or enjoyment. It was a being we see and yet do not see; it guided man and remained hidden; it was eternal and entered time; not spatial and yet it

16

appeared in space; unchanging but not rigid and immovable. Plato called it the being of ideas, 'ideal' being, the world of ideas (*kosmos noetos*). It revealed itself to him in connexion with Socrates' *daimon*, knowledge of value and conscience. He thought of it as the absolute for which both of them had been looking.

A close inspection of this ideal being would persuade us that it should not really be called being at all, at least if, as has become customary in modern times, we understand by being the being of natural objects: minerals, plants, animals as opposed to man who possesses intelligence and so is distinct from the rest of nature. It was man's intelligence which, in grasping values, came to know of those ideal standards Plato called ideas. And it was only intelligence which could know of such things as ideas. We can therefore say that the ideas had a spiritual-mental being appropriate to man in his uniqueness as a person of free moral spirit. This is a concept of being other than that applied solely to the things of nature. Wisdom, justice, moderation, loyalty, truth etc. have a being that is different from the being of a piece of iron, of a plant, of an animal. The fact that these things have being, however, shows that the concept of being was much wider in ancient philosophy than in modern philosophy. It was even used to embrace the being of God.

A second line of argument leading to the doctrine of ideas also started from the human person as an intelligent being, but concerned not value so much as mind in its grasp of the truth. This aspect of human intelligence was brought to Plato's notice – and after him to the notice of a great many other philosophers – by the nature of *mathematical thought*. A tangent touches a circle at only one point. Nobody has yet managed to see this, but we know it is true. Although the senses do not yield this knowledge, we ascertain it from another source, thought. Therefore, concluded Plato, there is no straight line, no true circle, no exact identity in the world accessible to the senses. They are all ideas which exist perfectly only in thought. As we see them in this spatio-temporal world, points are always extended, quantified, whereas the mathematical point is not.

17

As we draw them, circles are never completely round. There is nothing in the sensible world, Nicolas of Cusa was to say later, which cannot be more exact. It is only the mental circle which is perfect. In our tangible world, said Plato in the *Phaedo*, there are not two identical pieces of wood. Everything is in a state of transition. Every moment things are quite different. We could never therefore have acquired the concept of identity from the fluid material world. Therefore this concept originates in the mind in so far as the latter is pure thought.

Our concepts are not absolutely independent of sense-experience, because they come to us in our communion with the perceptual world. But their purity and truth is derived from the mind. As we should say today, they are a priori. Plato used the image of memory (*anamnesis*): we contemplated these realities or ideas in an earlier existence when we were with the gods. It is only an image, though. What he actually meant, the mind's rational insight into what must be true always and in all circumstances, is shown in the *Meno*, where a slave who has never learnt geometry knows, from his own resources and on the strength of reasoning alone, the length of the sides of a square which is twice the size of a square of given measurements. The slave does not measure out so many squares so that he can then say: the sides are this long; prior to any such experience, he works out, mentally, how long the sides *must be*. The a priori concepts that precede all experience do not include a handful of basic concepts only, like equality, identity, difference, opposite, unity, many, similarity, beauty, goodness, justice, which recur again and again in our thinking processes. Plato accepted the fact of ideas of everything which had an 'essence'. There were therefore ideas of people, animals, plants, minerals, and also of the products of human workmanship, tables, chairs and so on. Together they formed the so-called world of ideas, which contained the primal forms of visible things. The latter were derived from the former and so shared in them. In Platonic theory, the essence of the visible things of our spatio-temporal world depended on their share in the invisible primal forms accessible only to thought. The causality that brought them into being was therefore very much stronger than an impression or imprint, however dynamic. The latter applied only to spatio-temporal motion and change, whereas the share which things have in the ideas establishes their entire being in its essential reality. Plato's explanation of the world therefore moved from the top downwards. Just as we recognize and understand a portrait only if we know the original, the portrait otherwise remaining mute and uninformative, so Plato understood worldly things to be images of eternal originals, deriving our understanding of the temporal from a consideration of the eternal. This world of eternal forms was for him the world of true knowledge and true wisdom. It was also the world of true being.

If this explanation of the world was to be valid then it had to be possible for man, in his contact with the many visible objects of his sense-experience, to know, from within himself, what was eternally true. Plato accepted this. It prompted him to postulate the so-called *innate ideas*, or, more accurately, a priori knowledge of what must be. Plato did not deny sense-experience; but he thought of it as controlled – regulated and assessed – by a superior agent, mind.

The Platonic *theory of being* or metaphysics followed from this. According to Plato, being: (1) was mediated by man as a rational being; (2) was always in the process of becoming, despite Plato's emphasis on 'eternal truth'; (3) was concrete, despite the universal existence of real ideas behind everything, because we see the originals ('ideas') only in the copies ('things') and the two cannot be separated. Plato did not hold with a chorismos or separation of idea and reality in the sense of a duplication of the 'real' world in a world of ideas. One demanded the other, although the original was more powerful than the copy. Man, in whom the originals were preserved, did not, of course, create the world, but he was always more than the world, so that there was a world *for* us only *because of* us, and man could never be its slave.

(b) Man

If man shaped himself and his life according to the eternal ideas, he acquired his true being, his better ego, and discovered the right and the good. Man's nature followed from this. Plato described it in his *simile of the cave* in the seventh part of the *Republic*. Men, he said, were like prisoners in an underground cave chained there since childhood in such a way that they could look only straight ahead of them. They had never been able to turn round, so all they had ever seen was the shadows thrown on the wall in front of them by the things of the world. They took this world of shadows to be the only one. If they had stepped out of the cave into the sunlight, they would never have believed in the greater reality of the 'real' world. For Plato, the spatio-temporal world was the cave, and what he demanded of men was that they make an effort to pierce through the shadows and discern true being, the ideas, the originals, behind them, or, more strictly, in them. This was the proper function of *education*, whether self-education or tutelage under a teacher. All education must ultimately be a philosophical conduct of life: the vision of the essence of things. This vision was a challenge that never came to an end, because the essences led on to loftier and loftier forms of being and increasingly intertwined, and it was impossible to view the background and all the deeper interconnexions – the whole truth, therefore – of the ideas at a single glance. This process Plato called *dialectic*. (It might be useful to provide a fuller definition of this word here, given its importance in the history of philosophy. To the Greek it originally meant simply 'disputation', but its later aim was 'to discover the truth by successively presenting and refuting various opposing emphases and viewpoints until the truth, which embraced all their partial insights and yet transcended them in a fully coherent conception, was finally attained.' K. Ward: *50 Key Words in Philosophy* (Lutterworth Press). Its purpose is, thus, to clarify ideas and arrive at increasingly adequate judgements. Hegel's dialectic of thesis-antithesis-synthesis, in which the synthesis then serves as a further thesis, is derived from the Socratic method. In the Middle Ages, dialectic, as practised by a whole series of writers from Alcuin to John of Salisbury and Thomas Aquinas, was scathingly regarded by some as the instrument of increasing rationalization in Christian theology.) Unless one mastered dialectic, taught Plato, one could not attain the true interconnexions of being, one went no further than the appearances. One therefore remained as superficial as the cosmetician who, unlike the doctor, did not know what genuinely promoted man's physical fitness but merely that which produced outward show. Man was really his *soul*. In comparison with the soul, the body was a mere appearance, a shadow, a narrowing of the soul's opportunities; it was in fact the soul's prison. The soul was an intermediary between the world of ideas and the visible world. It was immaterial, indivisible and so also immortal. A strong soul could shape the body because noble things could fashion and mould inferior things and assimilate them increasingly to itself. Education therefore should not be content with childish pursuits and trifles and the satisfaction of irrational inclinations, but must lead us out of the cave – to the realm of true being, the world of ideas. Truth and value were the soul's food. Here in this world of mind man was free, and the more he cultivated his mental activity, the freer he became. With the myth of the *transmigration of souls* (metempsychosis) and fate, Plato showed that in himself man was free. When souls first fell from their stars and descended to earth, they had endless possibilities in front of them. They could choose any lifeless thing. If they were carried away by desire and deceptive appearances and their choice was a bad one, they could become entangled in the earthly world and sink deeper on the scale of being. Their desire trapped them and became their punishment. Eros did not die to all goodness, but it made it very difficult for reason to harness the steeds of passion. This was why man must arm himself with a knowledge of the truth and eternal values, and with these make his way in the world of space and time. He must not follow the promptings of inclination, desire or caprice, but do his 'duty' – which was whatever reason recognized as man's true essence. At its highest perfection, such a life was 'an imitation of God, to the extent that this is possible to us, that is, in so far as we can be holy and righteous by using our insight and wisdom' (*Theaetetus* 176).

(c) The State

For Plato the State was the organization of men on the way to the good. The need to be concerned over material things, work, economy, the social order, external and internal power, was taken for granted, but it was not an aim in itself, it was at the service of rational man. The best expression of this was the theory by which the guardians and philosopher kings in Plato's projected State were celibate and owned no property. They were denied the right to private property not so that they would all have the same (to offset the universal desire to keep up with the Joneses) but so that they might devote themselves entirely to the service of spiritual values without the obstruction of greed for material things. They would be guaranteed the means of subsistence, for which the third estate, the peasants, would be responsible. The second estate, the guardians, also called warriors, existed solely for the defence of the State. Even women could be guardians, provided that they were suitable. The education of the guardians was directed totally to the common good. For them spiritual nourishment was justice and truth, and not just the art of earning one's living as for the peasants. The guardian who particularly distinguished himself gradually became one of the chosen few who emerged from the cave, mastered knowledge and dialectic, gazed on the eternal truths and directed human affairs according to these values: he became a philosopher king.

Plato elaborated his theory of the *forms of State* with all this in mind. If a State was governed by an intellectual and moral elite, it was an aristocracy; if by an elite of one (so to speak), a monarchy. If, on the other hand, it was not an elite who governed but the ambitious, who prided themselves on their courage and on being hunters, sportsmen and soldiers, energetic practitioners, crafty tacticians and resourceful careerists, the State was a so-called timocracy. Its rulers had their own property and enriched themselves at the State's expense. They served less the whole and its welfare than their own aspirations. If a small group of wealthy men, out for more, took over the government, and their only concerns were economic power and privilege, in the service of which they were prepared to subordinate higher human values, their State was called an oligarchy. Of the three parts of the soul, reason (aristocracy), courage (timocracy) and appetite, the third was here predominant. If, again, it was the majority who ruled, so that every citizen 'lived for the pleasures of the moment and thought it an agreeable, free and happy life' (*Republic* 561), the State was a democracy. According to Plato, a democracy was almost as far from the ideal of order and justice as it was possible to be, because its concerns were not at all truth and justice, but mere subjective desire on which all the wider social issues were based. All citizens were equal. It was, to all appearances, an alluring concept of the State, anarchic, colourful, treating all men as equal whether they were so or not (558). The extreme degeneration, however, was tyranny. When freedom had lost all restraint, it became its opposite. 'Any excess is usually followed by a violent reaction, in the weather, in the growth of plants and animals, and not least in States (564).' To foster the universal desire to possess more, the masses needed a leader. And because they were used to 'placing one person at the top and coddling him and giving him supreme power' (565), it could happen that once a leader had tasted power, he succumbed to delusions of greatness and did all he could to stay in power. He abolished justice, the people became his slaves, bred other slaves, and finally 'the people realize just what a monster they have nurtured in their bosom and made great' (569). Tyranny, then, was the harshest possible slavery: the people were slaves, the tyrant's bodyguard was recruited from slaves, and the tyrant himself was a slave to his own passions. In the eyes of the philosopher bred to reason and truth, freedom and moral will, the tyrant embodied the most atrocious form of the State.

(d) God

In his analysis of the various forms of the State, Plato showed that man could, if he so chose, make himself the measure of all things. This was the famous thesis of the Sophists. Plato was not loth to lump together Sophism, democracy and tyranny. For himself, he preferred a contrary thesis: 'God is the measure of all things' (*Laws* 716).

The *existence* of God Plato derived from his doctrine of ideas. Occasionally he used the language of popular religion (polytheism), but where he relied on his own intuition, he was monotheist. His one God coincided with the idea of Good-in-itself, and was consequently the ground of all grounds, the form of all forms, the apex of the pyramid of ideas which emerged in the dialectical process. The dialectic of ideas was Plato's real path to God. It arrived at what Aristotle was to call the 'unmoved Mover'. At the start of a bodily motion, argued Plato, there must be something non-material at work, because the spiritual (for example, thought, will, design) 'precedes the length, breadth, depth and force of bodies' (*Laws* 896). Logically prior again to the act of thinking and willing was the possible object of thought, the content of the world of ideas. Plato always argued from the top downwards.

He was the opposite of a materialist. Soul and mind were not the products of matter, matter could exist only if there were already soul and mind. However, the spiritual-intellectual was only logically prior to matter, because the Platonic God did not create the world from nothing, like the Christian Creator: the demiurge found matter already to hand. The creation doctrine developed at some length in the *Timaeus* has had an enormous influence on western thinking on the world and the world's origin, at least until Galileo. The Middle Ages read the dialogue and absorbed it, and in general understood Plato's world-moulder as a genuine Creator. But that was interpretation.

Plato's thought on the *nature* of God must be deduced from his doctrine of ideas. We may say quite simply: God was truth. It is useful to read the *Laws*' justification of God in the face of evil in the world and its remarks on divine providence (899–905). Plato also knew of invoking God. The short prayer at the end of the *Phaedrus* (279 b–c) is one of his most characteristic texts: 'O beloved Pan and all the other gods of this place, make me beautiful in my inner soul. May my outward self harmonize with my inward being. May I think the wise man rich, and of gold may I have only so much as a moderate man may bear.'

3. Aristotle – Ideas in the World

Aristotle (384–322) has had an even greater influence on western thought than Plato. Where Plato created philosophy, Aristotle taught it. He was Plato's disciple for twenty years until he left the Academy – significantly. He was in no small measure critical of his teacher. 'I am a friend of Plato,' he once said, 'but a greater friend of truth.' The differences between the two men have frequently been overemphasized by their respective Schools, the Academy and the Peripatos, as well as by the Middle Ages and modern times. It is generally recognized today that there was more uniting Plato and Aristotle than dividing them.

(a) The Logician

Logic is the science of thought and speech (*legein* = to speak). Man used speech and thought for centuries without being aware of their different elements and rules, just as someone can wander through meadows and woods, looking at and recognizing plants and animals without suspecting that botanists and zoologists have reduced the extremely varied natural world to a scientific system. Aristotle performed this function for human speech and thought. He showed that the infinite world of the thinking mind uses no more than three simple basic elements: the concept, the judgement and the syllogism.

The *concept* is the mind's magic wand. The eye roves, it has to look at each thing separately, and it has to consider hundreds of things in turn; the concept can think of an infinite number of things all at once. We have to look at house after house, individually; the *concept* of house includes all (actual and possible) houses. The concept, consequently, makes the work of the human mind very much easier. Things themselves change, they are different each minute, because they are in time and fluctuate with time; in this spatio-temporal world, nothing is really completely and always identical with itself. The concept, however, grasps even this fluctuating world at a blow. It extracts the universal, that which is common to all the concrete individuals in a class or genus. The universal is, evidently, not the individual thing, but a part of it, the essential part, or at least what seems to man to be such. Socrates had already started from the praxis of conceptual thought; Plato had made a whole philosophical system out of it, since his ideas emerged from the Socratic concepts. Aristotle did not approve of such bold flight. Instead he became a specialist in concepts and their role in human thought – and in the process the founder of logic.

Aristotle discovered that concepts could be reduced to certain types called (by him) categories. Literally category means an assertion, statement or predicate. By analysing our speech – even so simple an example of human thought and language as the sentence: Socrates is pale – Aristotle demonstrated two things: firstly, that there is always something about which we are making statements, namely the subject or substance (*ousia*) which lies behind all the statements but which cannot itself be further expressed, in our case Socrates; and secondly, that we add to this subject predicates which, because they 'happen to apply', are called accidents. Either the categories are accidents which are a quality, a quantity, a relation, a time, a place or a position; or they express possession, action or passion. For example, Socrates is small (quantity), pale (quality), the husband of Xanthippe (relation), etc.

What Aristotelian logic prescribed for the artistically correct formation of a concept, its rules for so-called definition, have passed into the history of thought: the logician establishes the highest genus of a concept and then limits it by adding the specific difference which distinguishes that kind of concept from other kinds in the same genus. For example, the highest genus for man is living beings. His specific difference with regard to other living beings is reason: it is his reason which distinguishes him from the animals, plants, etc. The definition of man is therefore: a rational living being.

However important the concept might be for human intellectual activity, it has its dangers. The conceptual world of whole sciences, indeed whole cultures, can become encrusted and dusty and estranged from reality. The concept draws its being from reality. At the same time it depends on the knowing subject, his interests, his narrow or broad horizons, the age in which he lives, and not least on his will to power. Many do not notice this danger. They take the conceptual world in which they grew up, or which they somehow acquired, as the whole world. There is such a thing as scientific superstition which is critical of religious beliefs but which subscribes quite uncritically to its own scientific conceptual world.

Aristotle was aware of this danger, as can be seen in his doctrine of *judgement*. He defined judgement as a union of concepts which makes a statement about reality. Judgements should be true. Whereas for Plato truth was given with being, with the ideas (ontological truth), for Aristotle it was the property of judgement (logical truth); but for Aristotle too the actual facts were determinative of this property of judgement. Our judgement must be aligned on reality. 'Truth consists in saying that being is and non-being is not.' The concept of truth has undergone a good many variations in the history of philosophy. Truth has been defined in almost every possible way. Aristotle's definition established the norm which philosophers have never since then been able to ignore. His doctrine of judgement made another point of lasting significance: he saw that scientific judgement is fundamentally different from daily judgement. The latter concerns an individual entity only, say Socrates or Callias, while scientific judgement concerns something universal, man as a whole, for example, or life in general, or carbon in general. Science deals in universally valid assertions – establishes laws, as we should say today. With this simple logical thesis about judgement, Aristotle paved the way for the modern concept of science – although Plato had already taught that science's proper field of action was the universal, the essences of the *kosmos noetos*.

The third part of Aristotelian logic concerns the *conclusion* or syllogism. When we use the usual form of argument: All men are mortal, Socrates is a man, therefore Socrates is mortal, we are still speaking in the language of Aristotle. He recognized that this type of reasoning embodies something fundamental to human thought. This, however, was not the only thing about it he discovered: he observed and described in his characteristic fashion the typical variations of the scheme. He found three of them, called syllogistic figures, each one of which in its turn has four forms or modes. Any handbook of logic will give the details. It is still common teaching today.

The syllogism is a sort of conceptual mechanism. Three concepts (major, minor and middle terms) interlock: because Socrates (1) is a man (2), and because all men are mortal (3), Socrates also is necessarily mortal. The mechanism can prove or refute, because it can state with equal force that a thing must or must not be so. It is a valuable tool, but like the concept it has its dangers. It can degenerate into dialectical acrobatics in which (to change the metaphor) the logician juggles with words and loses sight of things, especially if he adopts the linguistic rules of particular schools and tries to work problems out that way.

Aristotle himself would have been the last to approve of any such procedure, as he was keenly aware that words must have an objective content if they are to be at all useful. We saw this in his theory of judgemental truth. He also expressed it in another context: his theory on the *origin of concepts*. According to Aristotle, concepts must be rooted in the real world accessible to sense experience. Human knowledge is not an inborn possession. If it (or part of it) were, Aristotle argued against Plato, we should notice it. No, the soul is like a blank writing-tablet on which images from the senses are then inscribed. Aristotle was much more positive than Plato in his assessment of sense-perception. He regarded the senses as instruments which transmit the essential forms that lie in concrete things and which shape their structural forms. The particular observations of the senses are, of course, individually distinct, but from them a universal idea may be extracted by excluding the incidental differences. It is rather like saying that although the seals made by a signet-ring differ from material to material, the form that impresses them is the same. The extraction of the universal form Aristotle called 'abstraction'. This word still plays a key role in modern philosophy, although its significance is not the same in ancient philosophy as in the British empirical school (for example). In Aristotle the process of concept-formation included the intervention of a mental force, later called 'active reason' (*nous poietikos*), which highlights the inner forms in sense-perceptions, just as colours are brought out by light. Because this active reason was automatic (spontaneous), sense perception was, for Aristotle, more a material than an efficient cause of knowledge, and in this he rejoined Plato. He was empirical, but not an empiricist. Both Plato and Aristotle could say, as Kant was later to say, that our knowledge indeed derives from the senses, but does not consist solely of sense-perceptions. 'Reason' gives us something over and above sense-experience.

(b) The Metaphysician

What is metaphysics? Just as logic studies the elements and functions of intelligence, metaphysics studies being and its essential properties. This definition embodies something new and specific. As well as being*s*, like minerals and individual plants and animals and people, and qualities such as vital and moral and aesthetic and religious values, there is *being* in the widest possible sense, common to everything that is. All particular cases of being share in it, it lies at their root, they embody it in their own individual way. Aristotle may be imagined as saying to himself: things that are, can be the object of particular branches of science like medicine, biology and physics; but there is no reason why being itself should not be the object of scientific treatment. This treatment he undertook in a work which came later to be known as the *Metaphysics*. For Aristotle, metaphysics was not strictly speaking the science of what lies 'behind' things, as is sometimes said, but, as modern investigation shows, the science to be studied after (behind) physics (which is the science of nature), because it takes us further than physics. Physics deals with a special case of being, namely being as it appears to the senses, whereas

29

metaphysics deals with the deeper 'underlying' being which appears in that appearance (so to speak). The relationship is like that of the reason to its consequence. To this extent the old understanding of metaphysics makes some sense: 'behind things' could mean 'behind the appearances', and metaphysics would therefore study that on which the appearances are based. The science of metaphysics does not imply an inaccessible hinterland totally cut off from the spatio-temporal world; its aim is to clarify the inner foundations or principles of being as we encounter it in things, being in other words as the essential core of perceptual appearances. Because these principles are, by definition, the most basic thing about beings, because they make the appearances possible (or, as we might say, because they 'keep up' appearances), metaphysics is also called 'first philosophy'. And because they themselves rest on a base, on an ultimate foundation or principle called God, Aristotle also called this first philosophy 'theology'; since his time the term 'natural theology' has been commonly used for this approach.

How are we to conceive of this universal being and what would its essential properties be? Is it not all rather dry and colourless? To some extent yes, but Aristotle succeeded in making some vitally important remarks, the most salient of which are as follows.

At the start of the *Metaphysics* he laid down the principle, against Plato, that being in its basic sense is not the idea, but the concrete perceptible individual thing, the so-called first substance, for example Socrates or anything from nature or from the world of technical or artistic things, in fact any concrete existing thing at all. The Platonic idea was universal, supersensory, spiritual, it was the principle of our perceptual spatio-temporal world, our real world existed only by gracious permission of the idea. For Aristotle it was the other way round: the world of space and time existed first, as a world of particular things. It was true reality, and the idea existed only if it was based on that. What Plato took to be true being was actually no more than a thought, later called a universal, and Aristotle justified it only as a reduplication of the earthly world. For Aristotle, the concrete thing, nothing else, was 'being' in the proper sense of that word; it was reality. For Plato, the idea was reality.

Aristotle's conclusion has had enormous consequences for western philosophy. Since his time, idealism and realism have continued to disagree over what true being really is. However, in Aristotle's discussion of the properties of being, of which the *archai* or 'principles' were the most important, it emerges that the difference between idealism (Plato) and realism (Aristotle) is not so great as at first sight appears. There were four principles: form, matter, motion and purpose.

Aristotle considered the individual substance to be basic, but not entirely so. It was itself composed of two principles, matter and form, which were more basic still.

Form was one of the most important principles of being, in Aristotle's view. If in nature there were different species, genera and typical forms – in modern parlance, different sets of laws – it was because being was divided up by a principle which was a form and which created forms. 'Man begets man' is a well-known Aristotelian axiom. It meant that the world's material, whatever its name, was controlled by an intelligible principle which ensured that like begot like. Form did not lie beyond things, nor did it exist on its own: it was in things, in the stuff of the world, it came to be as soon as matter was differentiated. It was not, however, a mere concept, not just a notion acquired by abstraction from things; it was active, operative. It was possible for Socrates to be a man only because, besides the matter of his body, there was what we call 'humanity', which formed the corporeal material so that it became precisely a man and not something else. Form was therefore 'substance', but this time second substance, so-called because it underlay the individual concrete substance as a universal essence. Here again, form approached the Platonic idea. Aristotle did say that form functioned not as such, in its universality, but only in concrete particular things which embodied it in space and time – in the case of Socrates it would be the humanity of the individual person who was Socrates' father. Even here, however, form as form was not a mere concept, but something real and efficacious; otherwise the universal form would be not a principle but a once-only material-mechanical agent which could explain the individuality of Socrates but not his humanity. For the former, *matter* was responsible (matter being equally a principle of being). When universal forms 'informed' matter, they became individualized, and this was true of human beings too: matter was their 'principle of individuation'. In Aristotle's theory, matter was as it were the permanently fluid ribbon of the space-time continuum in which the eternal forms were introduced, achieved a once-only position and so became individual things. In itself every being, even that which was already formed and which could be formed again, was matter. This concept of matter, however, concerned only relative (second) matter. Aristotle's real absolute concept of (prime) matter meant 'what cannot be designated as substance or quantity or indeed fitted into any of the categories'. Prime matter, therefore, was the absolutely indeterminate. It could not exist on its own any more than form could. None the less it has often since been thought of as a kind of unifying medium of the world out of which the forms construct the things of nature. When then, on the threshold of modern times, chemical elements were discovered and thought to be irreducible, the allegedly Aristotelian concept of matter, and his whole natural philosophy, came in for some devastating criticism. Aristotle's concept of matter, however, belongs not so much to natural philosophy as to metaphysics. It expresses the fact that in all our knowledge of the world by means of forms, concepts, laws and numbers, there is always something which is formed, conceived and reduced to mathematical relationships; that reality cannot be reduced to just numbers or concepts; that despite our progressive differentiation of concepts, laws and numbers and our gradual extension of forms as we discover more and more natural laws, there is always a formed residue. And because we cannot understand the world other than as the substratum of our statements, in other words as the ultimate subject of all predicates capable of an infinity of forms, Aristotle regarded prime matter as a principle of being. Because it had an essential connexion with human thought and understanding, it could also be called a logical (and not only a metaphysical) principle. Revealingly, Aristotle applied the term *hypokeimenon* (that which underlies) not only to prime matter but also to the subject of a judgement. If this is borne in mind, the theory of matter and form ('hylemorphism') is seen to be very much more than a theory about the structure of bodily reality and the nature of change: it is an entire metaphysics. A further remark may be made here: hylemorphism, as Aristotle understood it, gave priority to form, and therefore approached Plato's theory of ideas (without actually identifying the ideal or essential or 'formal' with the real).

The third principle was the *prime mover*. This was a specifically Aristotelian doctrine directed in large part at Plato, whose philosophy saw being in terms of the ideal but not of the dynamic. You cannot build houses with ideas, said Aristotle: there is also the first motion, the world's coming-to-be, which must be a separate principle. We could not understand becoming, change and movement without some such principle. What Aristotle meant was the passage from potency (possibility) to act (reality), or in other words the realization of possibility. The cause which realized ideas (possibilities) was something other than, stronger than, the ideas. Hence an Aristotelian axiom, the principle of causality: 'Act precedes potency' (*Metaphysics* 1049 b 5). This also served to establish his theory of God: God was the cause of all causes, the reality behind all realities, the beginning of motion who himself required no act, who preceded all possibility because he was pure act, that is, only and exclusively act. In his investigations into the nature of motion, Aristotle was all but forced to resort to formal factors: when he defined motion as the passage from potency to act (and ultimately every change could be reduced to this), there was form at the start and finish of the movement, and the movement itself could be understood only in terms of formal change. Hence we can say that Aristotle had not really broken with Plato's eidetic principles. This is even clearer in his fourth principle, purpose.

Purpose, for Aristotle, was that because of which something happened. By this he meant that everything in the world took

33

place for the sake of some goal. It was not only man who set himself aims and was aware of them because he knew his own intentions: nature too, according to Aristotle, had a goal. On this point he made no distinction between art and nature. This harmony of nature and man's free work arose from the fact that Aristotle could not imagine any motion without an aim: 'Every becoming is a passage from something to something . . . from a first mover, which already has a particular form, to another form or similar end.' Aristotle's theory of being was so stamped with the idea of purpose that even his concept of 'thing' included it. The essence (*physis* = what has become) of a thing was its relation to something else, its finality or purpose, and so Aristotle called it 'entelechy' (*en-eauto-telos-echon* = having purpose within itself). The Aristotelian notion of entelechy therefore applied not only to living beings but to all beings. Aristotle could therefore make the paradoxical statement that perfection stands not at the end of a process but at the beginning. Temporally, what is actual comes at the end, but logically and ontologically it comes at the beginning as the meaning or purpose of the process of change. The Platonic heritage appears here again: only an ideal being can precede the real and so, as a completed being, stand at the beginning. When Aristotle said that in all becoming matter was looking for form, he was thinking of this completed being, the ideal form which Plato posited, against which Aristotle argued, but which he could not in fact do without. The basically idealistic conception of Aristotle's philosophy of being already included the idea of purpose: purpose was part of the concept of form. He did not need to attach purpose extraneously to beings and events – as in Democritus' or David Hume's natural philosophy, where basically everything was separated from its neighbour. The forms were immanent in Aristotle's natural world. All forms stood in some sort of mutual relationship (even though it might be rather strained), and the whole world reality constituted a single cosmos of forms the coherence of which Plato studied in his dialectic and Aristotle in his theory about the order of forms and finality.

With the help of the four principles of being, Aristotle

elaborated his *special metaphysics*: his theories of the soul, the world and God.

Everything which was alive (which was its own mover) had a soul, according to Aristotle (and the Greeks in general). Man, animals and plants all had a soul. As in the movement of the cosmos, the source of the movement of individual living things was a particular form, and hence Aristotle's definition of the soul: 'the first entelechy of an organic substance'. The soul was therefore the principle of life. It is clear that form meant much more here than shape: it was dynamic, it was a force, 'a being capable of action', as Leibniz was to say later. It was not a mechanical, rather an organic, quantum of energy, a wholeness of meaning in which, by virtue of the *logos* of the whole, all parts received being and activity, were attuned to each other and drawn into the finality of the whole. There were different sorts of soul for the different levels of life: the vegetable or nutritive soul, which existed in plants and was responsible for growth, feeding and propagation; the sensitive soul, which added to the possibilities of the vegetable soul sense-perception, desire and the ability to move about: this soul was present in animals; and finally the rational soul, which was peculiar to human beings. Because of his soul, man was a 'rational animal'. As a living being he had the faculties of the vegetative and sensitive souls. The latter included, according to Aristotle, and still in the popular mind today, the five senses of sight, hearing, smell, touch and taste. Their acquired data were taken up into the imagination and so into thought. The sensitive soul also included the 'natural appetites' of the instinct to preserve and propagate life as well as 'natural passions' like ambition, courage, aggression, revenge, revolt, self-respect, self-assertion and thirst for power. The highest and properly human soul was the rational soul, with its intelligence, reason and free will. Intelligence was discursive thought that used concepts, judgements and syllogistic argument. Reason was the contemplation of the highest eternal principles of truth and goodness and was to that extent 'divine'. It could therefore be creative (*intellectus agens*), in other words, although the soul, as a *tabula rasa* was dependent on the data of sense-experience, it

35

could of itself extract timeless truths and values from things in a priori judgements on these 'experiences' because of its spontaneous vision of essences and power of judgement. While inferior souls were transmitted from progenitor to offspring, the rational soul was not, it was superhuman. It did not therefore die with man, it was immortal, not in its individuality but as spirit.

The *world* was the place of change and movement. Democritus had taken a purely mechanistic view of movement as the displacement of atoms. This was not totally foreign to Aristotle's view, although the mechanical-quantitative element was enhanced by an eidetic-qualitative control on the part of forms. Aristotle would have approved of the mathematical, quantitative processes of modern natural science, for example Galileo's laws of gravity, but he would have called them forms. And he would still have accepted the four elements of water, fire, air and earth, in theory to be understood qualitatively. Everything had its 'natural place', as part of its qualitative essence: fire went up, a stone down, in accordance with its 'form'. The ether was the fifth element (*quinta essentia*). It was the stuff of the stars, which were imperishable and subject only to purely local movement. The world was basically divided into two halves, the sublunary world on which men lived and which was changeable, and the 'beyond', the world of the eternal stars. The world was one, however, because everything in motion was moved by the prime mover. It was spherical. At the centre lay the motionless earth, surrounded by fifty-six concentric spheres (spherical layers) spinning on their own axes but dependent on the motion of the outermost layer, the sphere of the fixed star, the so-called first heaven. It in its turn owed its movement directly to the unmoved mover. Ultimately, then, motion was interpreted as a striving of matter for form. Movement, like time, was eternal, according to Aristotle. This followed from the fact that time was 'the measure of motion with respect to before and after'. Origin and decay affected only individual things: species were eternal. They did not come into being like Darwinian species, but were eternal like Platonic ideas. And there had therefore always been men, even though they might have been temporally more or less wiped out in great disasters.

The world was eternal, then, but none the less had a source, the unmoved mover, the Aristotelian *God*. The arguments which led Aristotle to accept his existence have passed into the history of philosophy as the five proofs. In a nutshell they read as follows. Everything which moves is moved by something else. This can happen in two ways. The mover can itself be moved by a third term, that third term by another, and so on; or the mover is not itself moved by anything else. In this case it is the unmoved or prime mover, God. We could not take our series of moved movers back in an infinite regression, because we should find ourselves reversing into non-reality (as one might say): if reality is determined, that is, if it exists and therefore has a last term, it must also have a first term. To explain the existence of reality at all, we have to postulate an *ens a se*, a being that contains no potency to be actuated and is pure reality (*actus purus*): this being must necessarily and eternally exist. Aristotle described God's nature as pure being, spirit and life. 'Life' meant self-initiating movement. The highest form of it was the spirit which thinks and the object of whose thoughts is itself, because it, the perfect spirit, needs nothing outside itself. All being apart from this perfect being needs the *ens a se*; it is *ens ab alio* because it exists by reason of another, it arises from the perfect being and is caused by it. Aristotle could therefore say that God was being, reality, substance; everything else *had* being, participated in it, represented and unfolded it fragmentarily, with the limitations of individual forms. God, however, was the being of beings, the reality of what was real, the form of forms. Plato had said of things which participate in the idea that 'they want to resemble the idea'. Aristotle said that in things matter strove for form. And he said of God that he moved the world as 'the object of the world's desire'. He did not move the world as if it were a piece of clockwork: he was the ideal finality of all formal becoming. As perfect being, then, he preceded the eternal world both logically and ontologically, he controlled its history and so gave it its meaning and its being. 'The heavens and nature depend on such a principle' (*Metaphysics* 1072 b 13).

(c) The Ethicist

If a person desires truth and being, he will also desire the good. By 'good' is meant the good we talk about when we praise and blame, respect and despise, the good often referred to as 'moral goodness'. Aristotle reduced ethics to a few rules, which were typically Greek. Q. When is a person good? A. When he or she acts judiciously. Q. What does that mean? A. It means when he or she does what right reason demands. Q. What is right reason? A. Right reason exists when our behaviour is 'beautiful', and it is beautiful when it observes the correct mean between two extremes. For example, bravery is the correct mean between rashness and cowardice, thrift between prodigality and avarice. To be sure of following the mean, it is desirable to have a sort of synopsis of the various human virtues, something like a table of values. In the *Nichomachaean Ethics* Aristotle set out to do just this by collecting and describing in some detail man's essential moral virtues: wisdom, prudence, valour, justice, self-control, generosity, liberality, magnificence, pride, meekness, truth, courtesy, friendship. Taken together these values embody the ideal man, his best and proper self. They are not derived from it, but are directly presented, in a kind of survey of value and essence, as imperative, beautiful, right and reasonable. They are only a preliminary, however, to a more central discussion of man's true nature. Ontologically speaking, human nature precedes the virtues. It is a moral principle and constitutes the metaphysical basis in which the virtues are rooted. Aristotle thereby gave his answer to the question of the essence of *eudaimonia*. All Greek ethicists started from this idea. And all ethics since then has asked the same question: what is happiness? (*Eudaimonia* is generally translated 'happiness'. A literal translation would be 'right spirit'.) Aristotle answered: not pleasure or enjoyment, not material possessions or reputation and authority in public life, but the perfect manifestation of human nature, which is unquestionably the most characteristic of human activities. What that means exactly is explained in the discussion on the various virtues. Possessions, public esteem, even pleasure are not excluded, but they are not principles, they do not constitute the specific character of moral goodness. That is the function of human nature, right reason, 'right spirit'. If that is present, the rest follows automatically. Here too form is superior to matter. The morally upright person does good not because it brings him pleasure or advantage, but for its own sake. 'It is clear that a person will be happy to the extent that he possesses virtue and insight and acts accordingly. God is proof of this. He is blessed and happy, but not because of any goodness outside himself, only because of himself and the quality of his nature.' Here again, in his *Ethics*, Aristotle arrived at the principle 'on which the heavens and nature depend'. The ideal of the morally perfect person was the wise man. Wisdom existed in God, who as spirit was the thought of thought, and thought of himself because he was perfect. Plato had said: we must be as like God as we can. Aristotle said: we must be wise, God is wisdom. In the *Ethics* too, God was the principle which moved everything as the object of the world's desire.

The perfection of earthly morality should be the *State*. Aristotle knew nothing of the modern opposition between politics and morality. The State, politics and power could all be good. Society was organized goodness on a large scale. With law man was the noblest being, without it the most savage of animals. Whoever first called the State into being created the very greatest values. The State, naturally, supplied the requirements of physical existence, economy and external and internal power for the sake of security, but its proper function was to safeguard the 'good' and 'perfect' life, that is, morally and intellectually cultured noble humanity. The State arose for the sake of life, but continued to exist for the sake of *eudaimonia*, of a moral quality therefore. It was one of Aristotle's principles that we work not for work's sake or for money, but to enable ourselves to enjoy leisure, just as we wage war for the sake of peace. 'The first role therefore falls to beauty, not to bestiality. It is not the wolf or some other wild animal that can endure a good fight, but the refined man. Those, however, who, in the education of their children, put excessive emphasis on bodily fitness and training in warfare, at the expense of necessary activities, are really Philistines.' Aristotle could consequently claim that the State came before the individual. Genetically, in space and time, the individual and the family came first: society and the State were formed from them. But families and individuals did not come together arbitrarily just to legalize with a social pact what they found mutually acceptable, as Thomas Hobbes maintained: they were following a tendency built into man's very nature. 'Man is by nature a social being', wrote Aristotle in the first book of the *Politics*. It followed that man's nature already demanded the existence of the State in its basic principles, and to that extent the State came before the individual and the family, 'given that the whole must necessarily precede the part'. The individual's basic rights and freedom were not safeguarded *in the first place* by the legal agreement of the majority, they existed already as part of human nature; a formal political agreement could at most acknowledge, promulgate and interpret them. Aristotle's individual remarks on the ideals of internal and external politics and the various kinds of State (aristocracy, oligarchy, democracy, tyranny) again testify to his depth of thought, his experience of life and especially his enormous knowledge of the constitutions and laws of the ancient world. At the same time they show that on many points he was a child of his time: he defended slavery as a 'natural' institution, abortion, exposure of children, and so on. He frequently argued against Plato's utopian State, often rightly, sometimes at excessive length. But basically his ethos of right, truth and morality, political and otherwise, was in the best Platonic tradition.

CHAPTER THREE: THE PHILOSOPHY OF HELLENISM AND THE ROMAN EMPIRE

In Hellenic times, people could look back on what was already a rich culture and a great scientific tradition. They could therefore afford to specialize. Philosophy accepted this tendency, and instead of embracing, as at the time of the Pre-Socratics, natural science, medicine, technology and metaphysics, it concentrated on the exclusively philosophical, which was considered to comprise logic, ethics and physics (where physics in actual fact meant metaphysics). One thing, however, it retained of a wider perspective: concern for man's religious welfare. At a time when the ancient mythologies and religions were breaking down, it became philosophy's function to attend to man's salvation – in its own way, of course. When Christianity appeared at the time of the Roman Empire, this function was taken over by the new religion; the schools of philosophy languished and closed their doors – the last one to do so being the great Academy of Athens, in 529, by order of Justinian. A rivalry grew up between philosophy and the Christian religion. In the early part of the patristic period, it is still noticeable; in the Middle Ages, when philosophy was under the aegis of religion, there is no trace of it; it flares up again at the start of modern times.

We must, regrettably, leave aside here minor philosophical schools like the *Peripatetics* (followers of Aristotle), the *Academy* (school of Plato), the *Sceptics* of various shades and the *Neo-Pythagoreans*, and say something on the more important of the philosophical schools, *Stoicism*, *Epicureanism* and *Neo-Platonism*.

1. The Stoa – Realistic Man

The Stoa is named after the location of its school, the 'many-coloured hall' (*stoa poikile*), in Athens. It produced some notable figures: *Zeno* from Citium in Cyprus, who founded the school in about 300 B.C., *Cleanthes* his disciple, and *Chrysippus* from Soloi in Cilicia (d. *c* 208 B.C.), who is often called the second founder of the school. Later names include *Panaetius* (d. 110 B.C.), *Poseidon* (d. 51 B.C.) and *Seneca* (d. 65 A.D.). Boethius called them 'sad old men' because of their strict ideas of virtue and harsh conceptions of duty. They are often accused of haughtiness. Nevertheless the writings of these men will never lose their interest. Too little attention has been paid to the influence that their philosophy, which became a school in its own right and common coin in human thought, exerted on the Middle Ages.

In their *logic*, the Stoics' main interest was in the principles of human knowledge. For them human knowledge was essentially a matter of sense-experience. Man was a *tabula rasa*, and all impressions must come from outside. They were received through the senses and even in concepts and judgements remained sense impressions. The Stoic was therefore a 'sensualist'; man possessed no a priori knowledge which would enable him to understand or judge his sense impressions; he was their prey, he had no choice but to reproduce them in his mind. The reproduction theory, which was predominant in the Middle Ages and accepted as Aristotelian, was in fact Stoic philosophy. Aristotle would not have agreed with it, because his *nous* was creative and superior to sense-perception, in both logic and ethics. To ensure an accurate reproduction, in other words to achieve an adequate image which would reproduce the object as it really was (naïve realism), the Stoic philosopher looked for a criterion of truth. He found it in so-called evidence. Evidence was provided if our sense organs were functioning normally, if the spatial and temporal distance between the subject and the object of perception was not too great, if the act of perception lasted long enough and penetrated far enough, if no obstruction came between the subject and the object, and finally if one's own and other people's repeated observations gave the same data. If these conditions were fulfilled, the resultant images 'seized' the human subject (were 'cataleptic'). One could not refuse one's consent. According to the Stoics, those ideas which occurred automatically, which were almost innate because they belonged to the stock of pre-formed rationality and shared in the world's *logos*, which were therefore called 'pre-conceptions' or 'common notions' (*prolepseis, notiones communes*), gave the same kind of certainty. (This is true despite the fact that the Stoic *tabula rasa* doctrine excluded anything like innate ideas.) It is on these principles that Cicero and the Middle Ages based their highly prized argument from the consensus of public opinion (*consensus omnium*) which was supposed to offer a sure guarantee of truth. Despite its attempts to establish a criterion of truth, Stoicism remained a naïve realism, because none of its precautions against error were really watertight. The logic of the Stoic school, especially its theory on the different kinds of syllogism, is on the whole more significant. It has not come in for serious examination until our own time, particularly from modern formal logic.

In *physics*, or more accurately metaphysics, the Stoics were materialists. Being or reality they identified with the empirical world. Truth was ultimately what could be grasped in sense-perception. This was sensualism (which inevitably goes hand in hand with materialism). Life too was explained on material-istic principles. The Stoics did talk about a separate life-force, which they called *pneuma* (breath), vital heat and fire, but whatever it was it did not rise above the material. All evolution was explained in materialist terms. Here again the Stoics readily talked about something non-empirical, the world *Logos* or cosmic reason, cosmic law and providence, Zeus and his dispensations, and fate (*Leimarmene*), but they had in mind nothing more adventurous than the infinite series of causes co-extensive with matter and its material laws. When they said that thoughts (the so-called *logoi* or seminal reasons) were responsible for natural change, they were referring not to ideas in any Platonic sense but to the laws of cause and effect and their necessity. And when they talked about a prime force or prime fire and called it divine and addressed it as Zeus, they meant no more than matter with its immanent laws. The Whole was experienced, reverenced and praised with religious fervour. But it was itself God. Materialism had been turned into pantheism.

The Stoics' *ethics* are important. As *Marcus Aurelius* wrote in his *Meditations* and *Epictetus* in his *Enchiridion*, the Stoic philo-sophy was the noblest way of life. It was hard. It laid great stress on duty. The emotions must be silenced, indeed ex-tinguished. The goal was 'apathy', unfeeling, with regard to the passions within and fate without. The ideal was 'resignation and submission'. Reason and the duties it dictated must alone be allowed to hold sway. A person who lived according to this ideal was a person of iron will, sacrificing himself in the service of public duty and persevering at his post whatever might befall him. St Ambrose and later King Frederick II of Prussia were inspired by this ethic, but it was above all medieval morality which learnt from it. The medieval theories of natural moral law and eternal law were taken directly from Augustine, but ultimately they derived from the Stoa. It was there that harmony with nature was turned into a principle of morality and raised to the level of an aim in life (*telos, finis*). Ambrose's preferred reading was Cicero's *De officiis* and *De finibus bonorum et malorum*. Long before Aristotle was translated and read in the west, the Stoic theories of right reason, insight, wisdom and natural law were current in medieval thought. The medievals drew their thinking on natural law from the Stoa and then passed it on to present-day ethics and philosophy of law. From the time of the Roman Empire, the Stoic ideal has exercised a beneficial and liberating effect on the human society of all ages.

The ethics of the Stoa were, admittedly, in insoluble conflict with its metaphysics. The former referred to moral imperatives: You ought, and therefore presupposed freedom; the latter excluded all freedom, because everything in life was fated. The Stoic metaphysics effectually debarred ideals. To think and live a moral life, the Stoic had to forget his metaphysics.

2. Epicureanism – An Ancient Philosophy of Life

By Epicureanism, most people mean its doctrine of pleasure. On that point it is at the opposite pole to Stoicism. While the Stoic denied himself, the Epicure indulged himself. His ethical principle was pleasure, in every shape and for its own sake. 'All choice and struggle has as its purpose bodily well-being and peace of soul; that is the aim of a happy life. Whatever we do, let us do it to flee pain and find peace of soul', we read in one of *Epicurus*' (314–270) letters. Others have spoken less elegantly than Epicurus, and their teaching is repellent, but as

Kant rightly pointed out, whether the pleasure looked for is sophisticated or base, the principle itself stays the same. It did not matter to Epicurean theory whether the pleasure was spiritual or bodily: it was pleasure as such that was the source of moral action. And although in this Epicurus was at least consistent, we should have to call it a theory of pleasure rather than an ethics, because if all one had to worry about was how much pleasure this or that could give, there were no moral laws (as Kant pointed out), only subjective and relative differences of taste.

Another thing Epicureanism has made famous is the Democritan *theory of atoms* resurrected by *Lucretius Carus* (96–55 B.C.) in his poem *De rerum natura*. For Lucretius as for Democritus, there was only empty space, atoms and eternal motion. What he added was the idea of chance. By some chance, individual atoms diverged from the straight line of fall, so colliding with others and bringing the world into being. On Democritus' theory, the atoms would have continued to fall in straight lines, and nothing new could have been created. The Epicureans hoped further that their idea of chance would free them from the eternal necessity of the Stoics' fate. The adherents of the theory of pleasure needed freedom, but only in a negative sense: freedom from. However, freedom from does not at all exhaust the concept of freedom, because freedom is a positive thing. But the Epicureans, regrettably, had little concern for deeper philosophical questions. They are to philosophy what comedians are to drama. Nevertheless Lucretius formed a bridge between ancient and modern atomism: Gassendi, one of the founders of modern physics, drew on him.

3. Neo-Platonism – Philosophy and Religion

Neo-Platonism was both a philosophy and a religion. This is not surprising. The Greek mind had always been open to religious thought. Orphism was a mysticism; Empedocles was a philosopher, priest and prophet; Plato wrote on piety and included it in the cardinal virtues; Aristotle wrote on prayer, Theophrastus and Eudemus on God and the worship of God.

The visitor to the Hill of Temples at Agrigento can see that the people were a pious people, even at the peak of their power.

The religious impulse in the philosophical thought of Hellenism received a strong fillip from *Philo of Alexandria* (*c* 30 B.C.–*c* 40 A.D.) at a period sometimes referred to as the 'dress-rehearsal of Neo-Platonism'. Philo was a Jew and drew on the revealed writings of his race. He interpreted them in the spirit of Greek philosophy, although the content of the Scriptures was sufficiently respected to exclude the possibility of falsification. He gave to philosophy basically scriptural ideas which influenced Neo-Platonism, patristic thinking, Arab and Jewish philosophy right up to the Middle Ages, the Renaissance period and well beyond.

The first of these ideas was God. Philo's God was more prominent than the philosophical God of the Greeks. He was absolutely transcendent, wholly other, better than good, more perfect than perfect – and personal. Another idea was creation. Greek philosophy had never taught that the world could be created from nothing. Philo, admittedly, explained his creation in the sense of a creation from eternal matter, as in Greek philosophy, but the word itself had been spoken and was to be repeated again and again. This was to have the greatest consequences. A third idea of Philo's was his doctrine of the Logos. The Logos was the idea of ideas, the force of forces, the highest of the angels, the representative and apostle of God, God's first-born, the second God, the wisdom and reason of God through which the world was created, and the soul of the world vivifying all that was. A breach was thus introduced between God and the world, peopled by intermediaries interposing between the world and the Wholly Other, who could not be grasped by the concepts of earthly time. This supplied a basic platform of Neo-Platonism and of later 'apophatic' or negative theology, which approached God by way of negation and was yet forced to make positive statements. It thus steered a middle course between transcendence and immanence, and reflected the Logos which as thought was pure spirit and had nothing to do with bodiliness, but which as sound and word could appear in the world of the senses and take on flesh.

With *Plotinus* (204–269 A.D.) too, the founder of Neo-Platonism, philosophical reflexion began with a strongly marked separation of God and the world. God was superbeing. No category could include him. Plotinus called him 'the One', in the sense both of the negation of the Many, the negation of concrete reality, and of the first one of all. He could also call him 'the Good'. God's transcendence was even more strongly brought out in later thinking, and philosophers arrived at a complete separation in which the particular mode of disconnexion, originally expressed by the idea of *chorismos*, was lost to view. Plotinus had, however, given this matter some thought: he defined the separation as the result of an emanation of the world from the transcendent God in which the world retained an essential connexion with God who remained immanent to it. This may be considered Neo-Platonism's greatest achievement.

This concept of *emanation* may be further defined as follows. All being flowed from the One, because, as the Most Perfect, this One must overflow. The nature of goodness demanded this. A well-known phrase from a later age was that 'goodness diffuses itself'. Plotinus himself used a number of different images to illustrate what he meant. Being issued from the One, he said, like water from a spring, a tree from its roots, light from the sun, an arc from the centre, the imperfect from the perfect, the copy from the original. The latter two comparisons fitted in best with the rest of Plotinus' thought, because they made it particularly clear how for him the emergence of being was from the top down, from the first, highest and perfect down to being which was, on the basis of this 'from the One' and 'out of the One', other. This being-other did not, of course, prejudice the dependent nature of derived being: the imperfect could be thought of at all only as a consequence of the perfect, just as the copy could not be thought of apart from the original. 'The One cannot be any existent thing, it is prior to all existents'; 'the Many are like the One, but the One is not like the Many'; 'the First must be simple, and it must precede all things . . . not be confused with what stems from it and yet in another way capable of being immanent to other things.' The transcendent was therefore both transcendent and yet immanent: 'in another way'. The entire thrust of Plotinus' philosophy was to understand this notion of being identical and not identical.

In comparison, the famous theory of the three *hypostases* (forms of being): the One, *nous* and soul, was no more than a particular application of the emanation theory. The One was God. The other two hypostases were both extra-divine, even though *nous* was often called divine (in the sense therefore of being like God). The One lost nothing of its substance. It remained always the same. The similes of the spring and the sun were therefore somewhat misleading.

The first creature to emanate from the One was *nous*. It was called the Son of God, was the image of the One, was the gaze with which the One looked at himself and posited himself as another, was a thought – an idea later incorporated into Christian trinitarian theology. The *kosmos noetos* was also *nous*, and therefore the totality of all ideas of which Plato had already spoken. As in Plato, the ideas formed the intellectual framework of the world, and *nous* thereby became the demiurge. It brought the world into being. Then the third hypostasis, soul, broke off from *nous*. Soul was like *nous*, and occupied a place between *nous* and the world, whether it was the world soul or an individual soul. Soul was the first step in the desire for becoming, in the Many, in extended matter, in time, in a word in nature. When the emanation moved further from its origin, self-initiating movement ceased. Self-movement was at its strongest in *nous*, was weaker in soul, and after that there was nothing but dead matter.

Even in the ultimate stages of emanation, the memory of the source remained, making the emanated matter conscious of its estrangement and nostalgic for the One. This turning back (*epistrophe*) to the One was not strictly speaking a return to the One in the same sense as one would speak of going back home after a journey. It was more the reverse side of the emanation, the source's consciousness of being in another, the presence of the identical in the non-identical. So much was true on the ontological level. If it was translated into ethical terms, the epistrophe meant knowledge of man's spiritual and intellectual home, his true being and better ego, knowledge of the perfect which raised him up to itself in *eros* and desire for the good. Plato's *Symposium* had already described this, and many of the Neo-Platonists, together with other thinkers from Porphyry and Augustine to Descartes, had developed the teaching in their theories about the ascent to the intelligible. All of them knew of the divine spark (*scintilla animae*) in man, the remembrance of the One impelling him to look into himself, to go apart from the Many and contemplate the One. This presupposed a process of purification (*via purgativa*) which allowed the divine spark to grow brighter (*via illuminativa*) and led finally to return to the One in union (*via unitiva*). The highest form of union was ecstasy. Plotinus must have experienced it many times.

Neo-Platonism gave rise to a number of *schools*. They are usually divided into: Plotinus' school, with *Porphyry* and others; the Syrian school with *Iamblichus* (d. 330 A.D.); the Pergamon school to which the Emperor *Julian the Apostate* belonged; the Athenian school, where *Proclus* (411–85 A.D.) taught; the Alexandrian school with the great commentators on Plato and Aristotle; and the Neo-Platonism of the Latin west with *Macrobius, Chalcidius, Boethius* and others.

Through Augustine, Boethius, Pseudo-Dionysius and John Scotus Eriugena, Neo-Platonism had a marked influence on the Middle Ages. Particularly notable was Proclus' *Elementatio theologica* and the *Liber de causis* which grew out of it.

PART TWO

THE PHILOSOPHY OF THE MIDDLE AGES

The term 'Middle Ages' is usually taken to refer to the period between the extinction of antiquity in the collapse of the western Roman Empire (476) and either the fall of Constantinople (1453) or the beginning of the Reformation (1517). Medieval philosophy, however, was to a large extent based on the thinking of the Fathers of the Church, and it is therefore useful to look briefly at the more salient features of patristic philosophy before considering the Middle Ages proper.

The Middle Ages were governed by the spirit of the Christian religion. Its whole intellectual effort can be summed up in Augustine's phrase, which through Anselm of Canterbury became the motto of the entire period: 'I believe so that I may understand' (*Credo ut intelligam*). The history of philosophy, therefore, has little to say on the period. It is the voice of faith not reason, of religion not philosophy, that is heard in the Middle Ages. And yet from some points of view this is something of a blanket judgement: it applies in the main, perhaps, but there are significant exceptions. We could compare ancient philosophy to a valuable cargo: the boat might be leaky, the cargo to some extent damaged, but the journey down river continues unaffected. The philosophy of ancient Greece and Rome was brought down the river of medieval intellectual life to the harbour of modern times. There were some medieval thinkers in whose hands the cargo suffered from the waves of religion: Augustine, for example, or Bonaventure or Nicholas of Cusa, although even here we have no difficulty in distinguishing the strictly *philosophical* ingredients in their thought which, as no one who is really familiar with their work will deny, were considerable. Other thinkers were more careful to preserve the cargo intact: Thomas Aquinas, for example. How successful they were must be decided in each case individually: it cannot be asserted in advance. We do not usually state without distinction that a Neo-Kantian or a Marxist philosopher is a priori unqualified to pass objective judgement. The Middle Ages at least made a fundamental decision in favour of intellectual freedom. It was standard teaching that a person must follow his conscience even when it was erroneous: this was already taught by the Fathers. Innocent III made it a rule that a believer who felt he had a clearer knowledge of a matter and therefore decided to disobey a superior's order was free to follow his personal conviction: ' "Whatever does not proceed from faith is sin" (Rm 14 : 23); and a decision that does not proceed from conscience leads to hell. No one may obey the judge against God, he must allow himself to be excommunicated if it should come to that.' This papal decision was incorporated into canon law. Thomas Aquinas and other Scholastics accordingly taught that a person falsely excommunicated must rather die outside the Church than obey a superior whose orders would offend his conscience: 'it would go against personal truth', which he may not abandon merely because of a possible scandal. Despite this theoretical declaration of intellectual freedom, the period did not appeal to the right all that often. It had insufficient understanding of it. But then has any period ever understood it? Here again it is a question of individual cases. It is therefore advisable to make a concrete study. The reader of medieval texts is astonished at the shrewdness, the accuracy, the cogency and the objectivity of their thinking.

CHAPTER ONE: PATRISTIC PHILOSOPHY

1. Early Christianity and ancient philosophy

At first the Fathers of the Church were reluctant to philosophize. They were still too much under the influence of their new-found faith. Paul was quoted: 'I will destroy the wisdom of the wise, and the cleverness of the clever I will thwart . . . Has not God made foolish the wisdom of the world? . . . to those who are called (we preach) Christ the power of God and the wisdom of God' (1 Co 1: 19–24). Paul also said, however, that the pagans had a natural knowledge of God (Rm 1: 19), and he himself in his speech on the Areopagus quoted from Greek philosophy to reinforce his Christian teaching. There were thus points for and against. Tertullian was very much against philosophy, Justin Martyr for it (hence his title 'The Philosopher'). In the end, mainly because of Augustine's influence, it was the acceptance of philosophy that won the day. As Augustine said, Christians spoke not only with the authority of Holy Scripture, but also on the basis of universal human reason (*ratio*) 'for the sake of those who do not believe'. If the philosophers have said something that is true, why should we not accept it? he asked. It can serve only to strengthen the faith and make it better understood.

The Fathers therefore started to read and exploit the philosophical texts, especially the Platonists and Neo-Platonists to whom Augustine owed so much and of whom he said: no one has come so close to us as these philosophers. Other influences came from the Stoics, Cicero, Philo and the Neo-Pythagoreans. Aristotle and the Epicureans were not much quoted. The Apologists were the first to set high store by philosophy: Minucius Felix, Aristides, Athenagoras, Lactantius, and then the three great Cappadocian fathers Gregory of Nazianzus, Gregory of Nyssa and his brother Basil, and finally and especially Origen, Clement of Alexandria and Augustine.

2. The main themes of patristic philosophy

There was a series of crucial problems which occupied the entire period. One of them was the relationship between *belief and reason*. At first it was the distinction, indeed opposition, that attracted attention, but gradually the two concepts were brought together in a tension that was more positive than negative. Belief and knowledge were seen as two ways leading to the same goal. The former, perhaps, was the royal way, but knowledge too was from God and led to God. The two were not exclusive, as is sometimes suggested today. Another crucial problem was the *existence of God*. The Fathers knew from their faith that God existed, but they soon began to reason to his existence 'from nature', with special reference to Rm 1: 19, which mentions a knowledge of God from his works with a spirit which is not yet the spirit of faith. They were also interested in the *nature of God*. Is he material, say light or something similar? Tertullian and Augustine had difficulties here, although it was not long before orthodox doctrine prevailed: God is spirit, he transcends the world, he is one, eternal, absolute, immeasureable, almighty. His work was *creation* and creation from nothing. This latter was a typically Christian concept and was never lost to sight. The Fathers began to inquire into its how and when. A favourite idea was the simultaneous creation of the universe and time. The doctrine of the *Logos* played a major role in creation (and other) theology. The Fathers drew heavily on Philo and the Neo-Platonists and enriched their synthesis with the biblical teaching on the divine Logos and divine wisdom. On *man* and the soul much more was known than ancient philosophy credited itself with. Every person was free. The Fathers proclaimed, as had never been done before: 'no one, by reason of the nature in which God first created man, is a slave of man or of sin', as Augustine put it (*De civitate Dei* 19, 15). The *soul* was a substance, immaterial and immortal. And the body was not a prison as it had been for Orphism and Platonism. The Christian doctrine of creation gave the body a positive role. Only about the soul's origin was there lengthy discussion: did the soul pre-exist, was it transmitted by one's parents, or was it created directly by God? The Christian doctrine of the soul was closely connected with that on *morality*. Nowhere was there so swift a synthesis between Greek philosophy and Christianity, philosophy and religion, as in the field of ethics, where Platonism and Stoicism had laid the foundations for Christian morality. The Fathers also willingly accepted the theory of ideas, of the Logos and of natural law, but immediately added that *right reason* was no other than the divine Logos who became flesh; the Logos was the natural law, not just a creature of flesh and blood; he was the Way, the Truth and the Life; and he showed what true human nature was. With the incarnated image of the revealed Logos before their eyes, the Fathers' ethics gained in concreteness and detail. This was true not least of their teaching on *conscience*, in which they were to some extent anticipated by the ancients from Socrates to Seneca but in these conscience had never been the locus of personal free independent decision to the extent that it was in Christianity. With its teaching on binding conscience, Christian doctrine made man free and 'master of his acts': nobody could henceforth dictate his decisions to him, he must make up his own mind according to the dictates of a higher norm.

3. Augustine – Teacher of the West

Augustine (354–430), in a sense, *is* the patristic period. Everything culminated in him. And he passed everything on to succeeding generations. He is the teacher of the west. His writings are vast and immensely important. From them we may select the most prominent philosophical themes.

(a) Truth

In heated debate Augustine wrested from scepticism the possibility of knowing the truth. The sceptics had said: there is no truth, everything is to be doubted. Augustine countered by saying: 'A man may doubt what he likes, but one thing at least he cannot doubt: his own doubt.' Truth *does* exist on one point at the very least, and scepticism is therefore refuted. Centuries later Descartes was to argue against absolute doubt in a similar way; and we are again reminded of Descartes when Augustine turned to mathematics for the prototype of truth. The statement $7 + 3 = 10$ is a universally valid statement for every rational being. Plato had already used a similar example; Kant was to use it again. It demonstrates where truth is to be looked for: not in the senses or the world of sense-experience, where everything is in a state of flux, but in the mind: 'Do not search without, look into yourself, truth is in man's heart.' In the insight which commands assent to the proposition that $7 + 3 = 10$ Augustine located the so-called 'rules', 'ideas', 'norms' which must be equally true for all rational minds and according to which we absorb, assess and also correct sense impressions. These rules are a priori, and they enable man to be superior, free and independent with regard to the world and its 'experience'. Without rejecting this experience, Augustine considered it no more than a material value of which man disposes as he sees fit and to which he is not a slave. Augustine derived this inner source of truth from an 'illumination'. The word refers to nothing given directly by God, it is not a theological theory: it does no more than register the a priori nature of the human mind. This is not to say that man owes his understanding solely to himself. That is not how Augustine understood human independence. Man is always under the rule of being, goodness and God.

(b) God

With the same emphasis with which he looked for truth within man, Augustine identified truth with God. He reached this conclusion by following an argument sketched out by Plato in his *Symposium*. Just as Plato proceeded from a consideration of individual things of beauty to the beauty in which they all shared, so Augustine argued from individual truths to the one truth on which they were all based. The argument was equivalent, for him, to a proof for the existence of God and a proof of what God is: the totality of truth, the goodness inherent in all good things, the being of beings. God therefore both is everything and transcends everything. No category can be used to define him, as Augustine professed with Plotinus. But we can know *of* him, because the world is his image and likeness. He is the locus of all original forms. The world was created on these ideas and is therefore God's image and likeness (=exemplarism). This reasoning was to exercise an extremely fruitful influence on the mysticism and mystical symbolism of later times.

(c) Creation

Creation is a theological not a philosophical concept. But in Augustine's mind it was fraught with philosophical difficulties.

If creation was an emanation, he argued, God would have to undergo change. The Fathers of the Church readily construed Plotinus in a pantheistic sense. Even if it were supposed that creation was the result of a free act on God's part and not a necessary process, as was often adduced against the emanation theory, when was creation created? Evidently outside time, because time came into being with creation; but then, if there was no temporal succession, creation must evidently have happened all at once (simultaneous creation). In fact Augustine interpreted the biblical account of the six days figuratively, not literally; but if creation took place outside time, then the world was eternal? Certainly not, said Augustine. God's decree was eternal, but not its realization, because, since it and time were coterminous, the realization could not happen in time. Finally Augustine put the question aside altogether. He saw that it was unanswerable in the spatio-temporal categories of thought at our disposal. God's years and days were not our time. Augustine did look for other forms of thought and language, but without success. It was not until he came to reflect specifically on time, which he did frequently, especially in his *Confessions*, that a fresh dimension opened up, leaving the conventional view of things behind and disclosing something almost transcendent, a mode of the subjective attitudes with which man views the world. Perhaps time is a mental self-extension, or, as we might say, a prospective enlargement of man's very mind, reasoned Augustine. Time, therefore, is quite distinct from eternity. Eternal being possesses itself once for all; temporal being is fragmented, it develops, it becomes. The concept of *matter* caused similar difficulties. Because of his sympathy with Platonism, Augustine would have liked to interpret matter as a shadow, but the Christian concept of creation would not tolerate such an understanding. Even though matter was created, for Augustine it remained 'next to nothing'. Only the eternal ideas were fully being. And with the eternal ideas Augustine's reflexion on creation came into its own. The forms controlled the universe 'according to measure, number and weight'. He wrote a whole book on this cosmic harmony – and the medieval view of the world as an ordered whole was born. Matter contained germinating forces, 'logoi', and these logoi led to an evolution which apparently stemmed only from matter, but which in actual fact was purposeful inasmuch as matter itself was created purposefully.

(d) Soul

In Augustine's writings on the soul, his delicate sensibility, his powers of observation and skilful terminology, his penetrating analysis and his many other gifts set him down as an outstanding psychologist. One has only to read the *Confessions* to appreciate this. For him the soul was a particular object of interest. 'God and the soul I desire to know.' The soul had a clear primacy over the body. The spirit of Christianity and its creation doctrine forbade any pessimism in considering the body, and yet for Augustine man really consisted in his soul. This doctrine was to persist right beyond the Middle Ages, even when the Aristotelian formula of soul-body unity was common theory. Man was soul, 'a soul which used a mortal body'. This is still widely held today, even though the terminology may not be quite so explicit. It all goes back to Augustine. He procured for the idea of the soul's substantiality the place it holds today in Christian philosophy. He argued to the substantiality of the soul – again with considerable psychological insight – from the fact that our self-awareness included three things: the reality, independence and permanence of the self. The self was not simply the sum of its acts, but as a real independent and permanent something was itself active. This, in the view of the Augustinian school, amounted to substantiality. Augustine tried to demonstrate the soul's immateriality and immortality in much the same way. His teaching is enshrined in the traditional Christian doctrines of the soul.

(e) The Good

When Augustine used religious language, 'the good' for him meant God's will, but when he inquired into why this should be so he equated goodness with 'eternal law' (*lex aeterna*). By this he meant the eternal ideas in the mind of God which, as in Platonism, were the basis of knowledge, being and goodness. They were an eternal order. Not only was man good, beings were good too and knowledge was true when things were aligned on this eternal order. We can achieve this alignment because the eternal law is imprinted in us. Its direction is the same as the underlying direction of our spirit (the reason for this being that we are made in God's image). The medievals were drawing on this doctrine of Augustine's when they called the 'natural law' (*lex naturalis*) a 'participation of the human mind in the divine light' and saw in it the metaphysical background of human conscience. The eternal law, however, was no longer a merely intellectual entity, as the Platonic world of ideas was. Augustine equated it with God's *will*. This was taken up by some of the late medieval thinkers who opposed Thomas Aquinas by voluntarizing the moral order. Occasionally they went so far that God became more will than reason and wisdom, and even an irrational will, a mystical God of power and anger to whom one could only submit in faith, not reason with on rational grounds. This contributed to the present-day tendency to substitute faith for knowledge. No such antinomy is to be found in Augustine, especially not (and not even) in his concept of the eternal law: that law is as much reason as will; the will is rational, the reason is willed.

Augustine allowed a prominent role to will and sentiment in practical morality as well as in theoretical principles of ethics. As in Plotinus, the soul not only thought, it also willed, loved, yearned with *eros* for the good and felt for it with what almost amounted to an instinct. The entire ethics of the ancients began with the idea of happiness (*eudaimonia*). Many feared that this meant subjectifying the moral good inasmuch as ideas as to what constituted happiness were so diversified. Augustine taught that all error and all striving resulted from a strictly objective concept of happiness, of universal validity, which was innate in man and which left his conscience in peace only when the error and searching were overcome and true happiness attained. The human heart had its 'natural place', the

One, who was both truth and goodness, God, to whom it gravitated. 'You have made us for yourself, and our hearts are restless until they rest in you.' If it was deep enough, man's love would find the right path. The heart too had its logic. These thoughts are part of the strongest and most lasting convictions of this great Church teacher.

(f) The City of God

Social, political and ecclesial life, indeed all world history, was much the same as the life of the individual: they displayed the same sense of search and struggle, the same mixture of truth and error, good and evil. People and peoples were equally creatures of will for Augustine, and both must model their wills on the ideal. 'Set justice aside and what are kingdoms but great robberies?' (*De Civitate Dei* 4, 4). From the point of view of ideal order and the disorder of false desire, human social structures could be divided into the *Civitas Dei* and the *Civitas terrena*. The distinction referred not to the Church on the one hand, earthly States on the other, but to the ideal Society which relied on God's eternal order and which directed all its activities to God, and the 'Society of the Devil', which the world wanted not to 'use' (*uti*) in order to come to God but to 'enjoy' (*frui*) in immoderate desire and disorder. This 'earthly Society' took the world to be its permanent home and indeed ultimately to be its god. World history would always be the battleground for light and darkness, eternity and time, the invisible and the visible, God and Anti-God. In his *De Civitate Dei*, Augustine used the (to him) well-known examples of the Old Testament world, the Greek and Roman empires to show how the powers of good must wage perpetual war against the powers of evil. The book is in effect a large-scale *philosophy of history*. It depicts the triumph of good over evil. The spirit of Christianity and its concept of God demanded such an issue. And so did Platonist philosophy, for which the perfect inevitably carried the day and was the only true and lasting good, and the imperfect lived off the perfect and was no more than a falling-away, a negation or a privation fundamentally without substance, however busy it tried to be and however successful its deception. In the evil man's heart lay the reproaches of the good, and his face was marked by the furrows of sorrow at true happiness lost.

4. Boethius – the Last Roman

In order of importance for the Middle Ages, Augustine is immediately followed by Boethius (480–524). He is significant particularly for his services as a teacher, in that a whole series of ancient philosophical concepts were passed on to the Middle Ages by his writings. Of Platonic philosophy, he passed on the theories of God, happiness, participation, a priori universals and the essential thoughts of the *Timaeus* on the constitution of the world. From the Stoa he took the concept of nature, the theory of natural law, the idea of a series of causes, the concepts of fate and providence, and especially the concept of reality: reality as the material external world. Of particular importance to Scholasticism, however, is the fact that Boethius translated and commented on Aristotle's main logical writings. He introduced Aristotle to the Middle Ages, even though it was only as a logician. Boethius' writings on logic, arithmetic and music were universally in use as handbooks of instruction in the so-called Seven Liberal Arts.

Apart from this rather technical apparatus, Boethius also bequeathed to the Middle Ages a number of important philosophical ideas which not only were milestones in themselves but contributed to significant advances in thought. To mention a few: *God* was the 'highest good including all good in itself, a good than which nothing greater can be thought'. In this Boethius spanned the arch from Plato through Augustine to Anselm and Descartes. *Man* was an *individuum*, that is, something which was independent, unique and self-determining. The concrete individual substance was contrasted with the universal idea and with society. Boethius therefore defined the person as 'an individual rational substance'. Despite the interest in universals, the Middle Ages appreciated the rights of the individual and never abandoned them. Boethius also talked about *freedom*. Despite a uniform cosmic order, man was free. Only creatures below man were constrained by the general order. Man experienced it as a moral imperative and to that extent binding, but even then he remained free. Freedom then was not just something negative, it had a positive side: the greater the level of spirituality, the greater the freedom. This is to say that the more a person raised himself above the non-spiritual, the material, nature, concupiscence, the more he fed on the One, truth, goodness and the greater, consequently, his freedom. And in that he would find happiness. Boethius' chief work was his *Consolation of Philosophy*, which he wrote in circumstances of extreme suffering, in prison and under sentence of death. Boethius found the courage to say that goodness was stronger and more satisfying than evil; its rule was true power and happiness. Evil was weak, despite its physical strength, and brought unhappiness; its unruliness enfeebled man and robbed him of peace. This for Boethius justified God in the face of universal pain and evil – the *De consolatione* is a miniature theodicy – and held out hope for man's salvation. Evil was overcome in the strength of the idealism which, Platonists and Stoics held, gave the world a new face that bore traces of the true essence of being from which it originated.

5. Pseudo-Dionysius – the End of the Patristic Era

The writings of Pseudo-Dionysius (early sixth century) mark a complete and powerful resurgence of patristic Platonism. In the language of Proclus, God was the Super-one, the Super-good, the Superperfect, the Superbeing. His otherness was taken to the extreme in the spirit of negative (apophatic) theology, not in order to separate God totally from the world, but to reveal true perfect proper being as the source from which finite imperfect being arose and to which it was constantly referred. Being was divided up on a hierarchical scale according to nearness to or distance from the Super-one: at the bottom was dead matter, which just 'was'; then life; then the soul; and finally the realm of the spirit. The further one moved up the scale, the more perfect became the being which lay at the heart of all things but was superior to all things, the 'nobler' and 'more powerful' it became, just as for Plato the idea of good-in-itself surpassed everything else 'in worth and power', was 'beyond' all essences but still was present in everything and so made being, existence and knowledge possible. The Good was infinite being which 'was' *per se*, while everything else shared in it and so was not being but 'had' being. Pseudo-Dionysius belonged to the great Platonists who wanted to reveal to men's eyes, beyond the variety of beings, being itself and its hidden depths.

The Middle Ages had the highest regard for Pseudo-Dionysius' writings and read them keenly. Medieval metaphysics, which owed so much to the tradition of which Pseudo-Dionysius was an outstanding representative, cannot be understood without a knowledge of Pseudo-Dionysius' doctrine. To view Thomas Aquinas, for example, from the sole view-point of Aristotle's influence, as the phrase Thomist-Aristotelian philosophy suggests, is to overlook an essential part of Thomas' outlook.

Pseudo-Dionysius stands at the end of the patristic period. Many other names come after him: *Cassiodorus*, *Isidore of Seville*, the *Venerable Bede*, *John Damascene*, etc. They were all avidly read by the medieval Schools, and so bridge the gap between antiquity and the Fathers on the one hand, the men and Schools of a new age hungry for learning on the other.

CHAPTER TWO: SCHOLASTIC PHILOSOPHY

General Remarks on Scholasticism

Scholasticism, the period between say Charlemagne and the Renaissance, is aptly called the Age of Schools. Learning was highly prized. A *magister* stood higher then than an industrial baron today, a manuscript was more precious than the car of a modern man's dreams. It was a time of knowledge in which the spirit not of technology but of metaphysics was predominant. Man was more important than machinery and money.

The Schools were originally attached to cathedrals and monasteries, but then grew into independent universities. The monastic schools, primarily intended for the novices, occasionally had pupils from outside, particularly from the nobility, and conversely courtly poetry enshrined ancient and Christian values. The medieval Schools based their curricula on the so-called Seven Liberal Arts: the Trivium (Grammar, Dialectic, Rhetoric) and the Quadrivium (Arithmetic, Geometry, Music, Astronomy). The structure was fairly loose: ethics, for example, could be included under rhetoric. In effect the scheme was based on Plato's four cardinal virtues which had been taken over from Apuleius, Macrobius, Cicero and Augustine. The teaching method in the medieval Schools consisted in the *lectio* and the *disputatio*, which today we should call the lecture and the seminar. From these certain literary forms developed: the *Summa*, the Commentary and the *Quaestio disputata*. The method of inquiry was geared to the idea of 'authorities': the Bible, official Church pronouncements and the works of thinkers, philosophers and theologians, for example, Augustine, Averroes, Aristotle. Since, however, the authorities were often mutually contradictory, there had also to be a process of reasoning. Scholarship therefore tended to be strictly rational and expressly logical, and drew extensively on the syllogism. Discussion and dialectic were immensely popular.

I. EARLY SCHOLASTICISM

1. The Beginnings

The beginnings of Scholasticism are to be found in the schools of Charlemagne. There was *Alcuin* at the court school of Aachen, *Rhabanus Maurus* at Fulda, *Paschasius Radbertus* abbot of Old Corbie on the Somme; and there was *John Scotus Eriugena*. The latter analysed being into its various modes, levels and species. He made a 'division of nature' that crops up again, metamorphosed, in Spinoza. First of all there was God, 'the uncreated all-creating nature', as the foundation of all that was. His self-contemplation issued from eternity in the ideas, those primitive and original bases of existing things, so-called 'created and creating nature'. Then, through them, came our spatio-temporal material world, 'created and uncreating nature'. Here again all that was, turned back, in its innermost essence and in all its becoming, to its source: it returned to its fulfilment, 'uncreated and uncreating nature', eternal rest in God the Lord. Some commentators have called Eriugena a forerunner of Hegel, but this is perhaps an exaggeration. He aptly illustrates, rather, the Platonic art of analysing being and going beyond appearances to pure being, pure will and pure goodness.

Of less importance in this period were the *dialecticians* and *antidialecticians*. Only one of the latter deserves particular mention here, *Peter Damian*, less because he was especially famous than because it was he who coined that celebrated phrase: philosophy is the 'handmaid of theology'.

2. Anselm of Canterbury – Father of Scholasticism

Anselm of Canterbury (1033–1109) is called the Father of Scholasticism because he launched the scholastic watchword *fides quaerens intellectum*. Faith, he said, must look for understanding, it must inquire into the deposit of faith from a rational, logical point of view. This does not, of course, mean that he resolved the faith into elements of pure reason, as Kant for example was to do. No, he was proposing no more, in effect, than Augustine himself had proposed centuries before. Augustine from the first spoke of a synthesis of belief and knowledge. Neither faith nor reason, if they are to remain human activities, can do without the other. They are two different ways to one and the same goal.

Anselm is even more famous for his so-called *ontological proof* for the existence of God, expounded in his *Proslogion*. It is often said that, as Kant and Descartes asserted, the ontological proof argues – impermissibly – to the existence of God from the concept of God. The latter tells us that God is the most perfect being. Now real existence must be an attribute of the most perfect being. One may therefore logically conclude, Anselm is imagined as saying, from the concept to the existence of God. This reasoning, however, continue Anselm's opponents, contains a vital flaw in that one may not pass from the logical sphere (concept of God) to the ontological sphere (existence of God) without further qualification. Every single idea we have poses the question of whether what we think really exists. This, however, is to misunderstand Anselm's argument. By essence or idea of God he meant more than a mere concept. God for him was the All of reality, the totality of being, being itself in which everything shared. Anselm did not need, therefore, to argue to a reality from a concept: his idea of God itself included the reality. Anselm was wholly committed to the spirit of Augustine and the Platonic viewpoint: all truths contained the one truth, and that in its turn contained being and God, because every imperfect being presupposed perfect being as its source and lifeline. Thinkers of a Platonist turn of thought, including Leibniz and Hegel, have usually accepted the ontological argument, while others, like Thomas Aquinas and Kant, profess their inability to understand it.

3. Peter Abelard – Medieval Subjectivity

Peter Abelard (1079–1142) stands out from the usual run of stolid Schoolmen both for the extravagance of his life and for two rather unusual theories: a nominalistic-type theory of knowledge and subjectivist ethics.

On the question of the nature of human knowledge, Abelard was faced with two alternatives. *Ultrarealism*, on the one hand, saw in universal concepts (the house, humanity) a universal reality which existed as such independently of individual concrete things (houses, men) and maintained that this universal reality already constituted the totality of concrete things so that the individual thing added nothing to it. *Nominalism*, on the other hand, regarded the universal idea as unreal and only the concrete individual thing as real. Applied to the Trinity, for example, this theory meant that only the persons were real, their common essence, divinity, was no more than a name. This seemed dangerous not only for theology but also for metaphysics. Abelard flirted with nominalism. We can trace in him a first doubt about what the old tradition had recognized as reality, as the 'inner nature of things', as Boethius had called it, the one truth giving substance to all truth, as Anselm had said. Abelard taught that the universals were only logical realities, that they gave no certain knowledge and that it was a matter of taste what was regarded as essential and what as unessential.

The same is true of his *ethics*. Up to then certain realities, norms, truths and values had been generally recognized. For the Schoolmen, the natural moral law was, to use Kantian terminology, a law binding on every rational intelligence. For Abelard, on the other hand, it was only an opinion. Everything boiled down to subjective intention. The actual deed, good or bad, was indifferent. Sin had no substance, he used to say, (mis)interpreting a phrase of Augustine's. (What Augustine had meant was that sin has no true being, it is a privation, a falling away. Abelard, however, was talking about personal conviction, which is certainly essential to moral activity but cannot accomplish everything.) Because the Middle Ages were in the main objectivist, Abelard found himself the subject of stern opposition. But it is a sign of the basic intellectual freedom of the times that his authority as a *magister* was high and he could count important figures among his pupils, including popes-to-be Alexander III and Celestine II and the author of that universal theological textbook of Scholastic times, Peter Lombard.

4. The School of Chartres – Medieval Humanism

Chartres is renowned not only for its cathedral but also for its School. The height of the latter's fame coincided with the building of the former – the twelfth century. And by then we are unmistakeably on the threshold of High Scholasticism. New ideas poured out, the literature of antiquity was the object of assiduous study, the so-called new logic, that is the up to then unknown logical writings of Aristotle (both *Analytics*, the *Topics* and the *Sophistical Fallacies*), was turned to account for the first time, Aristotle's physical writings were known too, seemingly, and the medical works of Hippocrates and Galen as well as Jewish and Arabic writings on natural science were keenly read. The School was concerned above all with natural science, while its basic philosophical orientation was Platonistic. *Bernard of Chartres*, who headed the School at its period of greatest success, was referred to by *John of Salisbury*, himself a member of the School, as 'the leading Platonist of our century'. Bernard's brother, *Thierry of Chartres*, belonged to that long line of philosophers, from Plato to Nicholas of Cusa, who tried to derive all being from the One in the same way that numbers are derived from one. Other famous members of the School were *Clarembald of Arras*, *Gilbert of Poitiers*, *William of Conches* and Bishop *Otto of Freising*.

5. Mysticism

Mysticism is part of Scholasticism. It is, in a way, its culmination. The technical, scholastic side is taken for granted without being especially cultivated, and the purpose of all Scholasticism is revealed in all its splendour: the spiritual life at its purest, even when it sometimes reaches the limits of the possible, for example in Joachim of Flora. The most famous name is that of the Cistercian *Bernard of Clairvaux*, Abelard's doughty opponent and an enthusiastic preacher of the crusades. With many others he was a living proof that ancient philosophy had not swamped the spirit of Christianity and robbed it of its essentials. Just as the Fathers had said that man's true nature became visible in the divine incarnate Logos, so Bernard added that true philosophy is the love of the crucified Christ. This was not just mysticism and theology: Bernard analysed the world and man in the light of the highest religious reality, demonstrated the continued existence even in man's crooked soul of his 'immortal greatness' which depended on the One and infinite Perfection, which yearned for God and longed to lose itself like a drop in the ocean, and showed that humility is great and pride small, that dialectic is often no more than talk and the truth can be plain and simple. This was all the purest philosophy of being and value, and assures the mystic Bernard a place among philosophers too.

Much the same may be said of *Hugo of St Victor* and *Richard of St Victor*, the greatest members of the Augustinian Canons' monastery outside the walls of Paris. To the former (or Conrad of Hirsau?) we owe that fine work on the virtues *The Fruits of the Flesh and the Spirit*; the latter was among those who taught the doctrine of the sparks of the soul. To the south, down in Calabria, lived *Joachim of Flora*. He proposed one of the many philosophies of history which, captivated by the idea of progress, imagined that time was shortly to enter a new Garden of Paradise. After the initial period of slavery and a middle period between flesh and the spirit comes the fullness of the times, the time of freedom and the spirit, the eternal Gospel in which all men find God, a visible Church is superfluous and everyone lives by justice in freedom and love. The single-minded abbot of San Giovanni was a utopian and an idealist who suffered from the excesses of his disciples. It was only after his time that 'Joachimism' came into real disfavour.

II. HIGH SCHOLASTICISM

With the twelfth century the Middle Ages came into something of an intellectual boom. There was a renewal to which three circumstances in particular contributed: the translation of Aristotle's philosophical works, the rapid growth of university studies and the increasing academic activity of the great religious orders. These three things made their influence felt universally in this period.

Aristotle, the Universities and the Orders

The (re)introduction of Aristotle to western thought was spread over several stages. Boethius had already been familiar with Aristotle, even though his acquaintance was limited to two works, the *Categories* and the *De interpretatione*. Aristotle's other logical works were introduced to Scholasticism as the

68

'new logic' by the School of Chartres. And then another channel altogether was exploited: Arab-Jewish philosophy. The *Arabs* had accepted and digested Aristotle's works very early on. Aristotle became known to the Middle Ages in translations from the Arabic. The two most significant Arab philosophers were *Avicenna* (d. 1037) and *Averroes* (d. 1198), and they became two of the outstanding medieval 'authorities'. The latter wrote commentaries on nearly all Aristotle's works. Since his commentaries were published with the editions of Aristotle, he came to be known simply as 'The Commentator'. Long before him, however, Avicenna had helped to spread Aristotelian ideas, but in the form of a Neo-Platonized Aristotelianism – this, as we know today, was not entirely false, inasmuch as Aristotle never in fact lost his Platonic inheritance. Two other Arabic works which went under Aristotle's name helped to encourage the Neo-Platonic interpretation of Aristotle: the *Liber de causis* (in fact a reworking of Proclus' Neo-Platonic *Elementatio*) and the so-called *Theology of Aristotle* (a compilation of Plotinus' *Enneads*).

Aristotle also became known to the medievals via *Jewish* philosophy. Here again the interpretation was Neo-Platonic, since the Jews were strongly influenced by the Arabs. The two most important Jewish philosophers were *Avicebron* (d. 1070) and *Maimonides* (d. 1204). The latter had a particularly marked influence on Thomas Aquinas' creation doctrine.

The third and academically the most valuable introduction of the Middle Ages to Aristotle, at least in a complete form, came later. It was through *direct translations from the Greek*, which seem to have begun in Sicily. *Henricus Aristippus* of Catania is the first recorded translator of Aristotle from the Greek. Others followed, of whom the most important was *William of Moerbeke*, who worked particularly for St Thomas. The entire translation of the Greek Aristotle was completed in the thirteenth century. To understand medieval Aristotelianism, it is always necessary to take Aristotle's original text as a basis. This condition has been observed for a long time. It is, however, equally necessary, and this does not happen quite so often, to include the Neo-Platonic influences which yielded in the face of the increasing popularity of medieval Aristotelian-ism. And because the Middle Ages had a penchant for combination, the historian must also try to assess the impact of *Plato's own works*. These included extracts from the *Republic* and the *Laws* in translation from the Arabic, the *Meno*, the *Phaedo*, the *Timaeus* and the *Parmenides* in direct translations from the Greek.

There were a certain number of *condemnations of Aristotle* (1210, 1215, 1263). Novelty is not welcome to conservative minds. They were, however, only passing skirmishes. In the end Aristotle won through: a knowledge of his entire works was required for the licentiate in faculties of letters.

The second great boost to High Scholasticism was the founding of the *universities* by popes and kings. At first there were only isolated faculties, of medicine at Salerno, for example, or of jurisprudence at Bologna. Gradually, however, in other great cities, the various faculties – of theology, jurisprudence, medicine, philosophy and 'the arts' (the Seven Liberal Arts) – were gathered into one *Universitas magistrorum et scholiarum*. Paris and Oxford were the oldest. Then came Orleans (1200), Cambridge (1209), Padua (1222), Naples (1224), Salamanca (1220), Toulouse (1229), Prague (1347), Vienna (1365), Heidelberg (1368), Cologne (1388) and Erfurt (1389).

Among the religious *orders*, of special significance for medieval learning were the Dominicans and the Franciscans. They had chairs in secular universities as well as in their own establishments. The Dominicans came down more and more on the side of emerging Aristotelianism, while the Franciscans went more for the older Augustinian-Platonic tradition.

1. Paris in the early thirteenth century – Theology and the Liberal Arts

As early as the twelfth century Paris was 'the city of philosophers', but to an outsider it was more the theologians that mattered. Famous names made the city a place in which *Peter Lombard* (d. 1160), who wrote that celebrated manual of theology the *Sentences*, could feel at home. In the thirteenth century *William of Auxerre* (d. 1231), *Philip the Chancellor* (d. 1236) and *William of Auvergne* (d. 1249) all taught there. Although they concentrated on theology they also wrote on a wide range of typically philosophical subjects: free will, natural law, goodness, the virtues, the soul, the cosmos, the first principle of being, and so on. These men are important particularly for having introduced into the Schools much of Arabic and Jewish philosophy. It was through William of Auvergne, for example, that the real distinction between essence and existence, which was to be the object of heated discussion later on, became current in Scholastic thought. At the same time he rejected outright other tenets of Arabic Neo-Platonism: the eternity of the world, the unity of the intellect, necessary emanation. In challenging the latter he insisted on God's transcendence. Things did not relate to God like water to its source: that would imply similarity. No, between God and the world there was only an analogical relationship. This was a clear affirmation of a principle to be heard time and again in Scholasticism. Aristotle's example had been the relation between health and healthy.

All in all, however, perhaps Paris, the city of philosophers, was even more important for later developments because of the *Masters of Logic* who were then active: *William of Shyreswood* (d. *circa* 1267), *Petrus Hispanus* (d. 1277), who wrote the most studied manual of logic ever published, and *Lambert of Auxerre*. They were called simply 'Masters of Arts' because they belonged to a faculty which taught the Seven Liberal Arts. They gradually drew away from the main university as, with the arrival of the complete Aristotle, the theologians found themselves unable to do the philosophical work simply because the material had become too extensive. This was the beginning of our present-day philosophy faculties.

2. The School of Oxford – Mathematics and Natural Science

Paris and Oxford together mark the beginning of High Scholasticism. At Oxford the old Platonic-Augustinian tradition

71

was still very much alive. This is important if we are not to succumb to the all too common fallacy that the entire High Scholastic period was little more than a slavish imitation of Aristotle. Oxford knew Aristotle. In fact the founder of the School was one of the great translators of his work. But it remained critical. This is why the Oxford thinkers turned rather to the Arabs for natural science, cultivated the patrimony of Chartres, practised mathematics and physics for which there was less interest at Paris. As has always been the case in British philosophy, they were empirically minded, although the background to their thought was Platonic. Idealism did not, for them, mean opposition to the study of experience: it meant merely that experience was used and controlled in a particular way.

The founder of the School was *Robert Grosseteste* (d. 1253), who was as famous for his 'metaphysics of light' as for his attempts to describe and measure natural phenomena in terms of mathematics instead of talking always about inner essences. Another important name in the School was *Roger Bacon* (d. 1292) who also combined idealism with experimental science and who had a number of things in common with his later namesake Francis Bacon. He wanted freedom from authority, called for scientific experimentation and warned against false idols which obscured truth. His pungent language did him much disservice.

3. The older Franciscan School – Augustinism

Conventional Augustinian tradition, most at home in Platonism and Neo-Platonism, also predominated in the Franciscan School. In fact the School was its mainstay. Certain of its tenets marked it off quite distinctly from all other Schools, particularly Thomism. They were: the primacy of will over intellect, the eternal basis of human knowledge in the mind of God, the concept of illumination, the concept of seminal forces in matter, the multiplicity of forms, the impossibility of creation from eternity, the concept of spiritual matter, a more or less total independence of the substantial soul from the

72

body, indirect knowledge of the soul in its essence and especially the concept of a Christian philosophy based not only on natural knowledge but also on certain revealed doctrines.

Prominent in the School as it emerged were, among others, *Alexander of Hales* (d. 1245) and *John of la Rochelle* (d. 1245). The greatest of them all was Bonaventure, the leading light of High Scholasticism next to Thomas Aquinas.

Bonaventure (1221–74) was properly a theologian, even a mystic, and the representative of a typically 'Christian philosophy', but he was also the most striking proof that exact philosophical work is still possible to a theologian. Our treatment of Bonaventure need be no more than brief here, because, as he himself said, he based himself consciously on tradition, and we have already given a sufficient account of Platonic Augustinism. A few main points stand out.

The nerve-centre of Bonaventure's philosophy, as it was for Augustine, was the *thought of God*. Where Thomas Aquinas said that being was the first object of knowledge, Bonaventure said that God was. We meet him in our souls. Augustine had already taught that truth reveals God, truth that is unchangeable, eternal and absolute, because God is the truth which gives truth to true things. The same applies to the moral life. We find God in goodness; he is the foundation of goodness, the good in good things, as again Augustine taught. And because, if we are not blind to it, value is visibly present, God is also present. If we accept that it is God's nature to be being, life, light and power and to encounter us as truth, then we must accept that our ideas pre-exist in God's mind. Bonaventure was much clearer and more emphatic on this than St Thomas. He also saw beneath the traditional words, that an idea is not merely logical but also dynamic active creative, and to that extent more being than other beings. Bonaventure reproached Aristotle for criticizing Plato on this. His arguments, he said, were worthless. Aristotle may have been the man of knowledge, but Plato was the man of wisdom. This is a very shrewd comment; and it also tells us something about Bonaventure. He too had that special faculty of seeing beyond the parts to the whole, the essential matter, the being behind the appearances, the force behind the effect. His philosophy of being therefore began with the perfect being, and proceeded to explain imperfect being from that. It also evaluated imperfect being by denying it a first place in the scale of values to which man owed allegiance; beings could never be an ultimate principle of goodness; they pointed beyond themselves; no number of them amounted to perfect being, adding them all up did not lead to God. Perfect being was directly grasped as the primary datum of human knowledge. 'It is amazing how people cannot see the first thing on which their intelligence alights and without which they could not know anything at all.' This was characteristic, because in fact all the great metaphysical thinkers have begun to philosophize with the perfect being as the primary datum. This enables us to understand what Bonaventure said about the *world*. The world could not be eternal. The concept of an eternal creation was a contradiction in terms. Everything was composed of essence and existence, matter and form. Even the soul had 'matter', potency: this was the significance of the concept of spiritual matter. There was no so-called prime matter in the sense of a complete lack of determination, because all matter already included seminal forces, the *logoi* of ancient philosophy. In beings, and especially in living beings, there were always several constitutive forms, even though one form coordinated them all – a point of view which better squares with the results of modern biological research than the usual Thomist doctrine of the unity of form. Bonaventure's forms were comparable to the ideas in the mind of God. The world for him was an appearance or symbol, an ocean of images pointing back to the eternal patterns (exemplarism). Human life was therefore a *journey to God*, if only man had the eyes to see and the ability to pierce beyond beings and values to their true divine core. There were *stages* in this vision of the truth-content of the symbols, and with this idea Bonaventure made a remarkable contribution to the doctrine of ideas: he introduced an antinomy by maintaining, on the one hand, the vision of the ideas, and by saying, on the other, that there was no end to the dialectical process and one should never presume to have

74

grasped truth. Bonaventure explained: there was a content of knowledge which was only 'shadows'; a content which already contained 'traces' (*vestigia*); and finally a content which was 'images'. These images were copies and therefore represented, inadequately, the divine originals. Since there was this difference, Bonaventure was not an ontologist. The difference was one of *analogy*. Scholasticism was extremely loquacious but not very lucid on the subject of analogy. Even the great St Thomas was ambiguous. Bonaventure, however, clearly grasped the essential point: analogy was analogy of likeness, of participation, or it was nothing. The shadow, the trace and the image were the various levels of this participation. In the light of this understanding of analogy, Bonaventure's *epistemology* becomes clearer. As he himself said: 'Things have a threefold being: in the knowing mind, in their own reality and in the eternal Mind. Our soul, then, to know things with certainty, does not need the truth of things in the soul or their truth in their own reality, because in both cases it is changeable, but rather it needs to reach out in some way to their truth as it exists in the divine knowledge.' The similarity to Augustine is evident: we need the eternal foundation of God's mind. This, for Bonaventure, was proven. But when he said 'in some way', we can see something of the strictly philosophical criticism with which he approached even that famous thinker.

Bonaventure had a *school: Matthew of Aquasparta, Roger Marston, John Peckham, Peter John Olivi* and others.

4. Albert the Great – the Universal Doctor

With Albert (1193–1280) the Dominican order, which contributed an enormous amount to the spiritual life of the Middle Ages, came to the fore. And with it the great renewal of the Middle Ages achieved its greatest breakthrough: Aristotelianism. Now medieval Aristotelianism was an independent system, or at least, shall we say, not identical, even in St Thomas, with the historical Aristotle. On every point there were differences. We have already mentioned the gradual infiltration of Aristotelianism and the partial flight of Neo-Platonism. But to sum up Thomas Aquinas or even Eckhart as Aristotelians pure and simple is to misconceive the matter grossly. Nevertheless the name does point to an overall if highly complex movement. And in that movement Albert was a decisive figure. His aim was 'to make the whole of Aristotle's philosophy intelligible to the Latins', and in this he was successful. The Scholastics were introduced to Aristotle's physics, metaphysics, psychology, ethics and politics as well as his logic. Arab, Jewish and especially Neo-Platonic ideas gave additional colour. Albert himself was the best example of it, just as he was the best example of critical Aristotelianism in the Middle Ages. His version was Neo-Platonic. The synthesis was the result of a conscious effort. 'You must know', he once said, 'that to be complete philosophy requires a knowledge of both Aristotle and Plato.' Albert is rightly called the Universal Doctor. He had an encyclopaedic grasp of things. Shortly after his death an anonymous chronicler penned the following tribute: 'At this time flourished Bishop Albert, a Dominican, the most distinguished theologian and the most learned of all *magistri*, compared with whom, after Solomon, there has been no greater in the whole of philosophy . . . but because he was of German nationality, he had many enemies, and his name was disparaged even while his works were used.' The encyclopaedist was by no means a bookworm. He was an outstanding student of natural science, a collector of natural science specimens and also a researcher in zoology and botany. One of his editors has written: 'If the development of the natural sciences had followed the path laid down by Albert, a detour of three centuries would have been avoided.'

Albert's *school* included *Hugo Ripelin of Strasbourg*, *Ulrich of Strasbourg*, *Dietrich of Freiberg* and *Berthold of Moosburg*. It became a home of mysticism. *Eckhart* and *Nicholas of Cusa* were influenced by it.

5. Thomas Aquinas – Christian Aristotelianism

St Thomas (1224–74) was the greatest figure of Scholasticism. He synthesized into an impressive and coherent system everything that had so far contributed to High Scholasticism. Although his teaching was not uniform in all respects – he was too much of a medieval to avoid eclecticism – the fact that his output was so varied raises him above the average Schoolmen and gives his work a richness and an influence it might not otherwise have possessed. His large output has been the profitable subject of research and analysis ever since, and has prompted a great deal of critical philosophical thought.

(a) Knowledge

Unlike Augustine and Bonaventure, Thomas did not begin his philosophy of the meaning and origin of human knowledge by positing eternal ideas in the mind of God. He claimed that the first object of human knowledge (in this life) was the essence of material things. Where Augustine had said that man must look for truth within himself, St Thomas said that he would find it outside himself. Sense-knowledge was correspondingly more highly valued in Aquinas than in Augustine. If we have bodies, argued Thomas, they cannot be totally without effect on our knowledge, and their role begins with sense-experience. The next stages in the argument are usually described as follows. According to Aquinas, sense-perception supplied us with images from the external world, called phantasms, without which (and this was maintained by Aristotle too) the soul could not think and from which the *intellectus agens* extracted the universal essence by a process of 'illumination'. This was how we came to possess immaterial and universal concepts. In this account, however, the essential point is omitted, in that the real question is *what* was abstracted: the average of the sense images or something more? If the former, there could be no such thing as universal concepts, because the content of sense-perception was always limited and could not justify a universally valid judgement: one may not argue from the particular to the general (runs an ancient maxim of logic). If on the other hand more than that – a genuine universal – was abstracted, the sense impressions could be only material not formal causes. In the *Summa theologice*

(Pars I, q.84, a.6), Thomas expressly stated that sense-experience was not the 'total and perfect cause of intellectual cognition' and that therefore intellectual knowledge was wider than the sense-derived phantasm. This means that abstraction for Thomas was not the same as abstraction for the moderns. If it were, Thomas would be a sensualist. In other words, the Thomist *intellectus agens* was essentially an a priori power. It was the same for Kant, although his form of expression was different: knowledge begins in the senses and is completed in the understanding. The latter, for Kant, was 'a priori' and 'spontaneous'; for Thomas there was an 'active intellect' which also (correctly understood) implied spontaneity; and if the word *agens* is translated as 'creative', then the idea of an a priori action emerges. But we do not need to use Kant (or anyone else) to interpret Thomas Aquinas, nor do we need to 'develop' Aquinas' theories. Our first duty is to take him as he stands, warts and all. Age and validity are not incompatible: philosophy is not like a dress-shop where only the very latest is worth stocking. This does not mean that it is impossible to clarify Aquinas' ideas by translating them into modern terms.

(b) Being

Thomas' theory of being was closely modelled on Aristotle's. As we noted earlier, Aristotle expressly applied himself to the consideration of being *qua* being, and Thomas, with the same intention, used the same four principles. But with Thomas the Aristotelian philosophy of being was subordinated to other considerations which stamp the whole with lasting originality and metamorphose Aristotle considerably. Of these the prime one was the typically Christian concept of 'created being', and it betrays the theologian. Aquinas the philosopher used it too, and in his hands it approximated to a transcendental (to use a Kantian term). To clarify it he used the concept of emanation: creation was the exit of being from the universal cause. He therefore differed from Avicenna who postulated an automatic necessary production. Thomas wanted to include God's free activity, but because, according to a Scholastic axiom, act always proceeds from and expresses a determinate being, and because, according to Thomas, the proper primordial essence of things 'pre-existed' in God and existed only 'improperly' in space and time, Aquinas' philosophy of being included the typically Platonic concept of *participation*. There is no need to lose sleep over the debate on the ideas as 'separated forms', which rests on a historical mistake. Participation is there, however, and gives a Platonic stamp to the whole of Thomas' theory of being. The reader has only to consult the *Summa* I, 44, 1: Platonism could hardly be more expertly expressed. Apart from the technical terms, particularly noticeable is the hierarchical structuring of being from the top downwards, from the perfect to the less perfect. Derived from this idea of participation, there follows another feature of Thomas' theory of being: the *concept of analogy* (as it is usually called). Being is predicated analogically. The best example of this is the predication of our concepts of God. We predicate things of God and man neither univocally nor equivocally, but analogically. Aquinas used the familiar example of health and healthy to illustrate his meaning. A medicine, a food and a complexion can all be described as 'healthy', the first because it restores health, the second because it conserves health, and the third because it indicates health. In each of these cases the word 'healthy' is used in a different sense, but there is something common to them all, namely the predication of the concept 'healthy' to indicate some reference to health. Ultimately the concept of health is derived from this common factor. To name one thing after another is, however, the Platonic formula for ideas (everything is named after the ideas and shares in them). Consequently the idea of participation is the origin of analogy. This emerges particularly clearly in what Aquinas called the analogy of similarity or proportion. The reader may consult, for example, the *Summa* I, 4, 3, ad 3. In tradition, however, as far back as Aristotle, there was another type of analogy: of proportionality. It included four terms: for example, two is to four as four is to eight, or the eye is to the body as understanding is to the soul. Such statements, however,

79

either are expressions of identity or are reduced to analogy of similarity. Analogy of proportionality is like a traffic accident in the history of ideas where the Thomists (among others) see nothing amiss. Thomas Aquinas himself used it, but it breaks the uniformity of his teaching. The last element in his philosophy of being was the *scale of value*, which fitted in with the basic Platonizing acceptance of a descent of being from God, as we have already described it. Aquinas found the doctrine in the Neo-Platonists too, especially the *Liber de causis*. Being was 'superior' or 'inferior'. 'This is immediately apparent from a consideration of the things of nature. The differences between things are graded: above lifeless bodies we find plants, above them irrational living things, and finally, above them again, rational creatures. Everywhere there is a scale depending on whether things are more or less perfect.' What was the standard by which the stages of this scale could be measured? The standard was the idea, or more specifically the greater or lesser distance from the idea of the ideas, namely from the One, as in Plotinus. Finally in Aquinas' philosophy of being, a fundamental role was played by the so-called *transcendentals* or determinations present in every being. They were 'one', 'true', 'good', 'thing' and 'something'. They were commonly debated in the Schools. Even more fundamental, however, because more characteristic of Aquinas' basic philosophical position, were the concepts we mentioned earlier: created being, participation, analogy and scale of value.

In comparison, the four principles of being developed with reference to Aristotle – matter, form, efficient cause, final cause – were of secondary importance. On these Thomas, at least in his terminology, was such a faithful Aristotelian that one hardly needs do more than consult Aristotle's treatment. St Thomas added nothing to Aristotle here. He accepted *hylemorphism*. Things are composed of matter and form. Matter individuates form. The resulting thing (first substance) is the 'real' thing and exemplifies the word 'being' in its basic meaning. Nevertheless Thomas also held that the universal form or essence (second substance) was not just a name or a thought or a concept, but an eternal idea in God's mind. Thomas too

80

held with the ideas, and with him too they formed the framework of things and of the world, only they were not 'separated forms' as the Platonists thought. We have already mentioned that he was perpetuating a historical error, although this does not effect the essential here. Efficient causality was interpreted as in Aristotle, and again it became a whole philosophy, the philosophy of *act and potency*, with, again, a parallel to the philosophy of matter and form. Through Avicenna, however, Thomas' act-potency doctrine was reinforced by the dual concept of *essence and existence*. Essence is a possibility (potentiality), a merely logical form. To exist it needs to be actuated by something already in existence. This is true of all created beings. *God*'s essence, of course, *is* his existence. Because he is pure act, God's essence is to be. In created things there is always a real distinction between essence and existence. As Thomas said in the *De ente et essentia* (and elsewhere), every created essence can be thought of apart from its actual concrete existence. 'I can think about the "essence" man or phoenix without knowing whether they actually exist.' And the distinction between essence and existence is universal in created being, even in the case of pure spirits (angels). Only God is exempt from this limitation.

(c) God

One of the best known passages in the *Summa* is the 'Five Ways' or five proofs for the existence of God (I, 2, 3). Because the word 'proof' too easily conjures up the type of demonstration familiar to mathematics, and that is quite foreign to Thomas' thinking here, 'Way' is probably a less misleading description of what he offers in the opening section of his *Summa*. The Five Ways are lines of argument designed to convince us that a thorough investigation into the nature of being can lead to only one conclusion: at the bottom of it all, there is one uncaused necessary and perfect being, 'whom everyone calls God'. The first Way starts from the fact of motion. Thomas followed it through in the same way as Aristotle (*Physics* VII and VIII). The second starts from efficient causality: every created cause is itself caused, and since one cannot argue back to infinity, there must come a stage when one reaches an uncaused cause – 'whom everyone calls God'. Like the second, the third Way is a variation of the first. It starts from the notion of contingency: created things need not exist; there is no necessary reason why they should exist. They are, in a word, *possible*, because they could or could not exist. And what could possibly not be cannot always have existed. If the world consisted entirely of contingent 'possible' things, nothing would ever have come into being in the first place. There must therefore be, somewhere along the line, a being who necessarily exists. The fourth Way is derived from the idea that there is a scale of perfection in creatures. It is typically Platonist (cf. *Symposium* 210e–211d). The imperfect, argues Thomas (following Augustine and Anselm), necessarily presupposes the perfect inasmuch as every finite grade of truth or goodness or heat or being implies an infinite idea on which it depends. The fifth and last Way is teleological in character: the universe gives evidence of purpose and intention, and it therefore demands 'an intelligence which directs natural things to their end'. Aquinas makes no use of Anselm's ontological argument.

The answer to the question of God's *essence* follows from these Five Ways. For Aquinas the philosopher, God was necessary being, pure act, the unmoved mover, perfect in every way.

(d) Soul

As a philosopher and Christian theologian, Thomas was particularly interested in the nature of the human soul. The essential statements of his psychology can be found in the *Summa* (I, 75–90; I–II, 22–48). They do not, as might be expected, propose a primarily rational, but rather an empirical, psychology: they offer a wealth of concrete observations on the psychology of sense-experience and volition, and their treatment of man's affective life is so broad in scope that not only the psychologist but also the pedagogue, the moralist and the aestheticist could learn from them.

Aquinas' *metaphysics* of the soul follows expected patterns. It is a Thomist axiom that *actus sequitur esse*: to every being there is an appropriate form of activity. Vegetative things have a vegetative soul, animals an animal soul, and man, whose activity is rational, has a rational soul. This rational soul is also responsible for man's vegetable and animal functions (growth, nutrition, reproduction, sensation, etc.). Although, according to Thomas, man is *one*, and therefore exists only as a compositum of soul and body together, the soul (the 'form' of the body) is a spiritual substance capable of living apart from the body (after death).

Man's spiritual soul is immaterial and immortal. But this does not mean, as for Plato, that it is imprisoned in the body and fighting to be released. In Thomist psychology, the body is the soul's presence to itself, to the world and to other people; bodiliness is an essential part of its proper functioning; it 'situates' the soul so that the person can develop in contact with other people. Thomas was much stricter than Aristotle in considering the unity of man: the matter (body) and form (soul) really constituted an indivisible entity reflected in a person's own awareness of being one.

(e) Morality

In ethics as in psychology, Aquinas' greatest achievement lies in his contribution to an understanding of man's concrete life. In the case of ethics, it lies in his analysis of the virtues, developed in the second part of the *Summa*. There he outlined the ideal of man's moral life with a rare sensitivity and insight. We can still learn much from him today on the phenomenology of value. His treatment coordinated Plato's cardinal virtues, Aristotle's ethical and dianoetic virtues, the Stoics' theory of duty, and the biblical and patristic teachings on Christian morality. The result is not, strangely enough, an exercise in academic abstraction, but a mini-handbook of realistic moral instruction.

Morality is based on human nature. Just as there are theoretical principles in logic, so there are theoretical principles in morals, and they are derived from the nature of man as a rational creature ordained to his Creator. Moral rules or norms are therefore binding on all rational beings. 'Right reason' consists in following them through, and conscience is an (intellectual) judgement on the success or failure of this programme. Moral norms are also known to everyone and cannot be totally stifled. They are to be followed because, as expressions of the 'natural law', they lay down what is right for human nature. In other words, they embody the eternal law as applied to human society, and in consequence they bring the happiness (both temporal and eternal) which follows from a correct functioning of that society. The *prime* motive of moral conduct, however, is obedience to the law because it is a law. In the spirit of Aristotle, Thomas derived the moral good from man's nature and so from being, which is to say that he derived it from God's will. But that is a later ontological interpretation. Logically prior to God's will and of decisive moral significance for man are the dictates of man's own practical reason.

(*f*) *Law and the State*

Man is concupiscent and tends to act arbitrarily. He therefore needs discipline, said Aquinas. This discipline is provided by the family and the State. The fear of punishment is designed to bring man to his senses so that he will then proceed to act in accordance with right reason. Although Thomas therefore saw law and force as in some way related, he did not identify the two. Law was of wider connotation: it expressed the ideal ordering of society; that was its purpose. It derived from an ideal social order, from the natural moral law, and ultimately from the eternal law. Natural right and natural law were two constitutive principles of Thomas' philosophy of law. Humanly enacted laws which contradicted the natural law were not binding. St Thomas attempted an outline of what, in his view, belonged to the individual's inalienable natural rights, but he could find no satisfactory formula. He had to be content with stressing that only the supreme and most general principles of natural law were absolutely certain. Of these again the first and most basic one was that good is to be done and evil avoided. The less universal the principle, the more time-conditioned and the more complex its application. The ultimate standard was one's own conscience, which binds the individual to what he or she thinks is right.

For Thomas as for Aristotle, the State fosters the moral good. It is there to enable its members to lead a happy and worthwhile life. Because it derives from man's nature, it cannot be manipulated at will: it cannot be used to impose obligations which deny man's basic rights. These rights are not determined by the State; the State exists to ensure that they are respected. Although political structures change from age to age and people to people, the State must never lose sight of this primordial duty. Man and the State are both historical and so subject to historical change, but their ultimate principle lies outside and above time in the realm of eternal law.

6. The Arts Faculties and the Averroists – the other Aristotle

A reaction set in against Thomist Aristotelianism: novelty, as always, aroused the opposition of the conservative-minded. Things reached such a pitch that in 1277 some propositions taken from Thomas' works and from the works of Latin Averroism were condemned by the archbishop of Paris. But the condemnation seems to have been sparked off by the new-fangled phraseology typical of some of Thomas' writings, while Thomas himself was very much more conservative than his vocabulary would lead some people to suspect. There was, in fact, no need to take up arms against Aquinas. Such was not the case, however, with the Masters of Art who dealt with Aristotle ex professo. In their faculties, the spirits conjured up by the enthusiastic mentors were soon out of hand. Aristotle's texts were adopted as they stood, but seen through Averroist spectacles: the Philosopher was inseparable from his Commentator. The Aristotelianism taught in the faculties of arts no longer served to encourage theological reflexion: it was pursued for its own sake. In *Siger of Brabant* (1235–84), for example, old

Aristotelianisms re-emerged: the world was eternal and pre-existed God's creative activity; divine providence was limited or even denied; essence and existence were not really distinct; there was only one rational soul common to all men; the individual was not therefore immortal; etc. The 'heterodox Aristotelianism' condemned by Tempier (archbishop of Paris) and Kilwardby (archbishop of Canterbury), which included some propositions of Thomas Aquinas as well as many of Siger, was not the Aristotelianism of Thomas. The condemnation did little to check the course of 'Latin Averroism' (as it was also called), for the latter flourished for several centuries. This is another proof of the tolerance of the Middle Ages.

7. The later Franciscan School – a Breakthrough

The founder and most important member of the later Franciscan school was *John Duns Scotus* (1266–1308). He was one of the leading lights of Scholasticism and did much to advance the theological and philosophical knowledge of his time. His ideas were more striking, his distinctions more exact, his proofs more cogent and his insight keener than anybody else's. The student of Aquinas would do well to make constant comparisons with Scotus. Scotus deserves his honorific title, *Doctor subtilis*. His criticisms were for the sake of truth. Scotus was familiar with Aristotle, but approached him with more reserve and circumspection than the run-of-the-mill Schoolmen, comparing him the whole time with traditional teaching – and Thomas – and acting to some extent as a bridge between Aristotelianism and Augustinism.

Scotus introduced a number of new ideas into Scholasticism. An example of this is his theory of the relationship between faith and knowledge. He allowed much less of a role to philosophy in our knowledge of God than Thomas had. He did not deny the use of knowledge altogether, but strictly limited it. Faith, correspondingly, was given greater prominence. Natural reason could not have a proper concept of God's essence. One could, of course, refer to God as highest being and infinite and so on, but these concepts remained 'confused'. Only faith and theology could discover what God was really like. It followed that the concept of 'natural law' was narrower than in Aquinas. While Aquinas had interpreted the Ten Commandments as directives of natural law, Scotus accepted only the first three as the dictates of reason. For the others to be included, said Scotus, a completely different world order would be needed. Augustine had said that the eternal law was God's reason and will: Thomas emphasized the reason, Scotus the will. As opposed to Thomas' so-called intellectualism, Scotus gave the primacy to will. He evaluated the human person much more in terms of volition than of intellection. In man's relation to God, love was more important than faith. In God himself the divine will was accorded more importance than the divine mind. Scotus did not reject the doctrine of divine ideas, but the ideas, he said, were 'conceived', even though from eternity. There were parallels in other writers to a lot of what Scotus was saying, but Scotus' contribution as a whole was unique. In his works we find the first glimmerings of the modern idea that will – whether the subject of it is God, man or the State – is power. Another favourite theme of Scotus' is also very much in favour today: the overriding importance of the individual. His theory of *haecceitas*, 'thisness', which he used to explain individuality, his theory of the univocity of being and his shrewd criticisms of the proofs for God's existence have all been much discussed.

8. Meister Eckhart – Mystic and Schoolman

In High Scholasticism too, spirituality of mind was accompanied by spirituality of the heart. This is seen particularly in its mysticism. Now mysticism was not a separate department of Scholasticism, a sort of annex frequented by the few. It was part and parcel of the whole movement. If the *Summas* on the whole show little evidence of being written by mystics or people interested in mysticism, it is only because they were designed uniquely as textbooks in the Schools. In actual reality heart and head went very much hand in hand (to mix the metaphor).

Scholasticism and mysticism overlapped, and Eckhart (1260–1327) is the best example. To understand Scholasticism properly, some knowledge of Eckhart is essential, just as no study of Eckhart is complete without a knowledge of Scholasticism. One has only to look at the apparatus of the first critical edition of Eckhart's works (promoted by the German Research Society) to appreciate how much of a Scholastic he was. The usual Scholastic sources re-appear: Aristotle, Avicenna, Averroes, Algazel, Maimonides, the Fathers especially Augustine, the *Liber de causis* and the Neo-Platonists, especially Pseudo-Dionysius. Eckhart also drew on the Scholastics and mystics prior to himself, especially Albert and Thomas. Eckhart was firmly in the Scholastic tradition. What a hasty reading of Eckhart might dismiss as pantheism and nordic self-consciousness, or what literary aestheticism might seize on as material for admiration and imitation is to some extent evidenced in certain formulas, perhaps bolder and more striking than others, but the impression is superficial. The solid background to Eckhart's thinking was the Scholastic doctrine of the Trinity and grace and the Logos speculation from the Fathers to Philo.

(a) The Ontologist

Eckhart the mystic was an ontologist, and this is important for a proper appreciation of his place in history. The way to his heart's desire, to union with the One, was through being, through 'true being'. Eckhart's ontology was that of Neo-Platonism. We must 'go apart', he taught, from the here and now, the this and that, the Many with their alluring irridescence which succeeds only in concealing the essential. We must penetrate beyond the appearance and look for truth and eternal being. As Avicenna said, everything is looking for being. That is why everything, even the physical world, is the object of the philosopher's investigation. The being of things has its yardstick in eternity, not in time. The mind, whose object is being, abstracts from the here and now and so from time. That is the path of wisdom. It is the path to a superior world, where nothing is taken up from below; rather, what is above reaches down and gives the visible concrete spatio-temporal world its true meaning. Man's physical make-up, even if he had his head at the north pole and his feet on the south pole, is of no relevance to his proper essence. The substance of humanity is guaranteed by an eternal essence, it needs no physical component. The same is true of everything else. That things are what they are because of their essence – 'everything white is white because of whiteness' – is a saying common to other Scholastics; but none said so with such conviction as Eckhart. With something near terror, he saw being in the varied and multitudinous world of beings, he recognized it as transcendent and other, and yet understood that it infused things as their true essence. Anyone who had spiritual and not just bodily eyes, he thought, could not fail to see things as he did; to be spiritual one had to have this vision of the truth of things. Eckhart was profoundly moved by it; his sermons were on fire with it. And he was constantly in quest of new words and images, not just to excite mystical sensations – even if that were possible – but to rouse people and lead them to true being. Eckhart was an ontologist like Plotinus. Like no other medieval Neo-Platonist he grasped the significance of Plato's philosophy. It was his constant endeavour to lead people out of the cave and confront them with the challenge of true philosophy. And from all accounts he experienced what Plato foretold would be the happy lot of anyone who tried to teach men to transcend the world of the senses.

(b) The Theologian

When Eckhart talked about being, he was really talking about God. And because being was analogical, embracing both the Many and the One, his relationship to God was analogical. On the one hand he could say that God was not being; on the other that being was God. His thesis that God was not being must be complemented with the phrase from his *Quaestiones Parisienses* that God was intellect and understanding. People in his own time were rather shocked, and people today scent medieval idealism. Both reactions are surprising. Aristotle and Thomas had defined God as understanding. They had defined God as being. So did Eckhart. What he refused to predicate of God was the being appropriate to created things. He did attribute pure being to God: 'When I said that God is no being and above being, I did not deny him being, rather I ascribed superbeing to him' (an idea familiar to the west since Pseudo-Dionysius). To specify this superbeing, he called God intellect and understanding. In this he was not simply substituting idealism for the old metaphysics: he accepted the old metaphysics, but concentrated on the ultimate ground of the being it proposed: ideas. And because, since Augustine's time, the ideas were thought to be in God's mind, God was intellect and understanding and being: being at its deepest. Eckhart's two statements were therefore not contradictory but complementary. It is surprising that this has ever been overlooked. An unresolved obscurity *does* appear when Eckhart interpreted the ideas in God's mind as the Son who is the Word with which the Father expresses himself, 'himself and all things'. In Eckhart's theology the Son cannot be created, but the ideas were said to be created. Eckhart was struggling with the same problem that had exercised the minds of the School of Chartres: how can the ideas in God's mind be eternal unless the world also is eternal; could God create the world in the same act with which he generated the Son? Late Scholasticism was to be very much preoccupied with this question.

(c) *The Teacher*

All his abstract and subtle talk about God and being and intellect should not lead us into supposing that Eckhart was a theological boffin. He set out to teach people how to live. He addressed the man in the street in countless sermons and provided sound spiritual guidance to a great many people. The everyday wisdom of which he was capable is shown in his famous teaching: 'It is better by far to hand food to a hungry man than to indulge the while in inner contemplation. And if a person were in ecstasy like St Paul and knew of a sick man

90

in need of help, I should think it a much better thing for him to leave the ecstasy and minister to the needy in a spirit of even greater love.' This type of Christianity in action occurs to Eckhart only because of his philosophy of being and God. In that philosophy he asks for a practical expression of 'God's birth in man'. God is born in us – so says an old Scholastic maxim which Eckhart made his own – when by grace we are born to a new better true and divine being and become the temples of the Holy Spirit. Behind that, Eckhart discerned another divine birth: when we are born again through God's grace, he said, God engenders his Son in us in his own likeness. 'Everything God the Father can do he engenders in the Son so that the Son can engender it in the soul . . . So the soul becomes a dwelling-place of the eternal Godhead.' Eckhart proceeded, with as much boldness as logic: 'I am a cause of the fact that God is God. If I did not exist, God would not be.' The reader will appreciate the possibility of a pantheistic misunderstanding here. Eckhart, however, was speculating on the nature of God. In God, he said, are our originals, our better egos. We are ideas in God's mind. Without those ideas the ego cannot become God. Such speculation is not idle theory. Because our ego is raised up into God, we are more than flesh and blood, more than space and time, and it is our duty to find our true being. Instead of divine birth, one could equally talk of the birth of being in man. Eckhart will be understood by the person who has experienced that birth. The being which is born is true being. It is born through our better ego. It is personal being, and the better ego achieves self-understanding in the light of true being. Even when he was talking theologically and ethically, Eckhart remained first and foremost an ontologist.

III. LATE SCHOLASTICISM

Late Scholasticism (fourteenth to fifteenth centuries) is often viewed as a time of decline and fall. Such a judgement, in my view, is oversimplified. The reputation of the Middle Ages suffered in the battles of the Reformation, at the time of the

Enlightenment and from overglorification by the Romantics. The truth can be established only on the basis of impartial historical inquiry. And that, it seems to me, is now bringing to light the many commendable achievements of late Scholasticism in philosophy, mysticism and natural science. As representative of the period, we shall say something on two men who had particular influence on succeeding generations: Ockham and Nicholas of Cusa.

1. Ockham and Ockhamism – from Metaphysics to Nominalism

The new *zeitgeist* that is just discernible in Scotus is fully visible in William of Ockham (1300–49). In his teaching on knowledge, understanding and reason, he suggested a very different role for sense experience from anybody else before him. The Thomist plea in favour of perceptual reality was not a serious realism: sense-acquired knowledge had still to be 'treated' by the spontaneous independent activity of the *intellectus agens*. The senses were no more than material causes of knowledge; the intellect with its powers of creation was significantly wider and drew on other, deeper areas. In Ockham, however, the senses became efficient causes. One needed do no more, he said, than view the external world through the senses and then reflect on the data they provided. We could almost imagine it were Hume here with his ideas of sensation and reflexion. Ockham, though, did not go quite so far as Hume: he was still convinced of the value of metaphysics. Truth grasped an in-itself, it was more than simply unravelling sense-derived phantasms. The categories of substance and quality referred to a transcendent something. Ockham, therefore, cannot be called a Nominalist without further qualification, although it would not be too wide of the mark to call him the initiator of a Nominalist trend. He rejected universals in things entirely; in human thought they were only signs, conventions, fictions. He dispensed with 'inner natures' altogether, because their only guarantee was the spontaneity of the human mind somehow working parallel with things. All knowledge was derived from sense-experience, and even though the categories of substance and quality were more than mere ideas, they were only gropings; the other categories were purely subjective. Ockham thereby prepared the way for modern subjectivism. His teaching influenced Gabriel Biel, Gregory of Rimini and Francis Suarez, and later Leibniz, who reduced even time and space to subjective entities, and Kant, for whom the categories were no more than subjective principles of cohesion.

In *Ockham's School* nominalism proper became the favoured philosophy. There was a conscious opposition to the *antiqui*, whom they called 'realists' because they maintained the real existence of universals in things. They called themselves *moderni* or Nominalists, because the universal, for them, was only a name, a concept, confined to the intellectual plane. The most important of the Nominalists were *Nicholas of Autrecourt, Peter of Ailly, Marsilius of Inghen* (the first rector of Heidelberg University) and *Gabriel Biel* (a professor at Tübingen). These men took Ockham to his logical conclusion. The categories of substance and quality were reduced to the ranks of subjective concepts, the notion of causality was rejected, the principle of contradiction was dismissed as mere convention. Nominalism had arrived. The root defect in the entire polemic of the Nominalists was that they had a mistaken idea of what was meant by a 'universal': they took it to be an individual reality. And of course a universal individual thing would be a nonsense. But universals, as they had been elaborated by the *antiqui*, reached beyond individual things. Philosophers had seen – or thought they had seen – that there were modes of being other than those meant when we say, there are apples, potatoes, etc. The Nominalists of early and late Scholasticism did not understand the Platonists' analysis of modality; but then neither had Aristotle (perhaps because he had not wanted to). Even many of those who talk about Nominalism today are not very clear on this.

However negatively the Nominalists' metaphysics must be judged, their physics and their achievements in the *natural sciences* are another matter. They broke with the Aristotelian notion of movement and tried other ideas: impetus, latitudes of form, mathematical measurements etc. They were still a long way from the modern natural sciences, of course, but none the less they laid the foundations. Significant names here are *John Buridan*, *Albert of Saxony* (the first rector of Vienna University) and *Nicholas of Oresme*.

2. Nicholas of Cusa – from the Middle Ages to modern times

The new *zeitgeist* we mentioned in connexion with Scotus and Ockham is also clearly visible in Nicholas of Cusa (1401–64). He had a high regard for natural science, mathematics and especially astronomy. At Bernkastel-Kues on the Moselle, the visitor can still see the instruments he used for his physical and astronomical studies, and his large library, in which all the great names of western culture are represented. Nicholas conceded much to the Nominalists. His assessment of the role of human understanding relied on the Nominalist theories of being as a world where only thought as concept or word could establish relationships and unities. But what particularly interested him was the human intellect. Nicholas was a philosopher of mind. He appreciated the advances in knowledge, but also had a profound respect for tradition. He understood the Middle Ages better than they understood themselves. He had a great gift for combining the insights of the ancients with the insights of the moderns, completing the old with the new, correcting and controlling the new with the old. Nicholas of Cusa is rightly regarded as the founder of German philosophy. His vision was of harmony achieved by the reconciliation of opposites, of union which did not destroy the parts that made it up. German philosophy too has pursued the unity of the Many in the human mind and tried to interpret the world of things as an unfolding of the One. The Cardinal's library at Cusa, which has been preserved with such affection and skill, stands today as one of the most venerable monuments of German culture.

The key to Nicholas' philosophy was the idea of *mind*. He expounded it in an imaginary conversation between a layman and a philosopher in a Roman barber's shop during a market in the Forum. The two could see the trades people counting, measuring, weighing. How do they do it, they asked themselves. Obviously by making divisions. And they do that by counting 'one' this or that number of times. Numbers, then, were made up of one. One itself was simple and could not be understood in terms of many. Nicholas was allegorizing: the mathematical unit represented the oneness of being. Being was the principle of things, things were composed of being, existed because of being. The Many were to be understood in terms of the One.

The concept of *One* was taken from Parmenides, Plato, Augustine, the School of Chartres, Eckhart. It was shared by Hegel and Schelling. It expressed the 'totality of being' (*omnitudo realitatis*). Human reasoning separated things, it created opposites. The intellect, however, which Nicholas distinguished from reasoning, went beyond the 'oppositions' established by human reason and integrated them into a comprehensive 'intuition' or 'apprehension' of the One. Differences disappeared in infinity. To use a mathematical illustration, as Nicholas did, the circumference of a circle protracted to infinite length is no longer distinguishable from a straight line, because the curve is so small as to be indistinguishable from nothing. Or again, if one side of a triangle is protracted to infinity, the others will coincide with it.

On Nicholas' theory, knowledge was asymptotic. That is to say, one could never fully know things. There was always something left to be known, and he expressed this by calling science 'conjecture'. This quality of human knowing is particularly evident when we come to consider *God*. We do have a concept of God – and yet we do not. We are for ever on the way to knowing him although we already possess him. The content of our statements about God is taken from space and time; it is therefore limited and incapable of reaching the infinite. But although God is in that sense unnameable (as negative theology had always taught), in another sense he is 'omninominable' (to use Nicholas' word). In the title of his most famous work, Nicholas called our knowledge of God 'learned ignorance' (*Docta ignorantia*). We can say that God is the *complicatio* of the world (he contains all things) and that the world is the *explicatio* of God (it reveals God). But there is still a difference between the One of reason and the Divine: reason has never finished reaching forward beyond its knowledge to the 'original' God. In some sense Nicholas subscribed to Protagoras' famous dictum (to which reference has already been made) that man is the measure of all things. This was to be the inspiration of the Renaissance. But then for him man was the measure of all things only because man was the image of the divine original. Only God was the measure in any actual and decisive sense.

Everything important that Nicholas had to say was included in his teaching on intellect. The intellect was man's theoretical and practical yardstick, and it was ultimately ordained to God. Nicholas was, one might possibly say, the purest expression of the Middle Ages. He developed its metaphysics in the spirit of Platonic and Neo-Platonic idealism, which was also the idealism of the Fathers. He was aware of the idealism of reason, but associated it with something greater: beyond the One of 'I think', he saw the eternal One, God.

PART THREE

THE PHILOSOPHY OF MODERN TIMES

Compared with ancient and medieval philosophy, modern philosophy is much untidier and less stereotyped. The historian almost despairs of bringing it to heel. On the other hand, a very close inspection discovers that there *are* certain themes which, while changing in formulation and treatment, remain substantially unaltered. For the most part they are the crucial and traditional themes of metaphysics: the One and the Many, being and appearance, God and the world, nature and the soul, freedom and immortality. Modern philosophy is only relatively new. The scientific philosopher will not go by the latest theories just because they are the most recent he can find: they too will be superseded in time. This is one of the most useful insights which the history of philosophy gives. What we have to rely on is our own thought, critical, scientific, open, ready to correct itself if correction is seen to be necessary. No school at whatever period need be without this basic openness.

CHAPTER ONE: THE RENAISSANCE

The Renaissance was a time of breakthrough. Everything was changing. People tried a bit of this, then a bit of that, rebelled then subsided, praised clarity of reason but confided in the mysteries of nature and the power of fate, put man on a pedestal but could not forget Christ on the Cross.

It all started, as the name suggests, with the rebirth of antiquity. The reunion of east and west at the council of Ferrara-Florence (1438), however shortlived, and the influx of scholarly emigrants from Byzantium (captured in 1453) into Italy provided the external stimulus. Internally, the medieval outlook had already made an effort to go back to the sources. In 1440 a new *Platonic Academy* was erected in the Florence of the Medici, and it could boast world-famous names: Gemistos Plethon (its founder), Cardinal Bessarion, Ficino, Pico della Mirandola. Platonists were heard again; Aristotelians, Stoics and Epicureans flourished. Humanism unearthed everything ancient. It called up not only the books but the very spirit, heathen though it might be, of antiquity. Heaven was brought down to earth, and man became a 'God on earth'. Where Dante had described a metaphysical 'other-worldly' order of things, the Renaissance seized on man as he was, with his tears and his laughter, his gravity and his humour. Everything about man was grist to the artistic and philosophical mill, just because it was 'human'. This was quite a departure from medieval practice. The Renaissance appealed to Nicholas of Cusa, who had said both that man was the measure of all things and that God was the ultimate primordial measure.

Different, although also typically Renaissance, was the fondness for *mysteries* and sciosophies, alchemy, magic, cabbalism, theosophy and occultism. *Paracelsus* (1493–1541), physician, alchemist and mystic, propounded a philosophy more like a secret esoteric lore than a genuine philosophy; he trafficked with the spirits of the elements and conjured them up like some wild Faust. *Reuchlin, Agrippa von Nettesheim* and *Trithemius* were really occultists; *Franck, Schwenckfeld, Weigel* and *Jakob Böhme* (1575–1624) are often dismissed as dreamers and pansophists; yet they all had no little influence in their own time and on succeeding generations. Paracelsus, who was a considerable physician, stressed the importance of experience and a field knowledge of nature, and instead of getting bogged down in details appreciated the significance of the whole, whether it was the human body or nature, man or the world. In many ways he was the forerunner of Leibniz. The others influenced the Reformers in their philosophy of religion. Böhme philosophized in a cobbler's shop, but his reflexions on personal experience, on evil and on God's relation to the world were taken up by Baader, Schelling and Scheler.

The Renaissance is particularly the age which witnessed the birth of *modern natural science*. The foundations were laid by some of the Italian natural philosophers, particularly *Giordano*

Bruno (1548–1600), although he was more of a visionary than a strict scientific experimenter. The real achievements were the work of men like *Copernicus* (d. 1543), *Kepler* (d. 1630), *Galileo* (d. 1642) and *Gassendi* (d. 1655), followed later by *Boyle* and *Newton*. Their method can be described as the inductive-empirical, quantitative-mechanistic observation of nature. Gassendi resurrected atomism, Newton canonized mechanism. The philosophers and scientists began to observe natural phenomena, recording and analysing their findings, extracting the essential factors and reducing them to a single mathematical formula which they regarded as universally valid. In other words, they set out to establish the laws of nature. The elements of the phenomena were all quantified, their basic features expressible in mathematical terms, and their functioning automatic-mechanistic. The success of this method was considerable. Modern technology derives from it. It first justified *Francis Bacon*'s (1561–1626) remark that 'knowledge is power' – as we know today, power to be both good and evil. Natural science must constantly draw on philosophy (particularly metaphysics and ethics) if it is to control the powers it has summoned.

The idea of power fascinated the people of the Renaissance, not only in physics but also in the new idea of *man and the State* as it emerged. *Machiavelli* (1469–1527) is the obvious illustration. His philosophy of man, of law and of the State was a quantitative-mechanistic observation of nature. *The Prince* is a handbook of the politics of power. Men were energy quanta, and the Prince an energy quantum. If he wished to stay in power, he had to exert more force than his opponents. If the methods he employed were morally good, so much the better, but if no morally good method lay to hand, any measure would do. Because men were evil, there was nothing to be done but to be evil with them, and if necessary more evil.

A light in this darkness was *Thomas More* (1480–1535), humanist, idealist and saint. In his *Utopia* he described with irony, caricature and real insight the ideal State as he conceived it. Machiavelli would presumably have replied that the question was not what man *should* be like but what he *was* like.

Otherwise one was asking for trouble. And Thomas More got it. But is it not true that a Machiavellian realism which declines to inquire into what should be is the real cause of discord in the world today?

Another bright spot in the picture was *Hugo Grotius* (1583–645), international jurist and political theoretician. His greatest work on war and peace (*De iure belli et pacis*) is a classic compendium of law and the philosophy of law. Perhaps his most lasting achievement was the attempt to counter positive law and the use of sheer power by developing a theory which would guarantee man's respect and freedom by appealing to a law higher than human law. However timid and reticent he may have been in some of his ideas, and however brittle his concept of nature, the attempt itself was something.

Scholasticism also persisted into Renaissance times. It would be very wrong to concentrate on the more spectacular side of the Renaissance at the expense of the philosophy which in fact easily predominated in the majority of universities in Charles V's empire, not to mention the Schools of religious orders and (the equivalent of) clerical seminaries. Scholasticism had soon recovered from the arthritis of Nominalism, especially in the universities of Spain and Portugal: Salamanca, Alcalá and Coimbra, and one may rightly speak of a new Scholasticism (not to be confused with the Neo-Scholasticism of the nineteenth and twentieth centuries). At the centre of the new effort stood the two Dominicans Thomas de Vio (1468–1534), usually known as *Cajetan*, and Francis Sylvester de Sylvestris (1474–1528), usually called *Ferrariensis*, and above all the Jesuit *Francis Suarez* (1548–1617), sometimes referred to as the Eminent Doctor (*Doctor eximius*). The Thomists had no love for Suarez because he denied the distinction between essence and existence. Others hold that his attempt to base knowledge on abstraction from a sensualistically understood sense-experience helped to spread nominalism. However that may be, he was one of the most scholarly academics in the history of Scholastic philosophy, and his two major works, the *Disputationes metaphysicae* (1597) and the *De legibus* (1612), belong to the finest works of philosophy ever written.

The achievements of these great names nourished the Scholastic philosophy of the sixteenth, seventeenth and eighteenth centuries. They were also exploited in Catholic and Protestant universities, and in the smaller seminary-type colleges of theology and philosophy run by the Jesuits in southern Germany: Ingolstadt, Eichstätt, Regensburg, Bamberg, Würzburg and elsewhere.

CHAPTER TWO: THE GREAT SYSTEMS OF THE SEVENTEENTH AND EIGHTEENTH CENTURIES

If the Renaissance was characterized by the multiplicity of new directions, the seventeenth and eighteenth centuries were dominated by the love of System. Grandiose philosophical edifices succeeded each other with startling rapidity. On the whole, and without too much distortion, they can be divided into two main groups: those drawing on rationalism and those on empiricism. The former was characteristic of continental philosophy, the latter of British philosophy.

I. RATIONALISM

Literally rationalism means the philosophy of reason. The idea is that the philosopher uses his reason (understanding, thought, concepts) in his analysis of being. This is not to say that he relies solely on deduction without drawing on experience. Even rationalists use their senses. However, and this is what distinguishes them from the empiricists, they believe that the power of the human intellect is more than a combination of sense perceptions, that reason and understanding have a strength all their own and can read, interpret and judge the data of sense-experience according to their own (a priori) laws. Three of the many rationalists of this period tower above their fellows: Descartes, Spinoza and Leibniz.

1. Descartes – the Father of modern philosophy

Modern philosophy begins with René Descartes (1596–1650). In many ways Descartes was still a Scholastic, and certainly a knowledge of Scholasticism is essential to a study of Descartes. But there was something about him which was new, different, and marks him off quite distinctly from the Schoolmen. That something was radical doubt, the point at which Descartes began his philosophy.

(a) Doubt

Philosophers before Descartes had learnt to think critically, but their critique had always used concepts and phrases that had not themselves been open to doubt. Descartes began with radical or absolute doubt. What, he asked, can we accept as certain and indubitable in our philosophizing? The convictions of everyday life? But fashions change, and then the French, the English and the Chinese have such different ideas! The accepted teachings of philosophy, then? But 'even at school I learnt that there is nothing so strange or incredible that some philosopher had not proposed it in the past.' Well, then, sense-knowledge: surely we can take what we see for certain knowledge? No, because what has misled us once can mislead us again. This is true of the syllogism, for example; even pure logic can go wrong. What if we reply that we accept the possibility of error in *individual* cases, but not in *all* cases taken together? There can be no doubt, for example, that extension, number, location and time are universal, that 2 + 3 always =5 and that a rectangle must have four sides. Well, replies Descartes, could it not be that an omnipotent God has so arranged matters that all these things we take to be universal facts are in fact delusory; that there is no earth or sky, no extension, shape, size or place; that everything is misleading? And if you claim that the reality of the external world is absolutely certain, then I can only say that the freshness and vitality of sense-experience, which you point to as a sure sign of the reality of that experience, are just as much a part of dreams. Dreams can be so vivid that you are convinced the incidents are perfectly real. Could not all life be a dream? Suppose, says Descartes, that we are being deliberately deceived not by God but by some cunning evil spirit. The air, the sky, the world, shapes, colours, sounds are nothing more than the vibrations of a dreamy sleep. My own flesh and sensations and thoughts do not really exist, I only think they do. What, then: has philosophy collapsed? Yes and no. Possible sources of deception have been shown up for what they are, but in the midst of all the doubt a new certainty emerges: I cannot doubt that I am doubting. It may all be a dream, but at least the thought that it is so is there, and I the thinker of that thought am there. 'I think, therefore I am' (*Cogito, ergo sum*). This most famous of sayings is not a logical conclusion from established premises, but an intuition, and as such an absolute and certain truth. Descartes constructed his system on it.

Like Descartes, modern philosophy also builds on this intuition, and this goes some way to explaining the distinctive stamp of much modern thought. There is only one trouble. The new 'truth' is one of inner awareness, subjective conviction. It is confined to the mind and has no reference to the external world. Descartes started from an inner awareness, but then proceeded to build up on that and make contact with the external world. Modern 'truth' has not followed him. Hence so-called immanent philosophy and its subjectivism. The whole of modern philosophy is to some extent infected with it.

(b) Method

Descartes regarded his newly discovered truth, the *Cogito*, as a 'clear and distinct idea'. This meant that the idea stood out as an independent thought distinct from anything else. Descartes drew an axiom from this: everything is true that I can see clearly and distinctly; and a method: philosophy must work with, and confine itself to, clear and distinct ideas. Then it would be a sure science, something like geometry, where ultimate simple quantities are worked out, combined and written down as mathematical equations. The mind must try to discover similar quantities for its work of philosophy. These quantities exist, according to Descartes: they are the 'innate ideas'. The three main ones were infinite substance (=perfect being which exists of itself and is called God), extension or bodiliness, and non-extension or consciousness. (Descartes called them the three substances: infinite, material and immaterial.) There were many other secondary innate ideas: number, time, place, motion, shape, everything which could be expressed mathematically and everything which could be reduced to an ultimate simple quantity. It followed for Descartes that all the sense perceptions which contained a shape, number or extension expressible in mathematical terms and which were clear and distinct were primary sense qualities. Sensations which did not verify these conditions, for example colours, sounds, tastes, sensations of heat and cold, were secondary. They were not false, they were true 'in a way', but they did not record things as they were, they were subjective, while primary qualities were objective. Objective in what sense?

(c) God and the external world

Before that question can be answered, we must say something on Descartes' concept of God. Descartes discovered God primarily as an innate idea, but if that exhausted his reality, God would be no more than an idea in our minds, qualified as 'infinite' no doubt, but still a subjective entity. So Descartes had somehow to go beyond the idea. He asked where the innate ideas had come from in the first place. They could in theory, he said, come from outside, or they could be our own invention. They could not, however, come from outside in practice, because so far in our inquiry we have not established contact with any outside (it must be admitted that Descartes' reasoning here is not devoid of confusion). And they cannot be our own invention, or at least the idea of God cannot be. The idea of God, the most perfect being, contains an infinite reality and so cannot be the work of finite beings like ourselves. In the words of one of Descartes' principles, which he took from ancient philosophy, a cause must have at least as much reality about it as its effect. In our case this means that the cause of our idea of God must contain as much 'formal' reality as we ascribe to God in our idea of him. Descartes therefore succeeds in breaking out of the solipsistic subjectivism to which his methodical doubt had led him. Descartes has managed to go beyond the thinking subject of his *Cogito* and establish the existence of something else which is not merely a thought but a reality: God. And because he has reasoned to God and recognized in him the most perfect being, Descartes cannot accept that God deceives us. If, consequently, we are faced with a clear and distinct idea registering some object extended in space, we can be sure that it is true. And if several primary qualities combine, they present things to us as they really are. Descartes can therefore accept the reality of the external world. Doubt has been overcome. It was not in any case intended to be definitive: it was a fiction of method designed to lead to an absolute certainty.

Descartes offered another proof for the existence of God, called the *ontological argument*. It was a combination of Platonic inborn ideas and Scholastic causality, and was an exercise, again, in pure ideal-realism. According to Descartes, the existence of God followed from the idea of God as the most perfect being. Kant objected that concepts, being entirely logical, could have nothing to say on actual existence. The passage from the logical to the ontological sphere was impermissible (as well as impossible). Descartes would have replied that the idea of God was no ordinary idea; it was not merely logical, but contained the entire ontic reality which lay at the root of things. Descartes was propounding the ancient ideal-realism of which Kant, 150 years later, had no understanding.

In God we encounter the concept of *substance* which was so important for Descartes and succeeding philosophy. His definition of substance was 'a thing which exists in such a way that it needs nothing outside itself in order to exist'. Because in Descartes' philosophy only God, of all existing things, did not depend on other things, there was only one substance, the divine substance. Descartes' definition of infinite substance differed from the definition of ordinary substance only in its greater breadth. Taken strictly, this understanding of substance would mean that there were no autonomous beings, no properly independent causality, no freedom and ultimately no human persons. The occasionalists and Spinoza in fact drew this conclusion, but Descartes did not want to. He therefore tightened his concept of substance by saying that only the divine substance fully existed independently, the other substances (body and consciousness) depended on God as perfect being. Inasmuch as they did not depend on anything else they could be called imperfect finite substances.

(d) Body and Soul

When Descartes called body and soul substances in this sense, he took a step of vast implications. If substance is something autonomous, needing nothing outside itself, bodies and souls exist independently of each other. In that case, how can the bodily organs of sense relay information to the soul? Forced by the facts, Descartes here accepted, in defiance of his own basic principles, a certain interchange between body and soul, but he refused to modify his philosophy of substance. If he were right, the soul could exist only as consciousness, not as the form of the body. Animals would lack a soul entirely, they would be mere bodies without sense-experience. Descartes held that animals did not see or hear or taste, but just acted as if they did. They were automata leading a life, like every life, of pure mechanical motion. The more Descartes thought of the soul as something independent, against any form of materialism, the more he thought of the body in exclusively physical terms. His concept of substance meant the total mechanism of the bodily world. That mechanism was geometrical, inasmuch as he thought of bodies as no more than extension, and bodily movement as a functional mathematical movement, even though we could not always find the exact formula that would describe it. The whole of nature was quantified and mechanized. The old doctrine of forms was gone. Materialists – for whom Descartes had no love because, as he explained in the second of his *Meditations*, the soul comes before the body – could yet take something from Descartes. From a

106

completely different angle he completed the atomism of Gassendi, and through Mersenne led to Thomas Hobbes.

A critical approach to Descartes would greatly profit by taking him in conjunction with *Blaise Pascal* (1623–62). Pascal started off as a follower of Descartes and had great hopes in the mathematical method. But he soon discovered that it laboured under severe limitations: it lacked all feeling for the concrete and the individual as opposed to the universal, and it lacked all openness to belief as opposed to the rationalism of reason. Pascal was a man of keen phenomenological observation and also one of the finest religious geniuses of all time. He saw that the God of religion was more than the God of philosophers.

2. Spinoza – the Philosophy of Identity

Descartes was completed, if a bit onesidedly, by Baruch Spinoza (1632–77). Although Spinoza's main work was called *Ethics*, it was in fact a philosophy of being and nature, knowledge and mind. The title is not, however, totally misleading. The ultimate aim of Spinoza's philosophy of being was ethical: man's happiness, which follows from true (that is, wise) humanity. True humanity was achieved when man was one with being and God in spiritual love. 'When experience had taught me that the usual content of life was idle and vainglorious, I decided to find, if I could, something that was really good.' For Spinoza true human nature was the highest good. The best a person could do in life was to tune in to nature. Spinoza's philosophy was an attempt to explain how one could achieve this and what the consequences were.

(a) God – Nature – Substance

In an early work of Spinoza's, the so-called *Short Treatise*, which set out the author's original ethical ideas, there is a reflexion which stands at the heart of his thinking. It reads as follows. Nothingness has no attributes. Attributes, therefore, must apply to something. To a finite something apply finite attributes, to the infinite or divine nature infinite attributes. God therefore is every something, that is, he is everything and everything is God. And because everything is being or nature, one can talk indifferently about 'God, nature or substance'. This is a famous phrase. It is due to Descartes that Spinoza replaced being by 'substance'. In Descartes' early thought, there was only *one* being, that of substance. Individual things were not really beings but something in the one being of the one substance. Descartes later abandoned this extreme view. But Spinoza did not. For him there was only one proper independent reality. Substance was all there was, bodily, spiritual, partial, entire, individual, universal. Only this One, substance, was of interest. And it was all, in that everything we see as existing things came from it. More accurately, only substance 'was'. Spinoza gave an unusually striking example: just as it follows eternally from the nature of a triangle that the three angles together make two right angles, so things come from God with the same necessity and in the same way. Spinoza was proposing a philosophy of *identity*. What, according to him, 'follows' from the nature of a triangle is the triangle itself. He was in effect identifying God and creation.

In antiquity and in Christian philosophy, it had always been said that God was all in all, that all things were in God and vice versa. There was a difference, however. Christian philosophy had always added after 'God is all in all' 'God transcends infinitely everything that is'. There was nothing like this in Spinoza, except the idea that basic being gave rise to consequent being, although the latter was not, as the triangle comparison made clear, really 'other'. Spinoza has therefore always been accused of proposing pantheism by destroying the distinction between God and the world and turning God into the world (or the world into God). He reads sometimes like a Neo-Platonic treatise, but he omits the conscious and emphatic analysis of the different modes of being which the Neo-Platonists never forgot. The 'is' applied by Neo-Platonism to dead matter, to life, to sensation, to understanding, to finite and infinite reason was not taken in the same sense every time. This use of 'is' was part of Neo-

Platonism's thought and speech patterns. Spinoza used 'is' in the same sense all the time. As Leibniz rightly observed, Spinoza was not exact, his concepts were ambiguous and more than ambiguous, and it was therefore a specious logic that gave his philosophy the appearance of tightknit uniformity. The apparent cogency of his thought was an illusion.

(b) Individuality – Freedom – Purpose

Despite this Spinoza has given philosophy some very important concepts and doctrines. The foremost of these was the notion of the absolute *necessity of natural laws*. The nineteenth century above all adopted it. However, the necessity of natural laws has never been and never can be proved. It is a theory based on nothing more than a blind acceptance of Spinoza. It suited Spinoza to look at nature that way, and there was no metaphysical or other reason behind it. The British have been more realistic on this point. They protested that natural laws could not be strictly demonstrated as laws, they were more like probabilities. Nevertheless Spinoza made a decisive contribution to the idea of *causal determination*: not only was every event caused – this had always been accepted – but every cause was itself determined by something else. There was thus no *free will*. Kant re-emphasized the concept of freedom. He introduced it somewhat by the back door, firstly by denying Spinoza's complete causal determination, and secondly by holding that there was such a thing as free causality, that is, an independent beginning of a causal chain. Spinoza could never have admitted such independence because substance itself was responsible for everything. This was in effect the end of all *individuality*. As Goethe once wrote in a moment of fervour for Spinoza's pantheism (or acosmism, as Hegel called it): 'And a divinity spoke when I thought I was speaking, and when I thought a divinity spoke, it was I myself.' In Spinoza's philosophy, again, there was no *purpose*, either in man's mind or in nature. Purpose presupposes freedom. And for Spinoza there was no freedom, because he wanted to erect a philosophy of necessity in which everything was strictly controlled. Kant opposed him on this point too. He saw that purpose was indispensable for an intelligent understanding of change in the world. We cannot imagine so much as the tiniest blade of grass coming into existence on a totally mechanical determination. Spinoza, however, had no time for the changeableness of being, for its grades, analogies or modes. His philosophy was violent, uniform, narrow and rigid. As the subtitle of his major work implies, being was to be 'demonstrated on geometrical principles' only.

3. Leibniz – Timeless Philosophy

'I have found that most sects are right in most of what they affirm, wrong in most of what they deny.' This sentiment is particularly characteristic of Gottfried Wilhelm Leibniz (1646–1716). His was a thoroughly positive mind. He had little time for critique and polemic. He had a large affection for what was true, wherever he found it. He was a thinker of encyclopaedic proportions, at home in almost any branch of knowledge, be it mathematics, physics, history or theology, and in philosophy too he sought the Whole, without forgetting individual things. His formula was the Monad.

(a) The Monads and Being

How did Leibniz arrive at his concept of monad? The mathematically inclined physics of Leibniz's time dealt uniquely with quantitative factors. Only one category entered its horizon: quantity. Was number not a quality then, asked Leibniz. What was counted was admittedly quantitative: one thing, counted out twice, three times, etc.; but what about that with which the quantities were counted, in other words numbers? Surely each number was a quality, a determined thing (*quale*) distinct from every other thing? The quantitative view of being, argued Leibniz, needed to be completed by a qualitative view. In the early stages of his philosophy, he had gone along with the quantitative-mechanistic approach to nature; but then, 'when I investigated the basis of mechanism and the laws of motion, I was quite surprised to notice that it was impossible to find them in mathematics and that I had to turn to metaphysics. My search there led me to the entelechy, the form, and I finally concluded, having improved and developed my ideas, that monads or simple substances were the only true substances, while material things were merely appearances, however well-established and coherent.'

Leibniz proceeded to examine this notion of coherence. Atoms, material things, life and its appearances, especially the human body and soul, must, he said, be interconnected. Mechanism and atomism tore everything apart, while for Leibniz the world must be a cosmos, a harmonious whole. He therefore created his celebrated notion of *pre-established harmony*. This notion he applied to the relationship between body and soul, but more particularly to the relationship between the multitudinous parts of the cosmos. Descartes' definition of substance as a totally independent entity had introduced a radical division between body and soul. And yet when a sense organ perceived something material, the soul had somehow to be informed. The problem was to explain the interaction of body and soul. Occasionalism had suggested that a superior spiritual power had superimposed the events of life so that internal and external activities corresponded. Two clocks would show the same time without either influencing the other. Leibniz applied this idea to the very smallest particles of the universe. The divine Spirit, to use another metaphor, had tuned them all to the same wavelength. The atoms, bodies, lives, souls, spirits of the world were so many clocks pre-established in harmony because a divine demiurge had so ordered them.

This is the more popular account of Leibniz's philosophy and does not really represent the most original part of it, which was his concept of *monad*. 'Monads', he said, 'are the true atoms of nature, in a word the elements of things.' Each individual monad, differing only qualitatively from its fellows, reflected the universe in its own way, so that the universe was a harmonious composition of an infinite number of different monads. Leibniz criticized the ancient Atomists for positing elements which, because they had shape and size, could not be the ultimate particles of reality. His own 'atoms' or 'monads', which he called 'souls' to express their spiritual and dynamic nature, were *really* indivisible and therefore simple.

Natural science had for quite some time before Leibniz talked about forces in the universe. Leibniz asked himself what exactly was meant by force. The only way he could explain it was to start from his own experience of spiritual acts, particularly volition, which verified the definition of force. For Leibniz there was no other means of arriving at the notion of *substance*. Substance was an independent self-acting reality. If, following Descartes, substance was thought of as extended, as in the natural sciences of Leibniz's time, then it was infinitely divisible. Every material entity that was an active unity was an aggregate of forces, and if that aggregate was to be real, it must be its own unifying force. If, then, that force again was extended as a corporeal atom, there was no end to the process, and there was no reality which could possibly initiate the exercise of force. Only a 'soul', an indivisible and dynamic entity such as we know from our own self-reflexion, could therefore be substantive. Hence Leibniz's definition of substance: 'a being capable of action'. His shorthand for it was monad. To appreciate Leibniz's point of view here, it is essential to understand the reasoning by which he reached his concept of soul. Modern man has difficulty in regarding bodies as any more than dead mechanical extended entities. Reality *is* the material extended world. For Leibniz such a view would be far too narrow. There are other modes of being besides matter: the immaterial or psychic, for example, and the spiritual. And in fact spiritual being is 'realer' and more forceful than matter. One of philosophy's first duties is to open our eyes to this realer being; Leibniz fulfilled it.

Further than this there were *grades of psychic being*, or modes of monadal existence. There were monads which possessed the power of representation only very inadequately, dead matter, for example; which were unconscious and obscure, as in plant life; which were conscious but confined to sense-experience, like the animals; and finally which 'thought', by which Leibniz meant monads capable of grasping more or less clear and distinct concepts, in other words human souls. Above them all stood the divine monad, who was pure thought and activity. Because Leibniz constructed the universe out of monads, and each monad, however low on the scale, was a soul, one may speak of Leibniz's philosophy as 'panpsychism'. At the same time Leibniz admitted the existence of bodies. It is not easy to see how exactly he could justify this admission on the premise that the world was composed of immaterial, unextended monads. Without going too far into that here, we can say that for Leibniz every corporeal reality with which our senses were confronted was an aggregate of monads of which one was dominant. In short, extended entities were aggregates of unextended monads.

On the basis of this doctrine of monads, Leibniz claimed to solve, or at least clarify, a whole series of philosophical problems. Unlike Descartes he had no difficulty in taking a mechanistic-quantitative as well as a psychistic-organological view of things. He explained freedom and necessity, individuality and cosmic wholeness, because – unlike Spinoza, whose philosophy Leibniz called 'miserable' because of its failure to posit individual freedom – substance was so free and autonomous that Leibniz could say: 'The monad has no windows.' Yet there were laws of being because all the infinity of monads formed a pre-established harmony.

In particular Leibniz succeeded in clarifying the problem of *God* as it was understood in the metaphysical tradition of the west. God was pure spirit and pure act, as Aristotle had said. This divine monad was being itself, because all other monads only partially existed. They had an in-built tendency to struggle towards purity of being (in other words, God), and God was therefore the 'adequate basis' (*ratio sufficiens*) of the world just as the ideas had been for Plato (for whom Leibniz had the highest regard). Leibniz therefore accepted the ancient proof for the existence of God. The summary of his 'proof for the existence of a single God, for his perfection and the origin of things' in the *Essays in Theodicy* (1, 7) could almost have been written by Thomas Aquinas. Leibniz also offered a version of the ontological argument, like the dutiful Platonist he was. And he affirmed the world, as the ancients and medievals had done. His theodicy, a justification of God in the face of the world's evil, culminated in the thesis that our world was the best of all possible worlds. This *optimism* did not deny evil, on the contrary it affirmed that evil belonged to this best of all possible worlds; but because this world proceeded from pure being, it was itself basically pure, evil was only a privation. For the perspicuous thinker, good was stronger than evil. Man must strive to raise himself above the obscurity of sense-experience to the clarity of reason – and he would see the true face of the world, eternal and good.

(b) *The Monads and Spirit*

The fact that the monads were psychic primal elements with the power of conceptual thought enables us to say something on Leibniz's philosophy of spirit. The main points are truth, law and holiness.

Because monads had no windows, knowledge was, according to Leibniz, an a priori process, at least in its essentials. Like Plato and Descartes, Leibniz accepted the existence of *innate ideas*. The mind was not a *tabula rasa* but a slab of marble which already contained within itself an 'aptitude' for the work of art that was to result. Leibniz praised Plato for his 'pure concepts', his doctrine that the eternal essences had a higher reality than individual things. 'The senses provide us with more error than truth; the mind is raised from matter, and so perfected, in the pure knowledge of the eternal truths.' The innate ideas were concepts such as unity, substance, identity, cause, perception, squareness, being and 'many others which the senses cannot give'. Sense-experience was yet not superfluous. One needed the senses, even though they yielded no more than grist for reason's mill. Leibniz made a distinction between truths of reason and truths of fact. It aptly illustrates the nature of Leibniz's innate ideas. If we were limited to sense-perception, we could know nothing other than what is happening here and now, we should have no knowledge of what must always and everywhere be so. Only reason can give us that. Reason has an exclusive faculty: insight into necessary essential connexions. In other words, the truths furnished by reason are necessary propositions based on the principle of contradiction. Euclid did not measure and tabulate what actually is, but demonstrated what must be. All his mathematical and geometrical information were truths of reason. They cannot be explored beyond saying that their denial would infringe the principle of contradiction. They are typically human. Animals have experience only of what is, and therefore 'the conclusions which animals draw do not rise above the level of the empirical', as Leibniz wrote in the foreword to the *New Essays on Human Understanding*. Leibniz did not engage in the dispute between empiricism and rationalism over whether we need the senses or only concepts; the discussion in his view was over *how* we use the senses: was their function limited to providing material data, or were they in some sense decisive? Leibniz firmly rejected the latter alternative. He wanted truths of reason, eternal truths, as the western tradition had always tended to do.

The eternal truths lead us to Leibniz's notion of eternal man, superior to the animals, like God because he is spirit. Leibniz postulated a *realm of spirits*. 'Spiritual beings can in a way communicate with God. God relates to them not just like an inventor to his machine, as he does to other creatures, but like a prince to his subjects, or better, like a father to his children.' 'To become spiritual' meant to approximate more and more closely to the image of God, and it constituted the perfection of man. The more perfect one was the more substantive, dynamic, free and individual and the more one fitted into the harmony of the whole. 'The greater the force, the more apparent the multiplicity out of and in unity, and the unity in the multiplicity. Now unity in multiplicity is the cosmic harmony, and because a thing is nearer to this than to that other thing, order results, and beauty, and love.' 'From this it is clear that happiness, pleasure, love, perfection, being, force, freedom, harmony, order and beauty are all bound up with one another.'

This realm of truth and perfection was also the realm of *law* for Leibniz. Law needed power, but it was not power. The truth and clarity of being, the wisdom and goodness of God and of his eternal world order were based on law. Leibniz explained this, against both Hobbes and late Scholasticism, as follows. If God's justice were held to depend uniquely on his power, then God was no better than a despot who imposed his will regardless of opposition and disagreement. To praise God for his justice would be the activity of a madman. And there would be no distinction between God and the devil: if the latter were really 'Prince of this world', he would have to be reverenced and obeyed, simply because he wielded power, even though his rule were literally devilish. If law were no more than power, a court could never pronounce an unjust judgement, and the purpose of law would be irreparably vitiated. And *religion* would be meaningless if holiness were only power. For Hobbes in fact religion was totally subordinate to the civil power. Leibniz rejected this opinion with as little ceremony as the Emperor Claudius scorning the pretensions of democracy. If everything was allowed, argued Claudius, then that included ill-manners, belching and the like; and Leibniz said that if everything, including the idea of God and the law, were an expression of power, then why should the State not turn belching and the like into gods?

Whenever power does become the be-all and end-all of politics, Leibniz's lucubrations are seen to be far more than empty theory.

II. EMPIRICISM

Empiricism marks the beginning of modern philosophy in that it represents the first radical break with Platonic-Aristotelian metaphysics which up to Leibniz had prevailed without exception in western history. Metaphysics is suddenly abandoned altogether, and with it transcendence and eternal truths. This is the decisive difference between empiricism and rationalism. From now on sense-experience is the unique deposit of truth. For rationalism the senses merely provide the

116

material on which reason works; for empiricism the ser.
themselves determine the truth and are the arbiters of valu(
ideals, laws and religion. Because sense-experience is neve,
complete, the world-process and knowledge never come to an
end, and there can be no such things as eternally valid truths.
Everything is relative to space and time; the human, and
sometimes the all too human, becomes the yardstick of reality.
Sensuality is superior to intelligibility, utility to the ideal,
individuality to the universal, time to eternity, desire to moral
duty, might to right, the part to the whole, the actual to the
necessary. At least that is the theory of it. The reality is a bit
different.

1. Hobbes – Modern Naturalism

Ancient philosophy was not a stranger to materialism and
naturalism: it had its Democrituses and its Sophists. But on
the whole the Platonic-Aristotelian philosophy was by far the
most influential. However, although the materialism of
Epicurus had practically no effect on Christianity and medieval
philosophy, it did raise disciples in the 'Epicurean atomism'
resurrected by Gassendi and unwittingly assisted by natural
science. With Thomas Hobbes (1588–1679) materialism and
naturalism first achieved solid status. To some extent Hobbes'
views drew on ancient Greek and Roman precedents, but for
the most part they were original. They in their turn stood
godfather to the materialism of the Enlightenment and in its
wake to the scientific and dialectical materialism of the
nineteenth century.

(a) Things and Thinking

Is it possible to start a philosophy with a theory of matter
and include logic in that theory? Hobbes did, and saw no
contradiction. He criticized Descartes for drawing an impermissible conclusion: I think, therefore I am a thinking –

that is, an immaterial – substance. Why, asked Hobbes, should a material substance, a body, not think? Much more recently than Hobbes, Stalin was to maintain that it was a grave error to hold that consciousness is not a function of the bodily matter we call the brain. The source of such views in our own times can be traced back to Hobbes. His theory of reality was a theory of bodiliness. 'Philosophy', he once remarked, 'is such knowledge of effects or appearances as we acquire by true ratiocination from the knowledge we have first of their causes or generation.' Effects and appearances were, for Hobbes, the work of bodies. Even the Epicureans had included three divisions in philosophy: logic, physics and ethics. Hobbes reduced everything to physics. His categories were categories of quantity. The investigation into nature must measure and enumerate. It is noteworthy that Leibniz had no objection to this in itself. With reference to Democritus, Epicurus and Hobbes, he had said that mathematical principles did not invalidate the philosophy of materialists. Bodily processes did happen according to the laws laid down by Hobbes and Epicurus. They were mechanical. For Leibniz they were mechanical too. But the point was that they were not *only* mechanical. This was Leibniz's objection. Hobbes' epistemology was consequently a form of *sensualism*: all human thought could be explained in terms of the addition and subtraction of sense data. Such a mathematical procedure was a bodily-mechanical act: this followed from the fact that logic was included in the theory of bodiliness. It was a modern version of *nominalism*. The only reality was that of bodies, material concrete things; the universal was no more than a thought. And for Hobbes even that thought was no more than a name, because, the logical being a function of the corporeal, thought had no existence of its own. Ideas were the paper money of mental activity: as long as the currency held, the pound notes retained a certain value; but once the currency collapsed, they were worthless. Truth was a mere convention. If for convention we read social conditions or political party, we see how close to reality philosophical theories can be. At a blow an entire system of concepts and 'truths' can collapse into worthlessness.

(b) Man – Citizenship – the State

In a philosophy like that of Hobbes, man could not be called rational in any very profound sense. He was body, a quantum of pressure and impact, a plaything of sense allurement and mechanical reaction. Hobbes' doctrine of the State was particularly revealing on this point. It included the two famous theories of the natural state of war and the Commonwealth, which were designed to show the nature of citizenship, the State and the 'mutual covenants' on which the State was based. The root of human life was the tension between man's self-centred passions and the dictates of reason which determined what was to be done for the preservation and comfort of life. Prior to the Commonwealth there was a *natural state of war*, in which men lived as self-seeking individuals driven by competition, mistrust and the desire for glory, without the ties of family, morality, law or religion. Men were by nature equal, in the sense that what one lacked in one area, say physical strength, he would make up in another, say cunning. In the natural state of war, it was a question of each man for himself and devil take the hindmost. The prevailing 'law' was the law of the jungle, as the Sophists had already held, and war (which 'consisteth . . . in the known disposition to actual fighting') was universal. In a famous sentence, Hobbes described man's life in the natural state of war as 'solitary, poor, nasty, brutish and short'. For reasons of pure egoism, men decided to form a Commonwealth based on *covenant*, in which the nastiness of life would be reduced to a minimum. The Laws of Nature persuaded individuals to sink their differences to the extent of bringing about peace, and with peace came trust, sociability, gratitude, and then ultimately morality, law and religion. Religion, then, was the concern of the State, according to Hobbes; and conscience, about which Hobbes had things to say in his *Leviathan*, was no more than the prudence of a man who knows what actions to avoid for his own comfort. We have already heard Leibniz on the subject. John Locke too criticized the covenant theory of the State because, he said, if man were really as savage and 'brutish' as

Hobbes made out, he could never bring himself to conclude a pact with his fellows. The will to abide by a covenant was a *moral* decision, whereas for Hobbes morality was the *result* of the covenant. There was, concluded Locke, an inner contradiction. And furthermore, men under a social covenant were the same men as before. Their contribution to the Commonwealth was egoism and self-seeking, and what Hobbes was pleased to call law and morality was no more than organized violence. Hobbes was a nominalist. A wolf is still a wolf even in sheep's clothing: 'citizens' do not change their natures under the covenant; wars continue. The 'naturalism' of Hobbes' philosophy of the State was not only an exposition of man's ill-treatment of man, but also a justification of it.

2. Locke – 'British Philosophy'

John Locke (1623–1704) introduced a development in thinking that has proved remarkably characteristic of modern philosophy: a special emphasis on epistemology. Philosophy now begins with the theory of human knowledge and its shape is determined by the results of that first investigation. In a sense it is to Descartes that modern philosophy owes this development, but by far the strongest impulse has been from Locke. He wrote (in 1690) the first great systematic treatment of knowledge, *Essay Concerning Human Understanding*. Leibniz replied with his *New Essays Concerning Human Understanding* (written in 1704, but not published until 1765). Others were to follow: Berkeley, Hume, Kant with his *Critique of Pure Reason*, Fichte with his *Theory of Science* and Hegel with his *Phenomenology of Mind*. This was the movement sparked off by Locke. Locke was also the typical figure of what is known as British philosophy: a concentration on experience and reality, the rejection of elaborate speculation, gravity of judgement, a peaceful coexistence of conservative and progressive thinking, and tolerance.

(a) The Origin and Significance of Knowledge

Locke based his investigations into human understanding on the *denial of innate ideas* (theoretical and practical). Human understanding was a *tabula rasa*. If we had innate ideas, Locke argued, even children would notice them, but they do not. Locke levelled against continental rationalism the same critique that Aristotle had levelled against Plato. Further, adults do not show any evidence of innate ideas: not even the first logical principles or the concept of God are always and everywhere identical. If there are universally accepted ideas, they are acquired; all ideas are acquired. Leibniz retorted with an argument already put forward by Descartes: Locke had misunderstood the nature of innate ideas. He imagined them to be actual developed ideas already present in the mind, like a poem learnt by heart, whereas in fact they were primordial aptitudes of the understanding, the a priori beginnings of the eternal truths of reason. They needed sense-experience and development, like everything else in man's life.

After this denunciation of inborn ideas, Locke proceeded to the positive part of his inquiry by asking how human knowledge arose. His answer was that it arose through sensation mediated by the bodily organs and through reflexion on the awareness of self in which we internally perceive that we see, hear, feel etc. Through both these channels we gain our ideas. The extensive treatment of simple and complex ideas, primary and secondary qualities, the degrees of knowledge (intuition, demonstration, sensation), the agreement and disagreement of ideas in judgement etc. which now follows in the *Essay* is a detailed anatomy of the human mind and an investigation into the factors and functions at work in human knowing. Much of the old metaphysics is transferred to the realm of consciousness, following the modern trend to concentrate on immanence rather than on transcendence: for example, Locke's division of ideas into substance, modes ('accidents' in old terminology) and relations, in which the ancient categories of *being* are transformed into categories of *consciousness*. The step was taken with as much ease and rapidity as the reverse step from consciousness to ontology today. Two of Locke's doctrines are of particular importance here: abstraction and the coexistence of concepts. 'Ideas become general by separating from them the circumstances of time and place and any other ideas that may determine them to this or that particular existence. By this way of abstraction they are made capable of representing more individuals than one; each of which having in it a conformity to that abstract idea is (as we call it) of that sort.' This is clear enough in theory; the only problem is how it is done in practice. How is the mind to know what is common to a number of different individuals? Surely there is a danger of seizing on the first thing that strikes us or on what interests us most? This is the weak point in the modern theory of abstraction. Abstraction, at all events, is a process which concerns consciousness exclusively; the result of it is an average idea (as one might say). It is clear that it cannot produce more than is contained in the sense data on which it is based, and it therefore provides no genuinely universal ideas or propositions. The most it can do is offer generalized concepts of particular, not universal, truth, whatever their pretensions to the contrary. This distinguishes it from abstraction in ancient philosophy, which not only was a process of consciousness but also had an ontological character, and which always exceeded the substratum of sense-knowledge because it was the work of a creative mind with a continual reference to being. The problem of the *coexistence* of our ideas is closely tied up with this. When we think of a thing, say gold, with its weight, colour, malleability, solubility in aqua-regia and various other properties, how do we know that all these ideas go together? Ancient philosophy appealed to our *intellectus agens* which in some degree participated in the divine *intellectus*, and thence drew a knowledge of essences, forms and substances. Locke, however, rejected the ancient concept of substance because he rejected the ontological-metaphysical thinking of which it was a part. His own concept of substance was restricted to the level of consciousness. And to the question of why we always combine certain concepts in the same way he had no answer, however hard he tried. Hume was to say that we cannot know whether the concepts belong together ontologically or not. The fact is they do regularly belong together in our own minds. It was not, for Hume, a question of being and truth, only of logic.

(b) Practical Philosophy

Locke studied human volition in his ethics and in his philosophy of law, the State and religion.

Ethics, as was (and is) usually the case in British philosophy, was eudaemonistic: the happiness, well-being, pleasure and pain of both individuals and society are the principles of good and evil. Locke defined good as whatever produced pleasure (mental or physical) and evil as whatever produced pain. His ethics can therefore be called hedonism. On the other hand, in his practical philosophy he offered a counterbalance. By admitting the ancients' 'natural law' and an 'eternal law', he showed that his hedonism was not thoroughgoing. And yet he still reduced ethics to the level of sociology by defining virtue and vice in terms of what society approved and disapproved. In other words, despite his theoretical admission of an eternal law, the empiricist in him proved too strong.

His *philosophy of the State*, like Hobbes', included the concepts of a natural condition and a social compact, but he was less radical than Hobbes. All men were equal, but they were not Hobbes' savages. There was a 'natural law', equivalent to the Scholastics' idea of the natural moral law, and without it no social compact was possible. Locke was emphatic on that point. But apart from guaranteeing respect for the covenant, the natural law was not significant. The reason for this was that, unlike the ancient philosophers, Locke saw in the State not a natural development but a product of the free will of individuals which was based on the idea of the general good and the desire to submit to the will of the majority in order to safeguard one's own rights. Locke's individualism and liberalism, however, could not tolerate more than the minimum infringement of an individual's liberties unavoidable in any social gathering. He therefore demanded a 'division of powers' in the State to prevent dictatorship, absolute monarchy and other allied forms of totalist non-democratic government. His two-fold division, legislative and executive, was later extended by Montesquieu into legislative, executive and judicative. (Locke did speak of a 'federative' power, but saw it as a function of the executive.) The supreme power in the State, the legislature, was 'entrusted' to the rulers by the people and could be taken back if their trust was belied. Locke's, and others', principles helped to shape the American and French Declaration of Rights.

Locke's *philosophy of religion* was pronouncedly conservative. He explained the relationship between faith and reason on the same lines as the Scholastics. Faith was an acceptance of a proposition on the basis of the authority which put it forward. Revelation and miracles were possible if they were 'super-rational' but not irrational. Although faith far exceeded reason, it could be rationally based. Because of the fallibility of human reason, revelation was even desirable. Locke accepted this from Scholasticism. What he rejected was a fanatic faith which was more like superstition.

3. Hume – Psychologism and Scepticism

Locke made innovations but was on the whole restrained in his thinking. David Hume (1711–76) took him to his logical and radical conclusion. Instead of merely doubting the value of metaphysics, Hume was a universal sceptic; for ontology he substituted psychology; the mind was a sensualistic and mechanistic function; ethics were exclusively utilitarian.

(a) *Human Understanding*

Hume's treatment of human understanding took over where Locke's had left off: at the coexistence of ideas. Hume had therefore no need to spend much time on showing that everything in the human mind had come from outside. His terminology, however, was slightly different. The content of sense-experience he called an impression, and the reproduction of it in the mind an idea. For both Locke and Hume the word that embraced both of these was perception. The question now was: how do ideas contribute to the concept of a thing or law? Hume put forward the theory of *association*. We group ideas according to the laws of 'resemblance, contiguity in time or place, or cause and effect'. When we see a picture, we automatically think of the object represented (association by resemblance); the idea of a particular room in a building attracts the ideas of the neighbouring rooms (association by contiguity); and when we think of a wound, we think of the pain (association by reason of cause and effect). Because Hume reduced the third form of association to the second, and restricted the first to the ideal comparisons of the mathematical-geometrical sciences, the entire world of experimental sciences was left with the association of contiguity. The latter was said to explain the whole problem, particularly the ideas of things and the concepts of law, including of course substance and causality. The process was purely mechanical. When ideas went together or followed each other several times, they were automatically associated in our minds. And if we remembered one of them later on, the other automatically recurred: lightning–thunder, wound–pain, fire–burning, and so on. Habituation was the important thing. It lay behind the laws of association. And it was therefore meant to explain human understanding and the mind, as well as experience, the central point of empiricism. Experience here expressed a reference to reality, but more significantly it countered rationalism by postulating a particular source of 'reality': sense-perception on the basis of a mechanical bodily function. It is little wonder that Hume's philosophy has been called 'a system of scepticism' and 'mental chemistry'.

Hume allowed a special role to the *truths of reason* in mathematics. They depended on pure comparison of ideas in accordance with the law of resemblance (=ultimately, statement of identity). Mathematics did hold necessary and universal truths, 'though there never were a circle or triangle in nature'. Mathematical propositions, in other words, were quite independent of experience; their truth depended on the meaning of the terms without reference to the facts of existence. In fact for Hume there were no circles and triangles, only ideas of circles and triangles. Mathematical truths, therefore, were of no ontological – or indeed logical – importance: they compared ideas, not thought content.

As well as leading to scepticism, this also led to psychologism.

And it also denied the value of the *experimental sciences*. For Hume the experimental sciences were not in touch with real being, even though, in his writings, he constantly referred to 'reality' and suggested that the perceptions of the mind, which strike one with varying degrees of 'force and liveliness', bore a reference to reality. Ultimately being was in the mind. There were more basic reasons, however: all concepts were relative, because they were coextensive with experience; all truths were psychological, because they were no more than comparisons of concepts; and all natural science was sheer belief because it was based on the habitual association of ideas. Hume effectively destroyed the very notion of science: there could be no universally valid propositions, only probabilities. Scepticism was the result. Kant was to agree with Hume's statement of the problems. He even admitted that Hume's questioning had jolted him from his 'dogmatic slumber'. But he disagreed with Hume when Hume denied the sciences anything but probability.

Hume's doubt was also applied to *metaphysics*. In fact metaphysics was the first thing to go. Here again Hume attacked the concepts of substance and causality. Substance was an aggregate of ideas, no more; it had no ontological basis. The soul did not exist, and personal identity was a succession of varying impressions and perceptions. Similarly with *causality*. Hume did not explicitly deny causality, but 'reinterpreted' it as the necessary connexion or regular succession of ideas. The adherents of metaphysics, who regarded causality as something ontological, clearly saw that Hume's theories effectively denied causality and had, to his own satisfaction at least, effectively done away with metaphysics. It was no longer possible to argue from the effect of the created world to a divine cause. Hume expressly set out to destroy what he called 'false and adulterate' metaphysics (as opposed to his own 'true' metaphysics).

(b) Moral Principles

While it is Hume's epistemology that is famous, he had a number of things to say on morality. The principle of moral good was pleasure and utility, both of the individual and of society. We know when a thing is pleasureable or useful by means of a moral taste, feeling or inclination, not by reason. Kant objected that this was to deny the possibility of universal laws. The moral command, the categorical imperative, brooks no ifs and buts. Hume was full of ifs and buts. If we find something useful or pleasureable, it is good. Kant replied that we are not asked: the moral law is absolutely valid, independently of every experience. Hume did not see this.

Hume's contribution (and that of other British ethicists) to the philosophy of virtue is perhaps more to the point. He had some interesting and important things to say on human conduct and character. His utilitarian approach to the quality of an action (whether or not it is useful/pleasureable to us and others) admittedly went a long way to excluding moral value; but he offered a miniature phenomenology of value which could be profitably pursued.

III. THE ENLIGHTENMENT

The key words of the Enlightenment were, among others, light, truth, knowledge, virtue, right, progress, happiness, freedom and morality. They helped to diffuse the work of the great systematic thinkers. It was a time of optimism, perhaps on occasions excessively so. It was also a time of idealism, if a bit superficial. 'Obscurantists' were not suffered gladly. But it is all but universally held today that the period witnessed significant advances in many areas of human civilization. This is not to say that there can be no criticisms against it. The so-called progress of modern science, which became almost a god to the Enlightenment, today threatens to become a deadly danger because of the undreamt-of possibilities of technology, and it would therefore seem that from the very beginning something was wrong. The real flaw was a forgetfulness of true being, a disorientation, a readiness to ignore the subject-matter of metaphysics which would have freed the Enlightenment from a slavery to materialism (that, I believe, is the proper term: matter is neither the first object of knowledge nor the prime content of reality; to engross oneself in it is bound to lead to distortions). Apart from this external threat, the Enlightenment also suffered from an internal threat no less dangerous: the constant temptation of freedom to degenerate into servitude. A word of explanation. Freedom was one of the Enlightenment's slogans. It did not primarily mean freedom from ideological and religious strictures, although that in effect was often the net result. No sooner had it gained sufficient strength than it set about acquiring more freedom by means of enslaving others. Liberalism did a great deal of good and could have had a genuinely and extensively liberating effect, but it did not seem to have sufficient faith in its own message: its actions were for ever those from which it claimed to want to free the world. Whenever it gained a foothold in colleges, universities and political administrations, it immediately denied freedom to those who disagreed with it. Liberalism propounded the view that its opponents had not reached the required standard; they were not progressive enough, not free therefore, still subject to prejudice, unscientific thinking, etc. It was liberalism's attempt to 'free' its opponents from their defects of character that led it to do violence to its own principles. Groups, even, indeed especially, in liberal democracies, placed themselves at the service of freedom and then attempted to exert pressure and impose their views on others. Pressure groups for freedom: I find this something of a paradox. The Enlightenment should have enlightened itself first, clarifying its own prejudices and presuppositions which were sometimes more dangerous than the old ones. Amongst them were its concept of freedom, its belief in progress and above all its belief in science, which took a great deal for granted. Both sides of the Enlightenment have to be borne in mind. And then the Enlightenment was not the same in Britain, France and Germany.

Two ideas became particularly characteristic of the *British* Enlightenment: deism and liberalism.

Deism claimed to believe in God, but in the God of creation not of supernatural revelation. God created the universe. This deists admitted. But then the universe continued to function without further divine intervention. The deists believed they owed this conception to their God, in the sense that any other course would have been unworthy of him. They therefore denied God the freedom to perform miracles or reveal himself. Modern science was so sure of itself that it thought it could define God and say what he could or could not do. The extraordinary element was taken out of religion; religion was 'naturalized', it became a matter of reason, not faith. The deists launched no specific attack on religion; on the contrary, they believed they were doing it a service. Christianity, they said, had now been proved to be as old as man, it had no mysteries, science could subscribe to it. Toland and Tindal put forward views such as these. Kant wrote his *Religion within the limits of pure reason* with a similar intention.

Liberalism, the other great inspiration of the British Enlightenment, propounded the inalienable rights of man. The idea spread rapidly, swept the Continent – through Montesquieu, Voltaire and Rousseau – travelled to the New World and ended up written into nearly all the constitutions of modern times as the Rights of Man. The influence of the British Enlightenment has on this point been thoroughly positive.

The *French* Enlightenment (*Siècle des lumières*) was somewhat different. It was negative, cold, hypercritical, sour and supercilious. It fought the authoritarian regime of the time, the 'restraints' of Christian dogmas and the 'superstition' of metaphysics. *Voltaire* (1694–1778) was typical of the movement. The greatest literary genius of 18th century France, he championed reason, tolerance and human rights, freedom, equality and brotherhood. Voltaire was neither a creative nor an exact thinker, but he knew how to captivate an audience. All he lacked was radio. In theory he was not an atheist but a deist. The whole of nature declared that God existed, he once said; but then he went on, 'If there were no God it would be necessary to invent him', and his deism is revealed for what it really was. For the deists the cosmic machine was itself God; science, reason, was God. Religion was something for the masses, an activity of the heart or, possibly, of moral sensibility. This meant effectively that it was not to be taken too seriously. Reality was revealed by the world of science.

Other French Enlightenment thinkers were more explicit in their atheism and materialism: Diderot, Lamettrie, Holbach, Helvetius, Condillac, Cabanis. 'Man is a machine', said one; 'man is a bundle of nerves', said another. The soul was an activity, not a substantial being. When we talk about psychic acts (=soul) we really mean corporeal acts, as Hobbes had already suggested. Physiology was a more accurate word than psychology. French materialism of the 'Century of Lights' stood godfather to the scientific and dialectical materialism of the nineteenth and twentieth centuries.

One of the greatest thinkers of the time was *Jean-Jacques Rousseau* (1712–78), Voltaire's rival and opponent of the Encyclopaedists. He too wanted progress, freedom and equality, but he proposed other means. Where Voltaire was rationalist and intellectualist, Rousseau was a man of sentiment. The unfeeling theories of rationalism and materialism had no attraction for him. He had had enough of culture, the State, society and religion and its institutions. For him they distorted natural man. Rousseau's idea of Nature was to become a new ideal. People cried, 'Back to nature!' Negatively they meant discarding history, society and culture. Positively they proposed a return to man as he had originally left the Creator's hand, man at his birth before the deforming influences of society and history. Unlike Hobbes, Rousseau regarded natural man as noble, displaying the qualities of freedom, equality and brotherhood. He lived by a *social contract*, which expressed man's desire to recognize his brother's rights and guarantee his freedom. The desire was 'natural' and therefore universal (*Volonté générale*). It was not identical with the sum of votes cast, even if the voting accidentally expressed the 'will of all'. Rousseau returned again and again to this ideal of the 'noble savage'. He used it to found his theories of the ideal State in which liberty, equality and fraternity would be upheld; and his theories of education; and his theories of 'natural' religion. He challenged Diderot's atheism, but he also opposed the old metaphysics and its idealistic proofs for the existence of God. Religion, he thought, was nature; it was a matter of feeling, a matter of the heart. His ideas influenced Kant almost as much as the concept of religion peculiar to British deism did.

The *German* Enlightenment can be divided into several periods. In the early part of it (*c* 1690–1720), the influence of British empiricism, psychologism and utilitarianism was particularly clear. The most notable figure was *Christian Thomasius*, important for the philosophy of law. He saw law as an ordering of the instincts and affections of man. Man he understood in terms of a material being seeking his own profit and capable of being brought to reason by appropriate, that is external physical means. Law did not, therefore, depend on a transcendent metaphysical order. Thomasius rejected metaphysics. In this he found an unexpected support from *pietism*, which suffered no interference of metaphysics in matters of religion, on the grounds that religion was an activity based on sentiment and experience, not knowledge. The second stage of the German Enlightenment (*c* 1720–50) saw a reversal. *Christian Wolff* was prominent here. Metaphysics proved popular again, but in a rationalist spirit. Book after book appeared with titles like *Rational Thoughts on* . . . Kant learnt metaphysics at the feet of his teacher Kuntzen, and continued with it until in his critical period he abandoned it finally and thankfully. The third and last period (*c* 1750–80) was characterized by the work of *Reimarus, Mendelssohn, Lessing* and others. The thinking was very definitely anti-Church. The French Enlightenment, encouraged by Frederick II at his court, was a notable influence. Helvetius, Voltaire and Rousseau were regarded as *the* authorities, and they helped to Gallicize the Prussian Academy. The literary high-point of the period was *G. E. Lessing* (1729–81), critic, dramatist, philosopher, theologian and epigrammatist. Everything was relative. The Bible and religions were stages in man's history, the history of reason. Only reason was eternal. This was the faith behind criticism, although it was not admitted in so many words. Lessing's philosophical drama *Nathan the Wise* put forward the typically Enlightenment view that religion was a matter not of dogma but of tolerance.

CHAPTER THREE: KANT AND GERMAN IDEALISM

With Kant and German idealism, philosophy left the superficialities of the Enlightenment and returned to the serious matters of rational investigation. Genuine philosophical thought came into its own once more. Big ideas and bold systems emerged, only occasionally spoiled by excessive speculation. Behind them all stood an ethical and metaphysical idealism. The metaphysical tradition of the west was continued, if in a slightly different form in that the Idealists accepted something from contemporary criticism, where they felt it was justified, and even contributed to that criticism themselves, especially Kant. However, compared with sensualism, scepticism and the trite utilitarianism of the Empiricists, German idealism set itself the conservative aim of reviving and reinvestigating the metaphysics, ethics and religious theory of the ancients.

1. Kant – Critical Idealism

Immanuel Kant (1724–1804) is often regarded as the greatest of all German philosophers, perhaps even the greatest philosopher of modern times. However his work is regarded, there can be not the slightest doubt that its influence has scarcely been equalled by that of any other thinker. He ushered in a new age. In his own time his philosophy was considered modern, as opposed to Descartes', Hume's and Rousseau's. Despite Thomasius and his disciples, the Enlightenment had faded out in Germany; Wolff and his school were reactionaries. Kant, however, the great Kant, seized the currents of modern thought and welded them into an astonishing system. The peculiarity of it is that he did not throw overboard interest in God, the soul, immortality, freedom, moral value and the suprasensory world, but set out to re-examine them. Although, as he himself said, he was roused from his dogmatic slumber by Hume and jerked into a critical frame of mind, and although he extended Hume's critique of the concepts substance and causality (which in a sense was metaphysics' death blow) to all concepts, Kant was at the opposite pole to Hume. Kant's question of how experiential knowledge was possible was equivalent to asking how *metaphysical* knowledge was possible. Kant was intent not only on working out an epistemology, but also on constructing a new metaphysics, and in his *Critique of Practical Reason* (which is to say, in his ethics) he diverged radically from the Empiricists. It is, of course, debatable whether Kant was as successful in his metaphysics and ethics as the ancients had been; but that he intended to investigate the metaphysical bases of being is beyond doubt. This being so, it is rash to be too free with adjectives like subjective and idealistic when describing Kant's philosophy. In effect his subjectivism was not individualistic, and his idealism did not deny the external world or objectivity. This will become clear, we hope, as we proceed.

(a) The Critique of Pure Reason

Kant's most famous work, the *Critique of Pure Reason*, was first published in 1781. A second edition, substantially altered and expanded, appeared in 1787. Briefly, the book set out to demonstrate what could and could not be known by the human mind; to distinguish therefore (the Greek *krinein* means to judge) between the possible and impossible objects of knowledge. Kant began with scientific knowledge: what, he asked, makes pure mathematics and natural science possible? He has become the theoretician of the modern concept of knowledge. And some critics regard him as no more than that. His real interest, however, was undoubtedly in what made *metaphysical* knowledge possible. And the solution to this problem was the culmination of his life's work. He found it in the a priori structure of human knowledge: 'Metaphysical knowledge', he wrote, 'must contain clear a priori judgements; this is demanded by the peculiarities of its source', and again: 'The main question is always what and how much understanding and reason can know independently of experience.' Such a priori knowledge was not to be merely analytical, according to Kant. That is to say, the predicate of a judgement must not simply explain what is already contained in the subject (as, for example, in the sentence 'All bodies are extended in space'). If it did, it would add nothing new to our knowledge. All the time we want to know something more about reality. Our judgements are judgements on experience or, as Kant called them, synthetic judgements (as, for example, in the sentence 'All bodies are heavy'). The main question of the *Critique* was therefore: 'What makes synthetic judgements possible a priori?' Philosophy prior to Kant had also investigated experiential judgements. British Empiricism gets its name from its efforts in that direction. It wanted to show how experience was possible, and its problem was to discover the laws which governed the connexion of concepts in a scientific statement. The result was meagre, however. Hume declared that the laws of association were questions of factual, or more exactly accidental, habit. Everything could be otherwise if the human mind, on which the conjunction of the various concepts depended, reacted otherwise. Hume (and Locke before him, if it comes to that) turned science into a system of *belief*, not knowledge. Kant, on the other hand – and on this point the rationalists find him congenial – wanted a strict science with necessary universal propositions. If Hume were right, this would be impossible, because our knowledge on his theory is limited to what comes to us from outside and is grouped into concepts and propositions following fortuitous laws. Kant proceeded the other way round. He wanted to show that our knowledge contained components contributed by ourselves prior to all experience. These components were common to every thinking mind and strictly necessary. This was his *Copernican revolution* in philosophy: 'Hitherto it has been accepted that all knowledge depends on objects . . . We must now see whether we do not make more headway in metaphysics by accepting that objects depend on our knowledge . . . The situation is like that in which Copernicus found himself. Having been unable to make any progress in his explanation of the movement of the stars by accepting that they all rotated round the observer, he began to wonder whether he might not do better to leave the stars where they were and spin the observer round. The same revolution can be achieved in metaphysics on the question of the observation of objects. If observation depends on the nature of the objects, I fail to see how we can know anything about them a priori. If, however, the object (as an object of sense-experience) depended on the nature of our observational faculty, I could quite easily entertain the possibility of a priori knowledge.' Kant objected to an 'experience' limited exclusively to the particular individual event of sense-perception: with only a posteriori knowledge, he said, the subject could never make a necessary universal assertion, because he would be constantly having to wait for the next event. One cannot anticipate experience, it was said; Kant intended to. The a priori content of the human mind, he declared, could to some extent anticipate every experience.

The whole of Kant is there in that intermeshing of the outer and inner worlds, of receptivity and spontaneity, of a posteriori experience and a priori anticipation. His Copernican revolution and a priori knowledge did not at all mean that our thought exhausts reality, that we project the world into empty space from the factory of our minds. Kant believed in things-in-themselves (he called them 'noumena'). They are the objects of man's sense faculties, he said. But he added that their outward appearance ('phenomenon') was formless matter that needed to be formed by knowing man: man's a priori forms gave shape to external things. He called these forms *transcendentals*. (Basically a 'transcendental' is something that goes right across the board, as we might say. It is a factor universally present in a given system or discipline.) His philosophy was therefore one of transcendentals, not transcendence as the old metaphysics had been. The latter claimed to know things in their transcendence, that is, as they were in themselves (as noumena). While Kant, however, agreed that there were such things as things-in-themselves, he denied that they were *knowable* in themselves: all knowledge of them on his theory was mediated through the a priori forms. His transcendental philosophy, therefore, was not an investigation into noumena, but an inquiry into the kind of knowledge we can have of noumena. It was obviously subjective, but not subjectivistic. By that I mean that its subjectivism was transcendental and logical and therefore applicable to all human understanding, unlike Hume's psychologism and subjectivism. Kant understood his *new metaphysics* in these terms. It was a theory of the transcendental-logical a priori laws of human and world reality, and an examination of the knowledge accessible to the intellect and reason prior to experience. Its aim was to enable the philosopher to say beforehand how the world and being must be constructed if they were to be the objects of human thought. Transcendental philosophy was therefore both an epistemology (in that it investigated the a priori and a posteriori components of experience) and a metaphysics (in that it investigated being as the possible and actual object of thought). Kant divided his treatment into three parts: transcendental aesthetics, transcendental analytics and transcendental dialectics.

Kant proposed his theory of sense-perception in his *transcendental aesthetics* (the word is here taken in its original sense of *aisthesis*, perception). Things-in-themselves are attractive to the senses. But they are just matter, a shapeless source of sensation, a chaos of unrelated parts. The contingency of sensation is overcome and order is imposed by the universal a priori forms of space and time. Kant proved that space and time were a priori by demonstrating that we cannot abstract them from things. His reasoning is of classic Holmesian simplicity. If we abstracted space and time from the contiguity and succession of things, we should have to presuppose them, in that the very notions of contiguity and succession are impossible without space and time. Kant showed that space and time are not strictly ideas but forms by saying that there is only *one* space and *one* time which are infinite, and although they contain individual stretches and periods they themselves remain qualitatively the same (like ideas in their exemplars). Space and time, therefore, said Kant, are 'empirically real', that is, objectively valid in the sense that they are pre-given to us, and yet subjective in the sense that they mould all human knowledge. The subjectiveness of space and time is not arbitrary: Kant called it a 'transcendental ideality', which in simpler terms meant an a priori condition inherent in all human understanding. This is particularly clear in mathematics which, as we mentioned earlier, was the springboard for Kant's whole philosophy. Mathematics gave Kant two model examples of synthetic a priori judgements. The proposition that a straight line is the shortest distance between two points presupposes the intuition or form of space and therefore a multiplicity of sense-experience; yet it is strictly necessary and intelligible a priori. Similarly the proposition that $7 + 5 = 12$ presupposes the intuition or form of time (in the process of counting) and therefore a multiplicity in inner understanding; but here again it is of necessary validity 'absolutely independently of all experience', to use Kant's own words. To put all this another way, human knowledge takes place in a subjective temporal framework.

Kant exposed his doctrine of categories (transcendental logic) in his *transcendental analytics*. Literally category means a statement or assertion. Kant used the word (as Aristotle had done) to denote the basic concept of thinking. Human knowledge did not exhaust itself in mere intuitions, but included concepts and then judgements about what is. For Kant, knowledge was intuition + thought. 'Our knowledge arises from two basic sources of the mind. The function of the first of these is to receive intuitions, and of the second to give knowledge of an object by means of these intuitions. The first presents us with an object, the second thinks about that object. Intuitions and concepts are therefore the component parts of our knowledge. Thoughts without previous intuitions are empty; intuitions which are not shaped by the understanding into concepts are blind.' Kant discovered his categories primarily by analysing the various forms of judgement. His 'metaphysical deduction' led him to posit twelve categories: unity, difference, totality, reality, negation, limitation, inherence and subsistence (accident and substance), causality and dependence (or effect), reciprocity, possibility and actuality, existence and non-existence, necessity and chance. Apart from these metaphysical categories, Kant deduced from the *Cogito* the category of *transcendental apperception*, which we might call the basic cell of the mind: the *Cogito* must be able to accompany all mental activity. Here we see at its clearest the Copernican revolution engineered by Kant: objects depend on us for their reality (as we see it), not vice versa. Kant also established that the categories' sole function was to shape and order the data provided by the senses; they did not apply to some transcendent world of ideas. And because the chapter on transcendental analytics demonstrates that even the forms of space and time are impossible without the unifying factor of transcendental apperception, it can be said to be the very cornerstone of Kant's whole system. The dividing line between aesthetics and logic is treated in the section on the *schematism* of concepts in which Kant shows how the mind passes from sensation to concept and how the concept ultimately corresponds to the particular sense datum. The passage takes time, time being the condition of inner as well as outer phenomena in that number (which reduces a multiplicity of sense data to one concept) is connected with the form of time. A particular temporal perception therefore corresponds to a particular category: for example, the perception of persistence in time to the category of substance, regularity in time sequence to the category of causality, and presence at all times to the category of necessity.

The most decisive section of the *Critique*, philosophically speaking, is the *transcendental dialectic*. Kant here completes his theory of the possibility and limits of human knowledge and his new metaphysics. Its themes are the themes of the old metaphysics: the world, the soul, God, freedom, immortality, but they are turned into 'ideas'. This is the original contribution of Kant's metaphysics. By 'idea' Kant did not mean what Plato had meant; nor did he accept the definition of the British Empiricists. No, he meant 'a concept from notions (= a pure a priori concept) which exceeds the possibility of experience'. Ideas determine the use of the understanding in experience according to certain principles. These principles are ultimate unifying thoughts on which (like foci) the lines which began with perception and thought converge. 'All our experience begins with the senses, passes to the understanding and ends with reason.' The process of reasoning consists, according to Kant, in looking for the conditions of what is conditioned. For example, the fact that Socrates is mortal is conditioned by the fact that all men are mortal. However, the principle that all men are mortal presupposes other principles which in their turn are conditions. These again are conditioned by others – and so on *ad infinitum*. Reason therefore is a search for all the conditions of a given thing, the world, for example, or the soul. Can we ever come to the end of the search? Kant said not. According to him the most we can do is act as if we had already reached the very last unifying principles of all conditions, and then allow ourselves to be guided by those ideas in further investigation. Ideas are therefore heuristic or 'regulative' principles, a kind of fiction or 'as if' which gives our search some sort of direction but no ultimate target. This is most obvious in our idea of God, who is the totality of all conditions and who for Kant as for Descartes was the *omnitudo realitatis*. Yet God was not himself a reality so much as the conceptualized totality of all the conditions of reality.

Here was the stumbling-block. Was God no more than a thought, then? people asked. And the world, the soul, freedom, immortality too? Criticism found this philosophy of Kant's too subjectivistic. God had always been reckoned the very realest of beings (or less inaccurately, being itself). It is true that according to Kant there was no visible object directly corresponding to an idea as there was to a concept. Concepts were constitutive principles, ideas only regulative principles. Many critics saw this as a weak point in Kant's philosophy. But the concept of heuristic fiction did not mean that the world, God, the soul, immortality, freedom etc. were 'fabricated' objects. It meant that we enjoyed no direct perception of what corresponded to these ideas as we did of the things of which we were accustomed to think in concepts. We did not know God, the soul etc. in the same way that we knew a house or a tree. Kant did not deny that God was the realest being, but he held that we could think only inadequately of this being and would never come to an end in our attempts to think of him.

God therefore was an 'idea', not a concept. This was no different from the old metaphysics. The latter was *verbally* different because it talked about a 'concept' of God, but it knew that God was not a conceivable graspable thing on a par with other objects of human knowledge.

By calling God, the soul and immortality 'ideas', Kant had no intention of denying their reality independently of human cognition; on the contrary. He believed that regarding freedom, immortality, the world, the soul and God as transcendent and not transcendental things involved one in erroneous conclusions (paralogisms) and contradictions (antinomies), the former in psychology, the latter in cosmology, anthropology and theology. In his theories on reason, Kant's philosophy was again transcendental. The ideas of reason, he said, were methods, not material objects. Reason even less than understanding could be properly understood in a transcendent sense. Man all too easily succumbed to the temptation to take the ideas as noumena, or, as Kant expressed it, man was too fond of taking the 'dialectical phenomenon' or appearance for actual 'hyperphysical being'. In fact the ideas of reason were no more than a conceptual framework in one's intercourse with the world. In his theory of reason Kant laid special emphasis on exposing the true nature of dialectical phenomena. 'If the critique of pure reason has done no more than focus on this distinction, it has contributed more to clarifying our concept of metaphysics and guiding our investigations in the metaphysical field than all the fruitless efforts to satisfy the transcendent functions of pure reason.' To encourage a breakthrough of transcendental thinking, Kant developed his theory of the four *antinomies*. He advanced four pairs of contradictory propositions (thesis and antithesis): the world is spatially and temporally limited – or unlimited; every composite substance is infinitely divisible – or not; everything in the world happens necessarily – or freely; there is a necessary being on whom the world depends – or there is not. All four of these propositions were demonstrable on the old metaphysics. But because the propositions are contradictory, the old metaphysics itself became involved in contradictions. Its impossibility would therefore be apparent. The reason for this was only that it reckoned to deal with noumena; it was a transcendent philosophy. If, on the other hand, one engaged in transcendental philosophy, one was dealing with the nature and capabilities of the human mind, and the antinomies were soluble. In the first and second, both propositions are false because the human mind cannot inquire into what lies beyond the phenomena. In the third, both propositions are true, if rightly applied: necessity refers to phenomena, freedom to reason. The same is true of the fourth antinomy: there is a necessary unconditioned ground of all dependent beings, but it is an idea of reason. Kant dealt with the conventional proofs for God's existence (ontological, cosmological, teleological) in this context. He reduced them all to the ontological argument, which concludes to God's existence from the concept of God as the most perfect being, and demonstrated its falsity: one may not, without further qualification, pass from the logical order, which exists only as concepts, to the ontological. As we saw earlier, the ontological argument did not in fact base itself on a concept and did not make the leap of which Kant accused it. He misunderstood it. He also misunderstood the other proofs for the existence of God, and indeed the entire significance of the old metaphysics. If the latter is understood in a deeper way than the mere wording Kant adopted from the Enlightenment philosophers, the difference between his new metaphysics and the old is not so large as might appear. Kant's critique of the proofs for God's existence did not deny that existence. It was only a critique of an allegedly inaccessible road to God, and intended to pave the way for a better account of the idea of God than had so far been proposed. Kant offered this better account in his ethics.

(b) The Critique of Practical Reason

It is probably true that Kant's greatest contribution lies in his services to ethics, or, as he called it, in his critique of practical reason. Against British eudaemonism and utilitarianism, which had had the effect of falsifying the meaning of moral goodness and submerging morality into the ebb and flow of historical and social relationships, so that they might more properly be called sociological than ethical theories, Kant determined to clarify once for all the purity and absoluteness of human morality.

Fundamental to his purpose was the proposition that man is a rational being and that reason implies two elements totally extraneous to the empirical world of phenomena: obligation and freedom. For Kant *obligation*, also called duty, the moral law, conscience and the categorical imperative, was an 'undeniable fact'. It 'belonged to man's essence.' At the same time he accepted it as certain that this obligation was a law in the sense that it was universally valid irrespective of time, circumstances and individuals: irrespective, in short, of 'experience'. It was a priori because it was nothing other than the expression of the mind, of reason itself, which can utter only what is timelessly and eternally true. Reason also implied *freedom*, either as a consequence of obligation, as Kant stressed in the *Critique of Practical Reason*, or, as he proposed later, particularly in the *Critique of Judgement*, as an element internal to reason. Because of his sense of obligation and his freedom, man as an intelligent being was distinguished from the rest of nature around him. Kant was therefore in the main stream of the old metaphysics of man.

Kant's ethics was based on his metaphysics. Because obligation was a universal law, the principle of moral conduct could be phrased as follows: 'Act in such a way that the intention of your will can always stand as a principle of universal legislation.' This has been called *formalism*. Kant did not begin his ethics by outlining a table of values, although he tried to demonstrate what the virtues, loyalty, for example, or truth or courage, meant in man's life, and although he referred to utility, well-being, cultural progress etc. All these are 'material' characteristics of man's life, he said, and material things, even ethical values, are empirical because one cannot know beforehand whether they are adapted to man or not. If morality depended on such empirical phenomena, it would be indistinguishable from caprice and would lose all credibility as a *law*. The moral law for Kant was a direct result of human reason, which was itself essentially both binding and universally valid. Moral good must be judged by reason. The fact that morality was universally binding did not depend on the nature of any particular material good. Rather the reverse was true: the good depended on its possible lawfulness. 'It is not possible to think of anything in the world, or indeed outside the world, which can be taken as good without qualification – except a good will.' And 'a will is good not because of what it does or because of its ability to reach any particular good, but because of its intention.' The will was good when it was 'pure', that is, when reason dictated the law on which it functioned. This constituted ethical *autonomy*. Kant used to say that reason is practical. By that he meant that apart from the empirical level of life, on which man is extended in space and time, the individual also experiences a higher level of activity as a rational being. On that level he himself knows what is good without the assistance of any external law-giver. In fact we should not submit to such in moral matters for fear of becoming his slave and lapsing into heteronomy. In his reason man is completely free and yet completely subject to the law: reason binds him, but it also frees him by raising him above everything which is not himself. Because reason is a law, man's autonomy is not to be understood as *total* independence and arbitrary self-rule. No, reason is like a god in miniature, not in the sense that man can aspire to divine autocracy, but because reason is a divine spark at work in him. Man, said Kant, can never be regarded as a means to an end: 'Act in such a way that you always use humanity, whether in yourself or in any other person, as an end, never as a mere means.' Kant was quite radical in following his ethical principles to their logical conclusion. Conduct was morally good if the action was done out of a sense of duty and for the sake of duty, in other words in obedience to the moral law. An action might still be 'legal' in the sense of materially conforming to the law, but if it was done because the individual felt inclined to act in that way or expected a reward or was angling for praise or was afraid, then it could not be 'moral' because it did not proceed from a sense of duty. This has been called Kant's *rigorism*. It was a logical development of his formalism. He wanted to exclude any consideration of one's own happiness, even eternal happiness, because if it ousted law as the basis of morality, he thought, humans would be reduced to creatures responding to promises of payment. None the less Kant had some place for it in his ethics: not as a motive of moral behaviour, but as a consequence of it. The life morally lived was worthy of happiness.

This brings us to the *postulates* of practical reason: immortality, freedom and God. Immortality is demanded by the consideration that man can never reach the moral ideal, but must continually work towards it. Only God is perfectly holy. All other beings are on their way to the good. Kant therefore postulated immortality, because without it 'the moral laws would be an empty fabric of the brain'. Freedom has been mentioned already in connexion with the theory of antinomies. It is at least thinkable, runs that theory, that conduct need not be subject to mechanical necessity. In the *Critique of Practical Reason* Kant regarded freedom as a precondition of obligation which we have only to make use of, even though here again he almost considered it to be a fact. The postulate of freedom means that it really exists, that it is not only thinkable. Kant arrived at the postulate of God by means of his reflexions on happiness. If we dare hope that moral conduct will be rewarded, we have to accept a supreme Reason which rules by imposing moral laws and is also a cause of nature, that is, is powerful enough to reward us with happiness. There is no equivalent in material nature. Because only God is the 'necessary combination of both elements' and because we necessarily belong to an intelligible world by virtue of our reason, we must accept the future world, God's world. Like Leibniz Kant referred to a kingdom of grace, with God the all-wise source and ruler at its head. 'Reason tells us that God and a future life are two inseparable preconditions of the sense of obligation laid on us by pure reason.' This is in effect a moral proof for the existence of God; and in fact Kant regarded it as the only valid one.

Basing himself on these ethical principles, Kant proceeded to suggest what *religion* was about. Religion, he said, must work within the limits of reason if it is to be genuine. By reason here he meant practical reason. In other words, Kant regarded morality and religion as all but identical. The only difference was that in religion the moral laws were also the commandments of God. Kant had little time for the historical side of religion. He thought revelation made sense only as an expression of reason and the idea of God, which latter, again, was no more than the ultimate consequence of moral obligation. According to Kant, then, the historical data of revelation needed to be sifted until the moral substratum was discovered. Despite this very narrow historical outlook, we must not forget that Kant made a genuine effort to get to the bottom of our thought of God, both in the *Critique of Pure Reason* and in the *Critique of Practical Reason*. And if after all that God is still only at the 'postulate' stage, we have to remember that for Kant so-called objective-practical reality was no less real than the data of the senses. In fact it was realer and should be called simply 'reality'. This is vital if Kant is not to be misinterpreted; he did not propose an inadequate subjectivism. It is, alas, all too common to express disappointment over his approach to what we should call 'things out there', but that point of view really rests on an insufficient appreciation of Kantianism.

Law and the *State* were included under practical reason. If Kant's philosophy of religion contained too much morality, his philosophy of law contained too little. Law was negatively defined as the 'essence of the conditions under which the will of one individual can be reconciled with the will of another in deference to a universal law of freedom'. Kant effectively reduced law to a matter of external measures of constraint. He differentiated it sharply from morality (the exclusive sphere of man's sense of duty). British empiricism's influence, especially Hobbes' theory of the social covenant, is very noticeable here. It had already penetrated Germany in the writings of Thomasius. Jurists have frequently applauded it as a fine achievement because it leaves them in sole charge of legislation. It leaves the field wide open for clarity of definition and detailed qualification; the law becomes its own master, subject to no superior power like conscience and sense of duty. The consequence of Kant's philosophy in law was legal positivism, and in practical life a sort of bookkeeping by double entry: people began saying: well, if law doesn't oblige me in conscience, I needn't bother with it; or: my conscience doesn't oblige me in law, so I don't need to obey it.

Kant's conception of the State followed from his concept of law. The State was 'a union of people under laws'. It was likewise a purely external institution. The individual's freedom was given room to move when force was held at bay by force. Kant accepted the division of power into executive, legislative and judicative. The idea of State had no positive content for Kant: its business was to keep the balance among the various social and political forces. The only valid social commandment was negative: do no hurt. If that were observed, freedom would flourish. It was the liberal ideal, and a poor one compared with the ancient concept of the State as the universal organization of human morality. Nothing else is left, apparently, in the present fragmented state of culture. Even so, Kant did betray a certain moral understanding of the State, inasmuch as the goal of world history was to be the establishment of an optimum State, a sort of League of Nations from which war was banished; and part of that was not only civilization but culture, of which morality was an essential part.

(c) The Critique of Judgement

Having investigated knowledge in the *Critique of Pure Reason* and will in the *Critique of Practical Reason*, Kant proceeded to investigate feeling in the *Critique of Judgement*. Feeling (pleasure and pain) Kant saw as in some sense a goal. Now a goal can be subjective (if it is proposed by man) or objective (if it is proposed by nature). Kant therefore distinguished an aesthetic and a teleological judgement (the critique of judgement being the proper philosophical place for a consideration of purpose). In both cases the world is seen from the point of view of freedom, since the idea of goal or purpose includes a concept of will, an attitude towards pleasure and displeasure.

The *aesthetic judgement* is concerned with the beautiful and the sublime. In this Kant's influence on German classical literature, particularly Goethe and Schiller, was enormous. Kant put forward the view that art is the contemplation of pure forms. If the perception of a form *qua* form is such that it arouses pleasure in the onlooker and inspires him with a sense of beauty, his statement 'I like an it' is aesthetic judgement. (A thing fulfils its purpose if it is adapted to certain ends.) Now a judgement is not just a statement, a verbal conceptual assertion, but an attitude. And an attitude of aesthetic pleasure does not coincide with personal comfort: comfort is a purely subjective thing; or with morality: the moral good inspires respect and esteem, not pleasure; or with desire: desire is just an appetite to possess. No, aesthetic pleasure is 'disinterested' agreement, and agreement with the objective content of the forms revealed in art. Kant therefore defined the beautiful as 'that which is recognized without the help of concepts as the object of a necessary satisfaction'.

The *teleological judgement* deals with the idea of purpose in nature, particularly organic nature. The parts of an organism are always in the service of the whole; they exist for the sake of the whole, and therefore also for the sake of each other. An organism is a model of purposeful cooperation. Not the tiniest blade of grass, said Kant, could be thought of without the idea of purpose or understood in purely mechanical terms. Once the individual organism is seen in this way, it is logical, Kant continued, to extend it to the whole of nature and see the entire world as a collusion of parts working towards a common goal. Mechanism and causal determination are subordinated to this goal. Further, the idea of purpose demands the idea of an intelligent being behind it. Does this turn teleology into theology? Yes and no. Purpose was not included in Kant's categories; it was a regulative not a constitutive concept. It was only an 'idea' and there was no corresponding object. We see not purpose but things as if they were purposeful; the underlying plan, the plan in the *intellectus archetypus*, we cannot see. If we had as clear a knowledge of objective as of subjective purpose, the goals of nature would be as transparent as our own. They are not, however. And the 'as if' remains; the idea of purpose is a regulative fiction.

Here arises a difficulty inherent in Kant's philosophy from the start. Purpose, freedom, immortality, God, etc. are ideas. Everything is seen 'as if' it were this or that. The fiction, however, must have some foundation 'in reality'. The ideas in our minds therefore correspond to something outside our minds, something real, something in itself. According to Kant, however, this something real is unknowable. But if it really is unknowable, it is hard to see how Kant can postulate it in the first place, even in his theory of categories. And then if Kant persists in postulating it, as he does, he must show, as ancient metaphysics had recognized, what justification there is. If his new metaphysics is a transcendental philosophy designed to expose the a priori functions of human consciousness in the process of knowing reality, it cannot simply refer to a thing as an unknown quantity and then confront the mind with it as if it were a definite something. Kant falls between two stools: he fails to explain the function both of sensation and of intellection. But then perhaps reference to things, substances, beings is mere talk, a metaphor and symbol for the mind which alone constitutes reality, which, with its language and dialectic, alone exists? Is there anything at all outside the mind? This was the problem to which German idealists, in particular Fichte, devoted their energies.

2. Fichte – Subjective Idealism

Kant was at fault, said Johann Gottlieb Fichte (1762–1814), in not taking his masterly vision of the creative human mind to its conclusion. He left the noumenon in place, attributed to it a power over our senses and made the mind dependent on it. Kant was too dogmatic and not critical enough. If his categories had been transcendent forms and not purely spontaneous, the mind would have been utterly free. There were only two philosophies, dogmatism and idealism. Only the latter made man free. The individual had to make his choice, because he could not embrace both at once. And 'a man will choose his philosophy depending on the type of person he is.' Fichte wanted to be free. So he opted for idealism. Mind meant much more for him than for Kant. For Kant it was something like a Platonic demiurge fashioning the world out of pre-existent matter; for Fichte it was something like the God of the Bible, creating a world out of nothing. Only the ego existed. The world came to be because of it.

Fichte described this process of creation in his *Theory of Science* or *Knowledge*. Knowledge was the process by which things came to be. Formerly philosophy had accepted the origin of experience and knowledge in sensation, thus the development of thought and reason began with sense data. This, for Fichte, was to enslave man to something other than himself. Consciousness, he said, needed no more than itself in self-contemplation and self-development. The prime datum of consciousness was one's own self, the pure I (cf. the *Cogito* of Kant's transcendental apperception). It enabled a person to say: I am I (thesis). But because an I cannot be thought of without a non-I (as right cannot be thought of without left), we are faced with what can become the world (antithesis). And because both position and opposition take place in us, both are tied up with a third step: the suppression of the contradiction and the unity of a higher I (synthesis). This so-called dialectical syllogism became an accepted pattern in German idealism. It was used to conclude from the Many to the One, in both thought and reality, and to subsume the Many into the One in consciousness. 'Thought corresponds to reality': this was the conclusion of philosophers who, after removing an inconsistency in Kant, imagined that the distinction between the two was more apparent than real.

Fichte held that the mind was more than just thought: it included action. His theory of knowledge was therefore also a moral theory; his dialectic was not an analysis of ideas, like Plato's, but progressive activity. 'In the beginning was the word' he translated as 'In the beginning was the deed'. Positing the 'I' was itself an act and a reality. And everything that was real, the whole of nature in other words, was our activity, or, more exactly, our duty, because activity was pure activity, pure will. Kant's ethics had accepted pure will as the only good thing in the world and as a creative force.

Fichte extended it beyond ethics: reality was reality and being was being only because of our activity and our sense of duty. Bare knowledge, as Descartes had conceived it, could doubt everything: there was nothing that could withstand the battering of methodical doubt, and so ultimately the whole world could be the merest dream. The only thing left standing was our will and its belief in duty, and on that foundation our knowledge of the world (and therefore the reality of the world) was built up. We know in pure will that this reality is not accessible to sense-experience. A reality which is no more than matter, said Fichte, a world in which man is at home, conquers nature and turns the earth into a paradise is unworthy of him. Being born to live the beautiful life and then die, leaving behind children who will do the same, is stupidity. To be meaningful, existence must be sublimated into a supra-sensory existence which is more than matter, power and enjoyment, which partakes of the eternal and divine, not only in the next life but in this. It is particularly clear in the early Fichte, but still evident in the mature Fichte, that the divine was engendered by right doing; religion was just morality; revelation was man's belief in reason; and God, even more than for Kant, was no more than a human thought. Fichte has consequently been accused of atheism.

In the late Fichte, however, the theory of suprasensory life, the concept of duty as the voice of God and the concept of the divine as the love of God in the Johannine sense show that, over and above the I, there was a genuinely transcendent non-I, which could, admittedly, be known only through our I, but which in its otherness was the superior being men needed if they were to be fully themselves. 'If we live truly in what is other and higher than ourselves, we shall have our own present fully.'

3. Schelling – Objective Idealism

Fichte had thought that there were only two possible philosophies: dogmatism, which accepted things-in-themselves, and idealism, which accepted only the content of human consciousness. One had to choose between the two. Friedrich Wilhelm Schelling (1775–1854) did not choose, but advocated both options at once. He saw that the subject called for an object, but denied that the one must be created by the other. No, what was needed was a *real* object (an object 'out there'). Conversely there must be a way from the object to the subject, because all unconscious things had a drive towards what was conscious. 'Our hearts cannot be satisfied with a merely intellectual existence. There is something in us which yearns for essential reality . . . and just as the artist does not rest satisfied with an idea in his head but wants to embody and clothe it, and a person consumed with enthusiasm for an ideal wants to reveal or find it in a palpable form, so the goal of all longing is the perfectly bodily as the reflexion of the perfectly intellectual.' This 'reflexion of the perfectly intellectual' was both nature and consciousness, according to Schelling, so that he was still an idealist. His idealism, however, can be called objective in that he postulated an orientation of consciousness to something not dependent on it. Fichte opposed nature to the activities of the subjective I, positive religion to religion that did not exceed the limits of pure reason, the God of myth and historical revelation to the God of ideas. There was still, however, in Schelling a temptation to reduce everything, including revelation and history, to a superior quasi-gnostic knowledge.

Schelling's philosophy developed as an antidote to Fichte's. In his *natural philosophy*, nature was not a creation of the active I any more, or the mere object of duty. It existed in its own right and preceded the human subject. It was infinitely full, and this very wealth proved its objectivity and its otherness to the I. One needed not only to act, but also to admire, learn and draw on. Schelling's greatest contribution in natural philosophy, however, was not perhaps this break with subjective idealism, but his insight into the *vitality* of nature. Kant had no category for living nature; his theory was mathematical and mechanical. In his *Critique of Judgement* Kant admittedly introduced the idea of purpose, but that idea was no more than a regulative principle and so of limited application. For

Schelling life and soul were constitutive principles of nature. And in their depths he discovered Mind. 'So-called Nature is therefore nothing other than immature intelligence. Its phenomena betray the characteristics of intelligence at a pre-conscious stage. Nature culminates . . . in the highest form of reflexion which is man or, in more general terms, reason; reason is Nature's turning back on itself, and that very process reveals that Nature is basically identical with what in us is known as intelligence and consciousness.' Nature, like Goethe's plant, is the 'form which in living fashions itself'. On the basis of this natural philosophy, Schelling was justified in saying that 'Everything strives with divine boldness to surpass itself'. Nature, therefore, was life, soul, and a path to Mind. Conversely one may pass from Mind to nature, as Schelling did in his *Theory of Transcendental Idealism* (a parallel to his *Towards a Philosophy of Nature*) when he showed, as Fichte had done, that the object can be discerned in the subject, and nature in Mind. Neither object nor nature, however, were posited by the I; they were discovered as a correlation in our examination of the significance and basis of Mind, just as Schelling had established Mind as the correlate of nature.

It is clear from what has been said, however, that Schelling effectively identified nature and Mind. The theme of his *philosophy of identity* was that they were basically the same. There was no distinction between subject and object, reality and ideality; nature was Mind in visible form, Mind was invisible nature. What difference, one may ask, is there between this and early Fichte? It reads like an even more presumptuous attempt to identify the Many with the One, the world with God. Schelling saw the danger and wanted to avoid any identification which would slur the concept of otherness. Unfortunately his efforts to disclose the presence of the identical in the non-identical without resorting to a dialectic that would efface all clear logical contours were too involved not to give rise to incomprehension in his readers.

In both his natural philosophy and transcendental philosophy, Schelling regarded the world as a divine work of art. In his *philosophy of art* he saw beauty in the fact that the infinite descended tangibly to the level of the finite and the finite was, in the unity of body and soul, nature and Mind, law and freedom, individuality and universality, a symbol of the infinite. One senses the Platonic theory of ideas somewhere at the back of Schelling's mind.

After his Würzburg period (1803–6), Schelling's optimism became less and less marked. In his *philosophy of freedom* and history, irrational elements became increasingly frequent: a will that was dark and unpredictable; an individuality that refused to submit to the whole and defied comprehension; a meaninglessness in history; evil at the base of reality, even God, distorting the world through sin. Even in all this misery, however, there was a gleam of hope: everything would come right in the end, world history and God himself would attain their true nature, light would banish the darkness for ever. '*Positive philosophy*' was intended to investigate this individualistic irrational purely historical element. Schelling hoped it would bring what he saw as a necessary corrective to other forms of idealism in that now the concrete was to be more powerful than the conceptually universal.

In fact, however, Schelling still inclined towards the universal. He struggled to capture it in what has rightly been called a gnostic-type knowledge. He found few sympathizers. Like Faust, 'with daring hopeful flight', he 'expanded toward infinity'.

In general, however, Schelling had considerable influence, particularly with the *Romantics, G. Carus, F. von Baader, F. Schleiermacher, H. Jacobi* and others, all of them thinkers to whom feeling, intuition, tradition and faith meant more than pure reason and merely conceptual thought. A similar current arose in France: *L. de Bonald, L. Bautain, A. Bonetty, G. Ventura, F. R. de Lamennais,* etc.

4. Hegel – Absolute Idealism

Georg Wilhelm Friedrich Hegel (1770–1831) is usually regarded as the culmination of German idealism. With an astonishing breadth of knowledge, genuine metaphysical insight and a tremendous power of thought, he set out to show that objects were manifestations of intelligence. In the beginning was the Logos; and not only in the beginning, but at all times. The Logos, confused neither by matter nor by the individual nor by freedom, was everything. This was not merely to identify the Logos with Nature: it was also to identify Nature with Mind. In other words, Hegel's philosophy was absolute idealism, or panlogism. The Logos evolved in the history of the world. Hegel regarded himself as the focal point of all previous attempts to see the world *sub specie aeternitatis*, from Heraclitus, Plato, Aristotle and Augustine to the late Middle Ages and finally to Spinoza's famous formula *Deus sive substantia sive natura*. At the same time his own philosophy was radically new.

(a) The Basis

Hegel's philosophy started where Kant had left off, at the thing-in-itself, the object, the noumenon, the material of the a priori form. Hegel accepted that the forms of objective knowledge were contributed by the spontaneity of the mind, but then proceeded to ask whether the object as it thus disclosed itself to man was really an object 'out there'. His answer was that although the categories might be constructs of the human mind, it did not follow that they were merely that and not also the fabric of noumena. Because Kant saw only one side, his philosophy was 'pure idealism without interest in content'. It was content, however, which guaranteed truth: it was an ancient conviction of mankind that truth consisted in thinking what really was the case, 'in itself'. Like his friend Schelling, Hegel achieved a breakthrough to objectivity, but it was neither to Fichte's subjective objectivity nor to dogmatism's realistic objectivity. In the former there was no genuine objectivity, in the latter no spontaneity. The only way out was to say that man's thought-process, where it was true (that is, where it reached being), was itself the thought-process of the cosmic Mind which created things by thinking about them (as Kant had also said) and in which thought, truth and being coincided. 'Everything rational' he said, 'is real, and everything real is rational.' Kant's idealism had been critical. Hegel pursued metaphysics, despite Kant's critique, and more boldly than ever before. Not only did he investigate the workings of the Absolute: he was conscious of the Absolute's working through him. God was the philosopher.

(b) Dialectics

Hegel's dialectic was designed to break away from the old metaphysics, with its talk about things-in-themselves, and also from Kant's new metaphysics, with its transcendental forms. It tried to see being, beings and the forms of thought as movements of the mind. The only reality now conceded to exist was this Mind, and the law governing its functioning, which was considered to provide a more than adequate explanation of the processes of nature and history, was dialectic, that is, the triple passage from thesis and antithesis to synthesis, which we mentioned earlier in connexion with Fichte. Ontology and transcendental philosophy were subsumed into dialectic. The central point of it was not the triple passage itself – that was only its technical expression – but the theory that being was nothing since everything was in motion and part of a continual flux in which the synthesis became the initial thesis of another dialectic. 'Something is in itself in so far as it has returned to itself from being-for-another.' The principle of contradiction becomes rather blurred here. The reader is tempted to go no further, because if in some sense a thing is itself only to the extent that it exists in something else, everyday experience, which is convinced that things are substantial and more or less permanent, is denied. Hegel replied in his *Phenomenology of Mind* by demonstrating that this alleged something is substantial and permanent only to the uncritical observer. In reality it fragments into countless states and relations to other things; negation is central to an essence, so that a thing exists only to the extent that it unfolds itself by absorbing the negation. To understand something, one would have to grasp in one mental operation its entire history and the many facets which it presents to different observers. 'The contemplation of everything that is, shows, in itself, that in its self-identity it is self-contradictory and self-different, and in its variety or contradiction, self-identical; it is in itself this movement of transition of one of these determinations into the other, just because each in itself is its own opposite' (*Science of Logic*). As Bertrand Russell pertinently remarked, if Hegel is right, no word has any meaning because we must know already the meaning of all the other words it presupposes. For example, if we are to understand the sentence 'John is the father of James', we must know who John is and who James is. To know that, however, we should have to know all their characteristics, and that again means knowing all sorts of people, things, countries, historical events, social conditions etc. Before we could know who John was, therefore, we should have gone into the entire universe. And in fact truth for Hegel was the universe. The objection raises important questions: is there a place in Hegel's system for individuality? in other words, are there boundaries marking one thing off from another, for example God from the world, the citizen from the State? are there such things as freedom and self-determination? etc. For the moment, however, we may more usefully concentrate on the background to Hegel's dialectic and try to see whether we cannot discover his true intentions.

(c) *Hegel's Philosophical Home*

The dialectic is based on a particular thought-form which Hegel made his own. It is usually referred to as *organological*. In organic life, birth (thesis) and decay (antithesis) together form life (synthesis). Hegel drew this basic idea from the Bible, in which opposites contribute to a third reality: 'Unless a grain of wheat falls into the earth and dies, it remains alone; but if it dies, it bears much fruit.' It was particularly in John's Gospel that Hegel found what became characteristic of his system: the equation God = Spirit = Truth = Life = Way. The Johannine Logos was in the beginning and it was God; it was responsible for creation; it was the light of the world, it came into the world, it became flesh so that all who believed might be children of God. Hegel said all this about his Idea. The Idea was in the beginning, it was Spirit, was God, became flesh, was the light and life of the world and wanted to take the world back to God. At the age of twenty-five, Hegel began to write a Life of Jesus. It started with the sentence: 'Pure reason, incapable of any fluctuation, is the divinity itself.' When, at forty-two, he undertook the formal elaboration of his system and wrote the *Science of Logic*, he gave as the definition of logic (in the Introduction): 'Logic is consequently to be conceived as the system of pure reason, the realm of pure thought. Such a realm is truth as it exists in and for itself without distortion. One may therefore say that its content is God as he exists in his eternal essence prior to the creation of nature and finite Mind.'

He called the point at which he came on the philosophical scene 'philosophy's Good Friday'. It was his task, as he saw it, to raise God to new life. Kant's alleged proof of the impossibility of metaphysics and of the proofs for God's existence had excluded God as an object of knowledge. God could only be believed, or, as Schleiermacher said, could be the object of sentiment only. Hegel opposed this view vehemently. Before Nietzsche he wrote: 'God is dead'. But, he went on, it is God's nature to die and live again. His system was to vindicate this living God. God was the soul of the universe and the life of its life. And Hegel's thought was at home in this 'life'. To understand Hegel it is important to bear these remarks in mind. His system respects both the individual and the universal, life being a synthesis of the two. The individualist falls short of reality as much as the totalitarian does, because they both hypostasize one side. Even if both sides were taken together statically, the result would be the same. Notions must be fluid, like everything else in life. But then fluidity itself, without further qualification, would be false, because the concept of it is incomplete unless it includes the notion of something static. Life is unavoidably a synthesis of the two. There are boundaries, therefore; there is this and the other, even if it is only so that they may be negated and overcome. There is freedom too in thought taken from life, because life is 'form'. The concept of form, which reflects the Platonic idea, always includes the Many as well as the One: everything wants to be like the Idea, but is not (is therefore free from the Idea) and yet is (because it participates in the Idea), and therefore there is a law even in freedom. *God* is not replaced by the world, but must be thought of in the world's being and becoming if he is not to remain a stiff empty concept. Nicholas of Cusa had also said that God was what must be named with every name, the 'omninominable'. Hegel also wanted to appreciate *Christianity* in its historical form and not simply as a religion of reason, despite his regard for philosophy as the highest form of truth.

(d) After Hegel

Hegel's influence has been almost incalculable. Here we can mention only the philosophy of religion, social theory and the philosophy of history.

As in all his philosophy, Hegel intended his *philosophy of religion* to subsume opposites into a synthesis. To fail to grasp that synthesis is to risk emphasizing one aspect at the expense of others. For example, stressing certain parts of his views on God, Christianity and religion, one could easily interpret Hegel as a theist. Stressing certain other factors, for example the superiority of philosophy over religion in his system, one would conclude that Hegel was a pantheist. And certain other critics would call him an atheist. So we find a Hegelian right (*Gabler, Hinrichs, Göschel, Bauer*) and a Hegelian left, which merges into materialism (the later *Bauer, David Friedrich Strauss, Feuerbach, Marx* and *Engels*).

In *social theory*, disciples maintained that all truth, philosophy, religion and law were mediated by social conditions. The net result was that the Marxists stood Hegel on his head and reduced all ideas to epiphenomena of industrial evolution. As Alexander Herzen (d. 1870) said, Hegel was the algebra of revolution because of his philosophy of eternal becoming and the dialectical transformation of one thing into its opposite.

But even the philosophers of the Prussian State appealed to Hegel, because he said that the State was God's access to the world and 'the reality of the moral idea'. They did not doubt he meant them. And when statesmen perceived fallings-off from the divine ideal, they could console themselves with Hegel's words: 'Every State . . . if it belongs to our created time, always contains the essential moments of its existence . . . The State is not a work of art, it stands in the world, in the realm of the arbitrary, of chance, of error, but still even the most despicable person, a criminal, a sick person or a cripple is a living man. The positive – life – persists despite its lacks, and we are here dealing with that positive thing.' Again one can appreciate the ambiguity to which Hegel's philosophy gives rise.

In the *philosophy of history*, Hegel has influenced a whole series of important philosophers: *A. Schwegler, J. E. Erdmann, K. Fischer, E. Zeller,* and a number of thinkers who have applied cultural morphology to history: *O. Spengler, B. Croce, A. J. Toynbee, K. Jaspers.*

5. Herbart and Schopenhauer – the End of Idealism

(a) Herbart

Johann Friedrich Herbart (1776–1841) was all but the last of the German idealist philosophers. He called himself a Kantian, but a Kantian of 1828. Times had changed. Criticism of Kant was more frequent and far-reaching than in any of the other idealists: Kant was explicitly not followed, although his idealism to some extent was. Reality, which Kant had said could be grasped only in conception, was reinstated as an object of knowledge. Such a statement left itself open to the objection that it rested on a misunderstanding of Kant. Herbart, however, understood him very well, although his procedure shows that Kant's transcendental philosophy was not so even as conventional Kantianism would like to make out. Herbart proves it, and he was typical of his period. We cannot here go into his theories of reality, the ego, the soul and beauty, or his influence in psychology and pedagogy, which, mainly because of W. Rein, extended to the smallest village school. O. Willmann was also influenced by him.

Other realist thinkers were *B. Bolzano* (1781–1848), the philosopher of mathematics, who maintained against Kant that 'he never understood or conceded that synthetic a priori judgements should be mediated through perception', and, much later, *F. Brentano* (1838–1917), who influenced the so-called Austrian school: *Marty, Meinong, Stumpf* and through them *Husserl*.

(b) Schopenhauer

Arthur Schopenhauer (1788–1860) was the declared enemy of 'Hegel and his gang' (his own words). He lost no opportunity to attack them and even resorted to abuse. He also criticized Kant, especially Kant's ethics. On the other hand there are similarities between Schopenhauer and Kant, and it is not totally distorting to include both among the German idealists. Schopenhauer's main work was his *World as Will and Representation* (1819). In so far as the world was representation, he agreed with Kant; in so far as it was will, he disagreed.

The world was *representation* (or idea) as far as its appearance or surface was concerned. Schopenhauer accepted from Kant that the world was the individual's subjective idea of it. This insight, he said, was the crux of philosophy. One was aware that one knew no sun or earth, but knew an eye which saw a sun and a hand which felt an earth. The world was therefore a collection of images or ideas. To this phenomenal world, however, Schopenhauer did not apply Kant's twelve categories, but substituted for them another form of mental ordering, the idea of basis, applied in four ways: as the logical base of judgements, as the entitative base of mathematical formulae, as motivation in the psychic field and as causality in natural objects. Like the Kantian categories, these forms of mental coherence were strictly necessary determinations, even in man's spiritual life. Schopenhauer was a rigorous opponent of free will.

The world was *will*, or force, as regards things. Schopenhauer accepted Kant's division of the world into phenomena and noumena, things-as-they-appear-to-us and things-in-themselves, but he also thought that we were not restricted to knowledge of pheonmena. The inner core of things was accessible. We could experience them. Through our will we could make contact with the world of things-in-themselves in an experience that was more intense than either sense-perception or conceptual knowledge. 'Man carries the ultimate secrets of reality in the depths of his being, and there he has untrammelled access to them.' The first thing we knew was our own will: in desire, hope, love, hate, grief, suffering, knowledge, thought, idea; and then, by a process of generalization and transference, the whole world. Will was at the root of all phenomena, from gravity to self-consciousness. Natural forces like centrifugal force, magnetism, chemical affinity, growth, instinct were all will. In man, will became conscious. Hegel had posited Mind at the root of reality, and in man a Mind that was free. For Schopenhauer will, even in man, was blind. It was unspiritual, mindless, pure desire and appetite.

Will necessarily suffered. Schopenhauer's philosophy was therefore one of *pessimism*. Man found himself thrust into infinite space and time, a finite quantum without an absolute when or where. He was for ever abandoned and threatened, his pilgrimage was a slow decay and his life a delayed death. Left to his own devices, sure of nothing but his own sense of need, man was everywhere pursued by cares. Life was a business whose output did not cover the costs. The world was a tragi-comedy. The real meaninglessness of it all was that despite everything things wanted to be there. In some anger Schopenhauer turned on Leibniz's optimism and Hegel's purposeful world, and claimed to speak in the name of Christianity: Christianity, like Buddhism, he said, preaches the nothingness of earthly life. In this, as in his pessimism as a whole, Schopenhauer was guilty of oversimplification. All he would have been justified in doing would have been pointing out the meaninglessness and pain in much of what goes on, without advocating a totally meaningless world. He offered no evidence for his views. Schelling too saw the blind will and the untruth in the world, but he avoided pessimism. Wiser than Schopenhauer, he saw life as a battle between light and darkness in which light was victorious. Light triumphed in history because the power of good was infinite, the power of evil finite. Genuine Christianity, without Schopenhauer's distortions, recognizes the finitude and painfulness of cosmic history, but breaks the power of evil in the ultimate triumph of God's kingdom at the end of time.

Nevertheless – and this was his only remedy against pessimism – Schopenhauer thought that one had to deny the world and will, or, more exactly, *deny individuation*, because in isolation and the ensuing egoism of individuals, will fragments and becomes an unhappy will that 'tears its own flesh unaware that it is injuring no one but itself'. Because space and time were the principles of individuation, the denial of will must be a denial of the world. It was achieved through sinking back into the All-One, into the 'stage of the cessation of perception and feeling' characteristic of Nirvana, until even self-consciousness was finally surrendered. Mysticism, whether Buddhist or Christian (for example, Meister Eckhart), was one way to this, art and its disinterested gaze, of which Kant had already spoken and which had also been the goal of the Platonic idea and the ancient *vita contemplativa*, whose wisdom consisted in raising oneself above space and time and their fragmentation, and gazing on the Universal, the One, was another.

Schopenhauer's thoughts on the *philosophy of art* are interesting from a number of points of view, particularly their metaphysical depth. The essence of art was seen at its purest in genius. 'Genius is none other than the most perfect objectivity . . . the ability to keep one's eyes open, to lose oneself in attentiveness and to withdraw the knowledge which is primarily at the service of life from that service, that is, to leave one's own interests, wishes, aims completely out of account and consequently leave one's personality totally behind for a time, so that one is a pure knowing subject, an all-seeing cosmic eye.'

It was in his *ethics*, however, that Schopenhauer gave his

clearest explanation of individuality. As part of his general pessimism, Schopenhauer's ethics were a morality of compassion commanding us to die to ourselves so that we could become one with everything else in a sort of Buddhist Nirvana and see our brother in everyone. Schopenhauer contrasted this material and empirical ethic of sentiment with Kant's ethic of reason and law. On some points he was favourable to Kant, but for the most part he rejected his formalism. Schopenhauer willingly recorded what he disagreed with and then successfully attacked it – a not altogether rare methodology in the history of philosophy.

PART FOUR

THE PHILOSOPHY OF THE NINETEENTH AND TWENTIETH CENTURIES

The later 1820's witnessed the collapse of German idealism. Since the time of Kant, German idealist philosophers had constructed a unique and more or less uniform conceptual system of grandiose proportions, and this suddenly caved in with hardly a whisper of regret. It was replaced with a series of philosophical trifles as thinkers attempted this or that current of thought without any overall coherence. No names could compare with the great figures of the 1700's, although many tried to salvage what was most lasting in the idealist system and in some way reproduce its grandeur. This is not to denigrate the nineteenth century entirely. Some sterling work was done. And if boldness in speculation is distrusted as a possible source of greater error, the modest but surer philosophies of the nineteenth century have a lot to offer. The number of founders of schools is large, and it is not easy to give a satisfactory outline of the main trends.

CHAPTER ONE: FROM THE NINETEENTH TO THE TWENTIETH CENTURY

1. Materialism – the Secular Revolution

It was for a long time customary to give but short shrift to the materialism of the mid-1800's. It was, said professional philosophers, not philosophical enough, not scientific enough, too trite and vulgar to be taken seriously. We can now see, from a slightly greater distance, that it was in fact *the* revolutionary movement of the time. It could possibly be said that it has been the nineteenth century's weightiest bequest to us, the most difficult to fight, however unpalatable that might be to scientific philosophy. The question is how such a wide spectrum of thought could be affected by materialistic theory and how materialism can be overcome. The answer must be so basic that it is irrefutable, and so simple and clear that it is evident to the man in the street – an eminently philosophical problem. The philosopher fails not only when he is too popular, but also when he is too sophisticated. In what follows we propose to divide our treatment into the dialectical materialism of the Hegelian left and so-called scientific materialism.

(a) The Materialism of the Hegelian Left

The Hegelian left wasted no time in turning Hegel's idealism into materialism. They extracted a part of the whole and developed it to the exclusion of the rest of the system. It was bad philosophy (was it philosophy at all?) because they engaged less in scientific thought than in journalism, politics and propaganda. They were inadvertently guilty of some level of philosophically constructive reflexion, but to refer to them as philosophers or to their output as a proper system is ludicrous. They regarded philosophy not as a primary challenge, a search for truth for truth's sake, but as a means to a higher end. This must be borne in mind by anyone approaching their writings. Even so central a concept as materialism was more a symbol of their political determination and a slogan for use against their political opponents than an impartially investigated philosophical principle. Their materialism was one of class warfare and had no use for philosophy apart from philosophy's tactical contribution by way of words and ideas. The same was true of the materialism of the French Enlightenment, which influenced them more than Hegel did, although they pretended their own version was far superior to crude Enlightenment materialism. The difference, however, was not great.

Ludwig Feuerbach (1804–72) was perhaps, of all nineteenth century materialists, the one with the strongest pretensions to strictly philosophical method. He sent Hegel a dissertation, but wrote on it that the 'self' of the Christian God must be dethroned. Later, when his thought had gained in clarity, he referred to 'that nonsense, an Absolute'. He rejected the theory that reality was posited by Mind, that concepts mediated reality, and said that only the sensible world existed because the mind was formed by the body and 'man is what he is'. The prime datum of consciousness was neither God nor being, but sense-experience, as sensualism and materialism had always taught. If one insisted on referring to a deity, it was none other than man himself. The State existed to minister to his needs. It was the 'content of reality' and 'man's providence'. Feuerbach was the harbinger of Marx.

According to *Karl Marx* (1818–83), the prime factor of worldly reality was matter, not Mind as Hegel had stated. Matter was decisive. All conceptual entities like morality, law, religion and culture were epiphenomena of matter. Because Marx accepted the dialectic, he was still a Hegelian, but 'tilted at an angle', to use his own phrase. He added something to Feuerbach's materialism: his own version was to be 'practical'. It was not enough to analyse the world as it was: one had to describe it as it should be. Feuerbach and the other early Hegelians had remained at the level of the existing world. All they had done, virtually, was to reinterpret it (in a materialist framework); they had not in any way altered it. They had failed to see that even materiality was a product of human activity. Man's relation to the world was not one of passive receptivity. Feuerbach had said that man is what he is; Marx retorted that this was the sentiment of the well-fed bourgeois. Everything was the historical product of common human activity. Sense-perception and the great intellectual systems of man were equally the result of social – in particular industrial – relations. The handmill resulted in feudal society, the stream-mill in industrial and capitalist society, in both cases with the corresponding spiritual and intellectual superstructure. In other words, philosophy, religion, art, culture, on Marx's theory, lost their traditional social and human justification, and became instead epiphenomena reflecting their material causes. There was no inquiry into the world as it was in itself. 'It does not require any very extraordinary insight to appreciate that man's ideas, views and conceptions, in a word, his consciousness, alters with every change in his material existence, social relationships and social life generally. The history of ideas proves that intellectual production changes with material production. The ruling ideas of any age are always the ideas of its rulers.' This made Marx the father of historical materialism (although he did not use that term himself). And it also made him a perpetual revolutionary, with a basis in Hegel: becoming is eternal, opposites continually clash. Inconsequentially, however, eternal becoming would cease with the classless society, when capitalism and the proletariat, those alienations of man, were overthrown and man had come to a new paradise. It is obvious here that Marx was not indulging in philosophy proper: his aims were political, not metaphysical. And it was almost foregone that the system would turn out atheistic. Religion was 'the heart of a heartless world' and 'the opium of the people', to quote a famous passage. Dialectical materialism (to use a convenient term as representative of many different thinkers) did not in theory reject metaphysics. But in fact, because the significance of 'being' was determined by man's active practical intervention, no science of being was possible. Marxism (again to use a convenient term) could properly be called nominalism (dialectical, if one likes) or even decretalism; this would be an accurate description.

Marx and *Friedrich Engels* (1820–95) enjoyed a lifelong collaboration. Engels' philosophy is hardly distinguishable from Marx's, except in so far as he seems to have concentrated more on dialectical materialism, Marx on historical materialism.

Ultimately the main exponent of the materialism of the Hegelian left was *Lenin* (1870–1924). Regarding Marx's and Engels' philosophy as a single theory, he made it his own and claimed to represent orthodox Marxism. His empiriocriticism opposed the alleged subjectivist individualism of Mach, Avenarius and their Russian followers. Against them Lenin defended 'objectivity' and identified the 'objective' or 'real' with matter. In this he was a naïve realist, because he believed that the scientific description of reality was a copy in the sense of a quasi-photographic reproduction. Lenin's confession of realism aroused a half-astonished, half-laudatory reaction in realists of other persuasions. In the *Philosophical Notebooks*, however, the concept of matter is ambiguous. Lenin saw that what is usually called 'matter' is perhaps less the object of the senses than the object of thought, and so could well be the product of an intellectual process. Commentators have often therefore distinguished a philosophical and a physical concept of matter in Lenin. By the latter is meant that which is extended or accessible to sense-experience (the materialists of the Enlightenment had used it in this sense), by the former that which is indeterminate in the sense in which Aristotle (to whom Lenin explicitly refers) used the word (as in 'prime matter'); this latter, in the mind of other naïve realists, was a point in Lenin's favour. As a matter of fact, Lenin's lucubrations on the subject of matter did the 'official' concept no good, because they threatened to turn matter into the goal and product of semi-spiritual (!) functions. This is why appeal to the *Philosophical Notebooks* by Soviet officials is so infrequent. The Russian leaders need not in fact worry: Lenin was saying nothing more than Marx when the latter proposed a practical materialism and subordinated sense-experience, the object of which was supposed to be extended matter, to factors arising out of the relations of labour in society. Lenin's theories are equally pragmatic – 'Marx and Engels were biased from start to finish', he once wrote.

The final authoritative summary of Marxism–Leninism was offered by *Stalin* (1879–1953). It was a concise account of historical and dialectical materialism, originally intended as part of the Party history, but then published separately and distributed to the people. It treated the subject under three headings: the significance of the dialectic, the concept of dialectical materialism as a philosophy of being, and the concept of dialectical materialism as a philosophy of history. Dialectic was explained as follows. Nature is a whole: everything in it is organically bound up with everything else and can be understood only as part of the whole. Being is in a state of continual development from lower to higher, simpler to more complex forms. Insignificant and unseen quantitative changes lead ultimately to qualitative changes. These suddenly break up, in accordance with the law of inner contradiction which, in the style of the Hegelian dialectic, demands the emergence of their opposites. Dialectical materialism was explained as follows. Reality is constituted not by Mind or consciousness, but by matter exclusively, and matter follows its own laws established by the dialectical method. Being is also matter. Consciousness is a derived or secondary form of reality. 'Thinking is a product of matter whose evolution has reached an advanced stage'; it is also 'a product of the brain', and 'thought cannot therefore be separated from matter without the gravest error.' Without noticing it, Stalin here abandoned the main lines of dialectical thought. Matter as he described it was the physical stuff of vulgar materialism. The old materialists, from Hobbes to Holbach, had unanimously taught that thought could not be separated from its material base and that thought was a product of matter (in particular the brain). Stalin adopted their language exactly: for him, dialectic did not describe the laws of matter; it laid them down, because, being a necessary mental methodology, it was logically prior to matter. If matter had any laws of its own at all, they were purely mechanical. This was clearly understood in official Soviet philosophy, but then (1931, 1947) proscribed because the slogan 'dialectical materialism', which had meanwhile come into favour, could not be changed. The initial attempt to go beyond the primitive physical concept of matter by applying human, social or other considerations, as we find it in Marx and Lenin, was abandoned by Stalin. Even for Marx and Lenin, however, the ideological propagandist implications of the word matter (drawn from the French Enlightenment) were more evident than the philosophical implications. In consequence Stalin based the philosophy of history on metaphysics and so derived historical materialism from dialectical materialism: 'Historical materialism', he wrote, 'is the extension of the theses of dialectical materialism to the investigation of social life . . . and to the history of society.' 'One will consequently look for the key to the investigation of the laws of social history not in men's heads . . .

but in the means of production . . . in the economy of society.'
But then, as Marx had maintained against Feuerbach, mind
precedes matter. And surely mathematical formulae and the
laws (principles of identity and contradiction) and basic
concepts (identity, difference, equality, unity etc.) of logic are
prior to everything material? Is this not necessary if we are to
be able to see and handle matter? Much more besides could
be adduced. But mathematics and logic are enough to disprove
the materialist proposition that all thought is a product of
matter. Finally, we must again point out that Marx and Lenin
only partially resorted to dialectic and Stalin not at all.

(b) Scientific Materialism

The Hegelian left received considerable support from so-
called scientific materialism. This was a branch of thought that
emerged in the nineteenth century parallel to the Hegelian
left and was more often than not proposed by natural scientists.
For myself, their endeavours simply go to show that if scientists
are not sufficiently alert to the limits of their discipline (whatever it may be), they too easily run the risk of mistaking the
part – the study of physical phenomena and their causes – for
the whole – reality – and of equating being with bodiliness.
Many scientists today are keenly aware of this danger, but a
group of particularly vociferous writers of the last century were
not. We may mention *K. Vogt*, who wrote *Physiological Letters*
(1845) and a polemical treatise called *Blind Faith and Science*
(1854), *J. Moleschott*, who wrote *Rotation of Life* (1852), *L.
Büchner*, the author of *Force and Matter* (1855), and *H. Czolbe*,
who was responsible for a *New Account of Sensualism* (1855).
For these scientists the world was force and matter. If the word
God has any meaning at all, they said, it refers to this corporeal
world, and the spirit or soul was (if conceded to exist) a function
of the brain. For none of them did it exist in its own right.
They all spoke about reason or understanding as distinct from
sense-perception, but the distinction was one of quantity, not
quality. Their concept of matter was naïve. Matter, for them,
was what man could directly perceive with his senses. It was

apparently beyond their powers of critique to consider whether there was a specifically human contribution in sense knowledge. Materialism, then, dialectic or no dialectic, is ordinary naïve sensualism. Both sorts of materialism are therefore monistic. The observer will not be deceived by the sophisticated vocabulary: 'new qualities', 'higher layers' and so forth. Pluralism is possible only if the higher forms of life do not automatically (whether mechanically or dialectically makes no difference) proceed from earlier stages but somehow come 'from without', as Aristotle so accurately and splendidly expressed it.

This monism is even more evident in a second wave of materialism of which *E. Haeckel* (1834–1919) and *W. Ostwalp* (1853–1932) were the main representatives. Haeckel did much to spread Darwinism in Germany, although it was a more radical version than Darwin's own. *Charles Darwin* (1809–82) shattered the universal convictions of milennia on the unalterability of species (polyphyletic pluralism) by proposing the evolution of all species from a single cell (monophyletic evolution) in his *Origin of Species by means of Natural Selection* (1859), and in his other great work on *The Descent of Man* (1871) he expressly included the human species. However, he contrived to hold that the primitive organisms from which everything else was derived were the product of divine creative activity. Haeckel, on the other hand, thought the world was eternal, that life emerged by itself (spontaneous generation), and that the various species, man not excepted, descended mechanically from the primal organisms. Man's immediate forebears were the primates. Hence the catchword: 'man is descended from the apes'. If a little more critical and accurate thought had been given to the question, things might have been different. The theorists should have been more nuanced. But they jumped straight from matter to spirit, ultimately because their monistic presuppositions identified the two. Haeckel's theories have been propounded almost universally in Marxist assemblies and the German paper *Forwards* wrote: 'Voltaire's contribution to the French Revolution should be applied, *mutatis mutandis*, to Ernst Haeckel. He prepared the German Revolution.'

2. Kierkegaard – Christian Subversion

The upheavals Marx sought in political life *Søren Kierkegaard* (1813–55) sought in the Christian life. He threw the old, the outworn, the fake overboard and called on Christians to evolve a new life-style. His early thought was stamped with a motif that was to remain with him all his life: action not theory, commitment not detachment. There was no sense, said Kierkegaard, in amassing vast amounts of knowledge just for the sake of it. The purpose of life was to perceive the truth, to enter into oneself and *exist*. 'What I needed to do was live a complete life, not one of theory only, and if I succeeded I knew my conceptual development would be based on something . . . which, together with the deepest roots of my existence, with which so to speak I grew into the divine, would cling to God, even if the whole world should collapse about my ears.'

He therefore challenged men to live fully, to *exist*. Kierkegaard's notion of existence did not yet carry the full weight of meaning attached to it by modern existential philosophy, but it was not far off. Existentialists frequently refer back to Kierkegaard. By existence he meant the uniqueness of the personal self and its decisions. There man is totally alone, and no theories, laws or concepts can avail to incorporate his activity into a higher unity, as Hegel would have wanted. 'All talk of a higher unity designed to reconcile absolute opposites is a metaphysical attack on ethics.' A second key idea in Kierkegaard's philosophy was that man needed courage to take an existential jump into *paradox*. 'The history of individual life is a continual movement from state to state. Each of these states is reached by taking a leap.' And in fact if theories and ideas are no use in pointing out our way, only the jump remains. This implies freedom, dread and nothingness. These are concepts we still associate with Existentialists today. In Kierkegaard's mind they were explicit antidotes to Hegelianism, which, as he thought, had nothing to say on individual life, however much it pretended to, but remained at the level of the abstract because for Hegel an idea was as abstract as it was for Schelling. Kierkegaard therefore demanded paradox instead of reason. Individuality had long been said to be inexpressible. Hegel wanted to say it, but he did not manage to get beyond universality. Closely connected with the idea of paradox was *faith*. Kierkegaard developed a somewhat oversubtle idea of faith as an obedience to God demanding the suspension of human reason. A paradox is not only something hard to understand, but humanly speaking something not understandable at all. Kierkegaard described this concretely in his analysis of Abraham's sacrifice. Again here he rejected Hegel's rationalization of religion, which turned religion into philosophy and so, in Kierkegaard's opinion, abolished it altogether.

It is not surprising under these circumstances that Kierkegaard waxed eloquent against the official religion of his country at the time, the Protestant Church of Denmark, and finally broke with it. He appealed for a new Christianity, for 'ministers who can separate people from the crowd and give them back their individuality; ministers who do not rely so much on study and who want nothing less than to rule; ministers who are as rich in silence and endurance as they are in eloquence; ministers who are as learned in refraining from judgement as in knowing the human heart; ministers who can wield authority and make sacrifices; ministers who are ready and trained to obey and to suffer so that they can soothe, exhort, edify, move and also compel – not with force, far from it, but with their own obedience – and patiently minister to the sick without losing their temper . . . the human race is sick and, spiritually, sick unto death.'

If one turns to the ascetic writings of the Church and reads in the sources what is demanded of the faith and its priests, one realizes that Kierkegaard was saying nothing new. His only contribution was an affected dialectic and an over-cultivated literary-aesthetic form that bordered on schizophrenia. His influence, however, was wide and disturbing, and his lead has been followed by many up to today, particularly in dialectical theology and existentialism.

3. Nietzsche – the Revaluation of Value

Friedrich Nietzsche (1844–1900) is the third subversive

thinker of the nineteenth century. Like Marx and Kierkegaard, he noted the decline of the bourgeois-Christian world and looked for new horizons. But he seems never to have bothered very much with Marx, and he began to read Kierkegaard only late in life. On top of that he regarded the former as too vulgar and the latter as too Christian. He preferred to think of himself as the great lone wolf, the most radical of thinkers, a turning-point of history. 'My name will be connected with the memory of some huge event, a crisis such as the world has never known . . . I contradict as no one has ever contradicted before . . . When truth battles with the lie of milennia, there is a convulsion, an earthquake, a meeting of valley and mountain such as has never been dreamed of.' The event that was Nietzsche has not, however, proved quite so cataclysmic. There was more wind than substance. According to Heidegger, Nietzsche was still hung up on the old metaphysics; he was not the nihilist he wanted to be; and the wholly new, the forgotten, the disguised, being itself, came to light only with Heidegger. Was this perhaps the result of Nietzsche's philosophical self-crucifixion: that although he did not usher in, at least he announced the earthquake, the wholly new?

(a) *The development of Nietzsche's thought*

In his early period, Nietzsche fought for a new educational ideal, the aesthetic-heroic image of man whose prototypes he saw in the tragic pre-Socratic age of Greece, in Heraclitus, Theognis and Aeschylus. To this period belong his *The Birth of Tragedy from the Spirit of Music* (1871), the essays on *The Future of our Educational Institutions* (1870–2) and the four *Unseasonable Reflexions* (1873–6) on David Friedrich Strauss, Schopenhauer as an educationalist, the advantages and disadvantages of history in life and Richard Wagner at Bayreuth. As these titles show, Nietzsche was strongly influenced at this time by Schopenhauer's philosophy and Wagner's vision. Severing his connexion with Wagner later on was all the more painful. In his second period (1878–82), he underwent a sudden transition to pure theory: he became what he called 'a man of learning', in other words he gave up his lectureship and restricted his activities to writing. This period saw his (conventional) attack on metaphysics, praise of free-thinking, belief in the law of nature and its causal determination. The reader of Nietzsche's works at this time could be forgiven for mistaking him for a writer of the French Enlightenment. He became what he had before abhorred: an intellectual and a Socratic. His works included *Human all too Human* (1878), *Dawn* (1881) and *Happy Knowledge* (1882). Then the motifs of his earlier period reasserted themselves, and in a more radical form, as the 'will to power'. This concept predominated in his third period, the period of *Thus Spake Zarathustra* (1883–5). *Beyond Good and Evil* (1886), *The Genealogy of Morals* (1887) and *Will to Power* (1884–8) were also published at this time. In this latter work, he expressed his theories on the reversal of traditional values to be engineered by the Superman, heralded by Zarathustra and symbolized by Dionysus. Nietzsche's insanity began in 1889 and is evident in his last works, for example in parts of his *Anti-Christ*.

(b) Down with Morality, up with Lfie

Nietzsche was happy to be thought an immoralist. He wanted to live 'beyond good and evil': a not unusual phenomenon. But he was not really an immoralist, because his intention was to replace traditional morality – idealistic, eudaemonistic, Christian, bourgeois-German, as he thought it – with the morality of life. This aimed at revaluing values. To that extent Nietzsche's whole philosophy was an ethic. The question is what he meant precisely by 'life', and, if the truth be told, his writings are far from clear on the subject. He was at pains to distinguish his own concept from that of the British, eudaemonists all, according to him, intent only on achieving the maximum happiness. But beyond that, he succeeded only in wrapping himself up in words. Life, he said, was the will to power. This he repeated in scores of different ways. But what was the will to power? There is good and bad power. Nietzsche said he meant the power of rulers, of the aristocracy, of big men. Traditional morality was the preserve of slaves, of the weak. It was the feeble who had praised love, compassion and submission, and called the strong evil. Their morality expressed their envy of men with more in life than themselves. Was lordship then something merely biological or physical, a muscular superiority? No. It was the life-style of Superman, a unique quality. 'The Superman lies close to my heart, *he* is my paramount and sole concern – and *not* man: not the neighbour, the poor, the greatest sufferers, the best.' 'God has died. Now we want the Superman to live.' What was meant by Superman: it is not enough to repeat the word without analysing more closely what actually constitutes the Superman and raises him even above the level of the rulers and aristocracy. Superman is he who gives the world its law. What law? The law which offers new values. What are these values? Here Nietzsche goes several times round the mulberry bush. Instead of giving some account of the new values and explaining how man's life might be modelled on them, he merely repeats that the Superman is a race apart, lives his own life, possesses an abundance of strength, beauty and courage, culture and good manners, has no need of moral imperatives because he can afford to do without, stands beyond good and evil, etc. The reader looking for eloquence of written speech will be satisfied; the reader looking for solid ideas is more than likely to be sadly disappointed. There is another idea of Nietzsche's: 'eternal occurrence', but that expresses not a value but the nature of existence as a process ruled by fate. 'My formula to express man's greatness is *amor fati*.' Man's constant attempt to fight down the pessimism and intractability of life will transform him into a Superman. If fate, however, *were* the overriding principle of life, all reference to values would be meaningless. Even the Superman would be meaningless, because he, after all, is a concept of *value*: strong men *should* strive after his ideal. 'One's aim should be to prepare a revaluation of values for a particularly strong kind of man, highly gifted both in intellect and will, and therefore gradually to free in him a whole gamut of instincts so far repressed.' Did Nietzsche really know what he wanted? Was he a philosopher, or just a writer? Would this explain his influence on many musical, non-philosophical minds?

(c) Germanity and Christianity

Nietzsche was loud – and abusive – in his attacks on Germanity and Christianity. 'I want to be known as the despiser of everything German.' 'Germany is coextensive with the ruin of culture.' 'The Germans are quite oblivious of how low they are.' Sentiments like these could be multiplied with no difficulty. Their tenor is universal, but in fact Nietzsche meant only the Germans of his time – another proof of the shallowness of much of his writing. His objections to Christianity were even more forceful: 'The God on the cross is the curse of life.' 'I call Christianity a great curse, a great inner corruption . . . a great stain on humanity' etc. There are, as always in Nietzsche, statements giving a completely opposite point of view – another proof that he must not always be taken too seriously. His writings have even been perused for a hidden theory of being, God and genuine Christianity. Heidegger interpreted his statement 'God is dead' in the sense that Nietzsche did not deny God but was looking for him. Nietzsche's undistinguished successors seem to go a stage further than their master, to their detriment: what in the master was still of some interest becomes insipid in the disciples.

(d) Nietzsche in the twentieth century

Nietzsche has suffered much at the hands of his interpreters. Despite its extensive talk of interpretation, our own age has little understanding of it. Its only concern is to explain *itself*, instead of giving a faithful and unbiased commentary on the text as it stands and as it was intended by the author. Commentators take a couple of ideas and use them to paint the victim in their own colours. There has been a whole series of Nietzsche interpreters. E. Bertram has given a George-style interpretation in terms of aesthetics and music. A. Baeumler prepared him for popular consumption under National Socialism. K. Jaspers turns him into a failed existentialist philosopher of his own persuasion. M. Heidegger appeals to him for support in denying everything philosophy had so far achieved because it was concerned only with beings, not being. All this and much more has been read into Nietzsche. And I suppose the process is not over yet, as long as commentators refuse to interpret scientifically and as long as they are happy to use Nietzsche as the springboard from which to rise to heights of fame themselves.

4. Phenomenalism and variants

We are on terra firma again with phenomenalism, which as its name implies based its inquiries on perceptible and verifiable phenomena. Since Kant, metaphysics had declined, ethics had been empiricized and the intelligible, on which Kant had placed so much emphasis, completely forgotten. In phenomenalism it was only the Kant of the critique of experience who lived on. From the many variations, we shall single out the positivist, empiricist and Neo-Kantian trends.

(a) French and German Positivism

The father of French positivism was *Auguste Comte* (1798–1857). He coined the watchword of the movement by proposing the *positively given* as the sure basis of all scientific knowledge. By 'positively given' he meant what appears to and is perceptible by the senses. The critical mind dare not rely on anything else. Unfortunately mankind had not always realized this. There had been a long development. Comte distinguished three stages (in the so-called 'law of three states'): theological, metaphysical and positive. The first was the period in which men ascribed natural events to superior personal powers (fetishism, polytheism and monotheism). In the second, men talked in terms of abstractly conceived powers, essences, inner natures, forms, ideas and so forth. Men were still un-critical, because they persisted in living in a world of fiction. They did not recognize the nature and purpose of science until the third period. Then it was that they concentrated ex-clusively on the 'directly given', which constituted and ex-hausted reality. The idea was to extract from the examined phenomena the constant factor (or scientific concept, as it was called), and then study the regular sequence of events, thus arriving at scientific laws. In other words, for Comte the purpose of philosophy and science was to investigate laws not causes, the how not the why of human phenomena. The concept of positive data was intended to be a principle of science, but it was not in fact. Alleged data contain a lot that is not given. The claim that only phenomena could be classed as real is actually a metaphysical statement, although that was not recognized until neo-positivism. Comte also opted for a 'positive' religion, with its own sacraments, feastdays and ceremonies. Its God was humanity. – Another important French positivist *Jean-Marie Guyau* (1854–88), however, specifically rejected all religion and metaphysics as distractions from positive data. His prime interest was in ethics. Ethics, he said, had nothing to do with duty or other suprasensory values, it dealt with life in society. Man just was a member of society for no particular reason and therefore stood 'beyond good and evil'. Guyau has been called the French Nietzsche. He agreed with Nietzsche in so far as the concept of life was a central one. He influenced modern vitalism, especially Bergson.

German positivism also concentrated on sense data, on the 'realities of experience', denied the usefulness of metaphysics, advocated the ideals of evolution and progress, and replaced religion with science, art and sociology. As opposed to the universal ideal of experience of other positivisms and em-piricisms, it stressed the critique of theoretical knowledge. Avenarius called his system empiriocriticism, and Mach offered an empiricist and idealist theory of science. Under German positivists we may include *E. Laas* (1837–85), *W. Schuppe* (1836–1913), *R. Avenarius* (1843–96) and *E. Mach* (1838–1916).

(b) British and German Empiricism

That British empiricism could hold its own in the nineteenth as well as eighteenth century is understandable: it was, so to speak, the philosophy of common sense. Who would not want to base knowledge and science on experience? British empiricism remained unchanged as the seventeenth and eighteenth centuries had shaped it. Kant had hoped to improve it by steering the phenomena of experience into strictly pre-established channels with his a priori forms. But nineteenth century empiricism would have none of it. It was determined to stake all on reality as it could be seen and touched. And its success was enormous. Many philosophers, some of them from very different traditions, agreed with its main lines and stated that we think realistically and empirically. It is a curious thing that Mill, Spencer, the Positivists, Lenin and the Neo-Thomists could all rally to the empirical standard. It says something for the power of words.

John Stuart Mill (1806–73) based all science on the perceptions of the moment. Only they were positively given. There were no such things as objective essences, or timeless authorities, or a priori structures and activities in the mind. All science had to do was work on the material provided by experience, not by respecting a priori rules, but by abiding by what experience threw up. In other words, science was purely inductive. For Mill induction was the key word. He wrote a *Logic* using it as his base. The book set out to explain how one could get beyond direct perception: after all, one could not stay at the level of the individual reality, but must proceed to the universal and the predictable. Hume had found this a problem years before; he had tried to solve it with his laws of association. Mill tried another line, taking a certain method of scientific reasoning and developing it into a general theory of knowledge. The concern of his *Logic*, as the subtitle suggests, was the basis of scientific demonstration and research. Whether the new method of science as proposed by Mill really stemmed ultimately from Hume is debatable. The same may be said of Mill's ethics. Mill propounded a utilitarianism just as if Kant had never existed. The Greatest Happiness Principle stated that the measure of right and wrong was 'the greatest happiness of the greatest number'. Mill owed this idea to *Jeremy Bentham* (1748–1832), a friend of his father's and founder of the English Utilitarian School.

The other important empiricist of the nineteenth century was *Herbert Spencer* (1820–1903). He is especially known for diffusing those famous nineteenth century words: evolution and progress. He discovered ethical values in amoebae and followed them through to the highest human values. For example, he associated human loyalty with the loyalty of a dog to its master. He also proposed a philosophy of history. History, he said, was coextensive with culture and civilization, and its purpose was to fulfil man's existence. Spencer had no time for idealism with its morality, rational commandments and suprasensory world. Marx and Engels, with their ideals of a human paradise ('lush meadows for the vulgar crowd', said Nietzsche), therefore found a fertile soil in old and new empiricism, and not only in French materialism.

In Germany *Franz Brentano* (1838–1917) was the most prominent representative of the empirical current. He was thoroughly acquainted with the writings of Aristotle and the Scholastics. He tried to use the concept of evidence to arrive at sure knowledge, and thereby derive from experience what Kant had postulated a priori. *C. Stumpf* (1848–1936), known particularly for his psychology, was influenced by Brentano.

(c) Neo-Kantianism and Neo-Hegelianism

However, there were thinkers in the nineteenth century who did not share the uncritical approach of the materialists and utilitarians, who did not support the otherwise universal appeal to experience, but who were also sceptical of the speculations of the idealists. A number of them in the 1870's – *F. A. Lange, K. Fischer, O. Liebmann* etc. – called for a return to Kant. They made critique the chief function of philosophy again, much more so than the positivists, who on other points shared many of their concerns. True to the Kantian tradition, their explicit interest lay in the formal and methodical. Transcendental philosophy became the order of the day, pure knowing, pure will and pure religion the watchwords. These thinkers opposed psychologism and any emphasis on pure factual experience, preferring to rely on a priori transcendental laws that make experience possible in the first place. Objects and essences were not 'out there', they were produced by the mind in accordance with timeless rules. Nevertheless divergences from Kant were very noticeable. For example, *Bruno Bauch* understood the contribution of sense-experience and the role of the idea in an almost Platonic way. The pure formalism of the other representatives of this tendency was certainly a major weakness; they were too abstract, too timeless, without any very solid content. The Neo-Kantian school enjoyed a rapid vogue in Germany. At the turn of the century it was the main philosophy in the universities. Method was the focus of interest. A centre of the Neo-Kantian trend was Marburg, where students of philosophy expended vast energy in investigating Kant's mathematical-scientific ideal of knowledge. We may mention *H. Cohen* (1842–1918), *P. Natorp* (1854–1924), whose book on Plato is still as readable as *R. Hönigswald's* (1875–1947) history of ancient philosophy, *A. Liebert* (1878–1946) and *E. Cassirer* (1874–1945). The other centre, the so-called Baden school, was more interested in the Kant of the *Critique of Practical Reason* and concentrated on the philosophies of mind and value. The school included *W. Windelbrand* (1848–1915), *H. Rickert* (1863–1936), *E. Lask* (1875–1915) and *B. Bauch* (1877–1942).

In France too idealism attracted famous followers: *C. Renouvier* (1815–1903), *O. Hamelin* (1856–1907) and *L. Brunschvicg* (1864–1944), among others. Hamelin was responsible for some important historical research, including books on Descartes and Aristotle. Brunschvicg was an emphatically methodical thinker. Next to Bergson and Blondel, he was undoubtedly the greatest French philosopher of his time. He wanted to develop both Kant and Hegel, but also followed Plato, Descartes and Spinoza, and in his philosophy of religion was particularly influenced by Pascal. His main works were

The Modality of Judgement (1897) and *The Stages of Mathematical Philosophy* (1912). What do we mean when we say 'is'? The 'is' of our judgements expresses the result of a process of thought or a transcendental connexion, as Kant called it. There are no things-in-themselves. Philosophy therefore is a philosophy of mind. This is true of Brunschvicg's philosophy of religion, in which he almost came to the point of saying that God himself was the content of philosophy (ontologism?). God, for Brunschvicg, was the copula of judgements, but not a thing-in-itself which we could know or love. He was not an idea either, as Kant had held. Rather he was the mind itself, which was equally connexion, copula, transcendental apperception and deduction. This was again 'pure' religion, a Third Testament, superseding and fulfilling the New as the New fulfilled the Old. For Kant it was the religion of reason, which was to interpret history and reduce it to morality. For Hegel philosophy was raised to the level of religion.

Neo-Kantianism was in fact a world-wide school. It had its representatives everywhere. Apart from those we have already mentioned, they included *A. Green* (d. 1882) and *E. Caird* (d. 1908) in Britain, the so-called Transcendentalists in the States, and *A. Chiapelli* (d. 1932), *G. Gentile* (d. 1944) and *B. Croce* (d. 1952) in Italy. The last two named are really better classed as Neo-Hegelians, but the distinction is not clear cut.

Amongst the Neo-Hegelians, therefore, we may mention Croce. He wrote important works on aesthetics, logic, practical philosophy and the philosophy of history. In all these areas he attempted a synthesis, not of opposites as in Hegel, but of differences, in which the differences were unified but not destroyed, and which was markedly positivistic. The more interesting of them were his synthesis in aesthetics, where he has been the leading light of recent philosophers, and his synthesis in history, in which he proposed an identity of philosophy and history: philosophy was itself a concrete historical event and therefore a growth, and conversely the growth apparent in history could be understood only on the basis of universal conceptual presuppositions. The synthesis of all syntheses was Mind. Mind was infinite growth, the absolute, and the substitute for religion, which in its historical forms was only a stage in the development of Mind.

Neo-Hegelians in Britain included *F. H. Bradley* (d. 1924), *B. Bosanquet* (d. 1923), *E. McTaggart* (d. 1925); in the States *J. Royce* (d. 1916); in Germany *A. Lasson* (d. 1917), *R. Kroner* (b. 1884) and the philosophers of law *J. Binder* (d. 1939), *K. Larenz* (b. 1903) and *W. Schönfeld* (d. 1958).

(d) Pragmatism

Pragmatism is another philosophy that deals in phenomena. Its purpose, however, is not just to describe them and verify them on logical or transcendental laws, but to control them, make them manipulable by man so that he can improve his material lot. Pragmatism, therefore, is a practical philosophy. We clarified this term in connexion with dialectical materialism. And in fact pragmatism is not far removed from dialectical materialism, although it stresses the freedom of the individual.

As a philosophy, it began with one of the founders of Neo-Kantianism: *F. A. Lange.* By defending religion against the attacks of materialists with the argument that religion was the locus not of truth and error but of man's need, and by seeing in this satisfaction of man's need the purpose and essence of religion, he effectively gave birth to the theory of pragmatism. Its most significant spokesmen, however, were *W. James* (1842–1910), *F. C. S. Schiller* (1864–1937) and the American philosopher and pedagogue *J. Dewey* (1859–1952). James made this illuminating remark: 'Ultimately our mistakes are not so very important. In a world where, despite all our foresight, mistakes are unavoidable, a certain measure of careless levity is healthier than an excessive nervous worry.' In practice it might often be possible to follow this recipe. But the principle itself means ignoring the question of truth and acting only on personal preferences. Such a principle cannot be held to be valid, because beyond the level of 'I should like' and 'I need' there is a right and a wrong which impose duties on man. Truth may not, as Dewey's instrumentalism would have it, be turned into a tool and symbol of our pretensions and requirements. Objective truth is superior to all subjective expediency. The proper fulfilment of man's existence can be sought only within the limits laid down by truth and right. Mere desire leads only to disorder.

5. Inductive Metaphysics

Despite the general overemphasis on phenomenalism, the nineteenth century did manage to produce a metaphysics. But because of the overwhelmingly empirical trend of the times, that metaphysics was of a rather special kind: it was inductive. Relevant names here are Fechner, Lotze and Hartmann.

Gustav Theodor Fechner (1801–87) set out to elaborate a metaphysics which would clarify the nature of religious belief in a way that was more than just creating concepts in the service of some pragmatic world-view and which, without abandoning critical thought or endangering the scientific conscience, would be acceptable to the natural scientist. His metaphysics was intended to be an investigation into reality as a whole. It started from experience, was inductive, and claimed to go beyond experience. In classical metaphysics, the ideal structure of the world enabled the philosopher to say, 'This is how things are and must always be', but in Fechner's metaphysics, the result of induction was only an anticipation of further experiential data, to avoid an otherwise necessarily fragmented approach. In reality, then, the Fechner brand of metaphysics did not advance beyond sense-experience. All one could do was hypothetically anticipate data by means of generalizations and analogies. One could not say, 'This is how things will always be', but only 'Things will probably continue like this'. Basically, then, inductive metaphysics was empiricist, but in so far as it claimed to include the 'whole of being', the title metaphysics was justified. The inductive form has been popular in the twentieth century. Fechner also did great services to psychology, which he developed on a natural science methodology and interpreted in the style of psychophysical parallelism.

Rudolf Hermann Lotze (1817–81), like Fechner a metaphysician (although he styled himself a 'finalistic idealist'), went back beyond Kant to Leibniz and adopted something like Leibniz's panpsychism. He accepted the scientific concept of causality but developed it in another context. Whereas Kant thought a causal subordination was possible but unknowable, Lotze defended it by maintaining that because of a basic inner coherence of the cosmos, all causality was included under a universal causality in (a spiritual and personal) God. On other points too Lotze had no scruples in ignoring Kant: the concept of substance, for example, or the freedom of the will. In ethics he ranks as one of the founders of the modern theory of value. For him values were objective authorities like the Platonic ideas, which Lotze also interpreted as objective authorities.

Karl Eduard von Hartmann (1842–1906) elaborated a system which, in his own words, was a synthesis of Hegel and Schopenhauer (with a decisive preponderance of the former) on the principles of Schelling's positivism and concept of the unconscious from his first system. Also included were an individualism derived from Leibniz and a series of basic propositions from modern empiricism. That is why Hartmann can be numbered among the inductive metaphysicians. He is best known for his 'unconscious spirit' in which logical 'thought' and illogical 'will' were one. Like Schopenhauer he described will as an irrational force, and the representation or intellect as a powerless idea – two thoughts later adopted by Scheler. Existence, again as in Schopenhauer, was given a pessimistic interpretation. Non-being was better than being. The function of ethics was to achieve the triumph of this conviction and redemption from the will to be. Future world religion was therefore to be a mixture of Buddhism and Christianity.

6. Neo-Aristotelianism and Neo-Scholasticism

Apart from inductive metaphysics, the nineteenth century was also no stranger to classical metaphysics. The Neo-Aristotelians and the Neo-Scholastics were its partisans.

A prominent member of the *Neo-Aristotelian* school was *A.*

Trendelenburg (1802–72), who made significant contributions to the understanding of Aristotle's philosophy, not only historically, but also systematically. He was not carried away by the latest theories, but looked for the truth as an artist for beauty. Not every thinker, he said, need start from scratch and work out a new philosophy. Philosophy was already at hand 'in the organic world-view based on Plato and Aristotle which had only to deepen its grasp of basic concepts, both in isolation and in dialogue with the real sciences, and so perfect itself.' These basic concepts included purpose, organic whole, the mind and its logical rules, the fulfilment of the mind in a divine world-spirit, and an eternal law which provided an objective criterion for all other positive laws. His best-known work was his *Natural Law on the Basis of Ethics*. Trendelenburg's followers included *F. Brentano, G. von Hertling, O. Willmann, G. Teichmüller* and *R. Eucken*.

Willmann and Hertling form a sort of bridge with the other school of classical metaphysics, the *Neo-Scholastics*. These referred back directly to the Middle Ages, some to Thomas Aquinas, others to Augustine and Bonaventure, but they were all ultimately rooted in Aristotle. An awareness that Aristotle derived his thinking in large measure from Plato could have invigorated the whole spirit of neo-scholasticism, but it was too slow in making itself felt: Aristotle had become something of a rallying-point, and there was little interest in Plato's work. Neo-scholasticism was influenced by some of the trends in modern philosophy. Just as some said, 'Back to Kant', so others called for a return to the classical Schools. *J. Balmes* (d. 1848) was a pioneer here, followed by *Z. Gonzalez* (d. 1895). Other names are: *M. Liberatore* (d. 1892) and *T. Zigliara* (d. 1893) in Italy, *K. Werner* (d. 1888) in Austria, *C. von Schäzler* (d. 1880), *J. Kleutgen* (d. 1883), *A. Stöckl* (d. 1895) and *K. Gutberlet* (d. 1928) in Germany. From the start the most important centres of neo-scholasticism were the Institut Supérieur de Philosophie at Louvain, founded by *Desiré Joseph* (later Cardinal) *Mercier* (d. 1926) (the Institut was originally a school of Thomism: today the curriculum is quite general), and Quaracchi, the centre of the Franciscan Order, now known only for its exemplary editions of theological and philosophical works.

Neo-scholasticism took two forms, historical and systematic. To the historical form we owe the editions and researches which have contributed extensively to an accurate knowledge of the Middle Ages (the prejudice and invective of the Reformation and Enlightenment had completely obscured, and the enthusiasm of the Romantics had overestimated, the true value of medieval thought). At first, particularly in the schools of *C. Baeumker* and *M. Grabmann*, the researches were confined to establishing accurate texts and plotting the actual development of ideas. Today, in the light of modern philosophy and the Neo-Scholastics' contact with it, the problems are more speculative and philosophical. The so-called systematic form of neo-scholasticism tried to perfect a *philosophia perennis* by extracting the eternal truths from the various philosophical tenets. There is such a thing as truth, it says; there are such things as eternal truths; man's knowledge is conditioned subjectively, but is not exclusively relative to the subject: it is directed at being and so has an objective side which is more important than the subjective side; being itself is therefore knowable; it can be analysed into created and uncreated being, substance and accidents, essence and existence, act and potency, model and image, bodily, living, psychic and spiritual being; man's soul is immaterial, substantial, spiritual and immortal; man is therefore essentially different from animals; morality, law and the State are controlled by eternal norms, even though they can be based on man's subjectivity; the prime cause of being, truth and value is the transcendent God. As always in philosophy, individual members of the 'school' differed considerably on basic questions as well as on details of interpretation. It would be quite unjustified to accuse the Neo-Scholastics of a lack of originality because they all allegedly said the same thing. No school is totally uniform. Like the Neo-Kantians or the Empiricists or the Phenomenologists, the Neo-Scholastics shared a point of view, but the real question is how they acquired it. If a school simply takes over somebody else's views, we cannot strictly talk about genuine philosophizing. If on the other hand a group of thinkers together elaborate a way of looking at things, each making his own contribution to the whole, we can talk about a philosophical position or trend without drawing attention to anything exceptional in the history of philosophy; on the contrary. And if schools can reach a sceptical or atheistic or Marxist philosophy without attracting unfavourable comment, there is no apparent reason why others should not come to an objectivistic, theistic and even, as German idealism shows, Christian position. Nothing can be decided as to the genuineness or not of a philosophical school simply by counting heads. Each case has to be taken on its own and examined for originality and invention. It is original and inventive thought which makes for philosophy, nothing else. Our times have more than enough paid functionaries in other areas.

CHAPTER TWO: TWENTIETH CENTURY PHILOSOPHY

The roots of contemporary philosophy can be traced back to the trends of nineteenth century thought, which we could, I suppose, have continued to our own day. But then the development of those roots has produced certain typical concepts which have proved central, and phenomenology and existentialism are exclusively characteristic of our century. We shall try to explain the main trends by taking in turn five of the most typical catchwords: life, essence, being, existence, logos.

1. Vitalism

At the turn of the century, especially in Germany and France, there appeared a trend which soon swept the academic establishments and captured the academic imagination: the philosophy of life, or vitalism. It occupied then the place existential philosophy occupies now. Its proponents differed, of course, in matters of detail, but their common concern was Life: they opted for the fleeting, the unique, the individual, the irrational, the experiential, as opposed to the static, logical, universal and schematic. We may distinguish French vitalism, German vitalism and naturalistic vitalism.

(a) Bergsonism and Blondelism

Henri Bergson (1859–1941), a prominent writer and a Nobel prize-winner, gave an immediately coherent and popular shape to the new trend. Unlike Nietzsche's effervescent impetuous vitalism, Bergson's was academic, lucid and well thought-out. Its key idea was the *élan vital*, or vital impulse. He intended it to counter mechanism, materialism and determinism. It was false, he said, to concentrate exclusively on the external extended sphere, on mathematical and physical bodies, and then attempt to squeeze man into the scheme. Is there no inner sphere which shapes the outer? which endures although it is in time? which has its own time that is not clock-work, that is lived, that grows with the subject, that incorporates the ebb and flow of life? Bergson called it 'duration' (*durée*), which he defined as the time of the psychological ego or 'the form taken by the succession of our states when our minds refrain from establishing a separation between the present state and the previous state'. It characterizes all living things. To exploit life to the full, more is needed than the thinking appropriate to mathematics and the sciences, which is mechanical, schematic, analytic. Intuition – which Bergson defined as 'the sympathy with which one transports oneself to the interior of an object in order to coincide with those elements of it which are unique and therefore inexpressible' – insight into the whole of reality and feeling are all required if the inner areas of experience and the once-for-all-ness of life's moments are to be properly appreciated; knowledge and freedom are needed if man is not to succumb to mechanism and stifle the spontaneity of his nature. Spontaneity and freedom cannot exist without a soul and consciousness. Life, therefore, is superior to matter. Consciousness, thought, soul have a physiological correlate, the brain, but they cannot be interpreted, as in materialism, as mere cranial functions. No, they have a potency all their own, and they are more powerful than matter. If being is life, and life soul and consciousness, then being is consciousness; and by 'consciousness' here is meant not thought in a narrow sense, but a self-awareness which is experience, impulse, duration, freedom, inventiveness, 'spiritual energy' (to use the title of one of Bergson's works, published in 1919) and dynamism all in one. This opens up metaphysical insights: nothing simply 'is', everything 'becomes'. And it 'becomes' on the strength of the creative freedom and 'creative evolution' (Bergson published a book of this title in 1907) characteristic of the dynamic surge of life. Man 'is' not, he 'becomes'. Even God can be said to be a becoming being, ceaseless life, pure activity, pure freedom. Schelling is behind this, and Scheler was to follow. Bergson adopted similar reasoning in ethics and religion, rejecting externality, law, duty and valuing innerness, freedom and creative will. The corresponding concept was love impulse (*élan d'amour*).

Although *Maurice Blondel* (1861–1949) had certain points of contact with Bergson, he disagreed both with him and with vitalism generally. He would tolerate no alogical impulse, he wanted 'action' (the title of his doctoral thesis, 1893), which he equivalently approximated to thought. 'By action I mean that which produces and develops individual thoughts. Thought is not primary, it is not exclusively representation or light; it is a force, an impetus in the dynamism of intellectual life, and one must study the conditions which make it possible.' The conditions of the mind were those of life – including history – and to that extent Blondel was a vitalist. But since they also included the 'cosmic thought' as a presupposition of action, life for Blondel was 'more than life' and the philosophy of action intended as an antidote to vitalism. In *religion* Blondel supported Catholic modernism. If action is asymptotic – 'by his own voluntary action . . . man cannot satisfy his own needs'; action remains 'this side' of its objectives – the intelligent man recognizes his need for God to 'complete' his action.

(b) Vitalism in Germany

Unlike Bergson, German Vitalists did not take life in a cosmic or metaphysical sense, but studied its forms in the history of thought. They gave important interpretations of intellectual phenomena in philosophy, psychology, pedagogy, history and poetry. Their main representative was *Wilhelm Dilthey* (1833–1911). He set out to understand life without any a priori or metaphysical or other standard prejudices. He promoted an understanding (a key word in Dilthey) of the 'human sciences' as opposed to the natural sciences (in 1883 he published his *Introduction to the Study of the Human Sciences*, in 1907 *The Essence of Philosophy* and in 1921 his *Analysis of Man*). The natural scientist is interested only in universal laws. Understanding too draws on universals, the 'structure' in psychology and the 'type' in the history of thought, but only to go beyond them to the unique shape of the individual and let *that* live. The individual gained an increasing hold on Dilthey's thought and eventually led him to a relativism of viewpoints with which he was not himself entirely happy, inasmuch as he was as keen to transcend the viewpoints as to promote an understanding of them. His research into structures and types proved fruitful, and a school of followers emerged: *G. Misch, B. Groethuysen, E. Spranger, H. Leisegang, A. Dempf* and others.

Two other writers who took an active part in the vitalist discussions were *Rudolf Eucken* (1846–1926), like Bergson a Nobel prize-winner, and *Ernst Troeltsch* (1865–1923), both of whom pointed out the danger of relativism in vitalist philosophy. The sharpest critic of vitalism, however, was undoubtedly *Georg Simmel* (1858–1911), who said: 'Life, which in itself is formless, can become a phenomenon only if it is formed', and must therefore be 'more than life'; it cannot consist in pure becoming, as the Vitalists tended to think.

(c) Naturalistic Vitalism

Nietzsche – a onesided, biologistically interpreted Nietzsche – was again the inspiration behind the naturalistic branch of vitalism. Two names that can be picked out are *Oswald Spengler* (1880–1936), whose *Decline of the West* offered a (pessimistic) morphology of world history, and *Ludwig Klages* (1872–1956), who, like his friend T. Lessing, also announced the decline of the world because of Mind, Mind being the adversary of life and the death of everything which innocent Nature produces. Klages' concept of mind was a gross distortion, and after an initial success, his books causing something of a stir, he has subsided into semi-obscurity.

2. Phenomenology

According to Kant, man has no direct contact with the noumenal world: his experience and reasoning are confined to phenomena. 'As appearances', he wrote in the *Critique of Pure Reason*, 'objects cannot exist in themselves, but only in us. What they may be in themselves, and apart from all the receptivity of our sensibility, remains completely unknown to us.' Our own century has seen a return to objects and essences. This trend, assisted by the decline of Kantianism, is associated particularly with phenomenology, which has made a genuinely new contribution to modern philosophy and has had remarkable success. The phenomenological method is now applied to every conceivable field, not only philosophy. Its triumph is due to the fact that it is only a *method*, capable of almost endless application. It may be defined as the art of disclosing and describing the actual state of affairs. Back to things as they really are, say its adherents, who are dissatisfied with what they see as the jaundiced vision and rigid formulas of the schools. This movement back to objective essences is apparent in literature, art, aesthetics, ethics, pedagogy and religion. The question is: what are things? what kind of being do they have? is there an intellectual insight into reality as it is or is reality confined to human consciousness and its activities? Because, however, the phenomenologists show widely divergent views, depending on the particular set of experiences studied (the 'logical' and 'cognitive' experiences for Husserl, the emotional experiences for Scheler, etc.), one must avoid too glib a reference to a return to essences.

The founder of the school was *Edmund Husserl* (1859–1938), whose *Logical Investigations* appeared in 1900. He performed the same demolition of psychologism as Kant of Hume: he overcame the limits of the merely relative and individual in human thought by demonstrating the existence of necessary factors of timeless validity, not by postulating transcendental a priori forms, but by suggesting necessary essences. For example, that $2 + 2 = 4$ can be thought of subjectively in many different ways (*noesis*), but the content, the objective thought as such (*noema*), constitutes a necessary essence. Husserl wanted to demonstrate essences of this kind in a wide variety of areas so that he could arrive at the basic structures of reality. He called this aim one of fundamental or regional ontology. Essences are 'viewed' in the process of so-called phenomenological reduction which brackets off the incidentals, the merely factitious, in an effort to grasp the essential. The end product of reduction is not the essential as a mere universal – which was the aim of abstraction without ever needing to leave the psychological field – but as a self-validating *eidos* with an objective intentional thinkable being. Husserl's theory has met with a lot of criticism. If essences could be viewed in this way, it is said, Kant's logical empty forms would be attributed with material existence. The question would remain whether these essences had a transcendent meaning or not. Especially in his late period, Husserl answered this question in the negative.

Max Scheler (1874–1928) perfected phenomenology by stepping outside the rather narrow bounds of Husserl's immanence philosophy and applying it to the great themes of value, man, the world and God. At least, he *appeared* to apply it, whereas in fact, in his fear of the transcendent, he fell back on the activities of consciousness, however much he may have spoken about values, essences and absolutes. According to Scheler, when we look at the absolute, we do not see it as it is in itself, we see our own thought of the absolute. Every religion has an absolute: but not *the* absolute, only *its* absolute. Similarly, values are merely qualities of our psychic acts. Value, however, was one of the great themes of Scheler's philosophy. He turned Husserl's contemplation of essences into a contemplation of values. Values are essences, even though they qualify only our acts. They are implemented as essences: they become the material, the necessarily a priori goal, of our moral activity. They do not depend on notions of duty, they are ideal imperatives in their own right, waiting for realization in human activity. Scheler can therefore be considered the creator of a material ethic of value. He rehabilitated virtue in the face of Nietzsche's misguided sneers, and challenged the formalism of Kant's ethic of duty by maintaining that universally possible laws depended on value, not vice versa. His critique of Kant was shrewd but not always pertinent. He sharply differentiated value from the being of things. This explains his most famous theory, the theory of the human person. Personhood, it runs, cannot be defined as the basis of continued existence (hypostasis, the ancients called it, from the Greek for basis or foundation), because that would not distinguish man from things. Nor is it the sum of psychic acts, even with an intelligible or empirical ego, because these are means the person uses, not the person himself. The person is constituted by values. He is a continual activity, an *actus*, which is not subordinate to causal determination, be it heredity of character or class, but which rather grasps in freedom the world of values – as a person. Persons 'are' not, they 'become' as they concretely realize values. They therefore represent a mode of being which cannot be objectified: the human personality is accessible only by means of an intellectual-voluntative-affective participation, that is, as an *actus*. Basically this personal 'act' is loving which corresponds to the heart's intimate disposition, and in the last analysis this love, as a share in the world of values, is a share in the primordial Person, who is God. This leads us to Scheler's philosophy of religion. Like all values, the value of holiness is *sui generis*, something independent of metaphysics. The God of philosophers is not the God of religion. Religion and metaphysics are neither partially identical, as in scholasticism, nor totally identical, as in Hegel. That, at least, was the theory of it. In actual fact Scheler's 'system of conformity' ultimately identified the God of religion and the God of metaphysics, but the idea that religion was self-justifying and had no need of metaphysics found a ready audience. It sounded very much like an exposition of Christianity (from which in fact Scheler borrowed some of his more sonorous terms). However, when one considers that values and truths, even holiness and the absolute, have little substance of their own on Scheler's theory and need inferior but more powerful strata of being for their authentication – God himself comes to self-possession only after a process of numerous disorders and afflictions and is God only at the end of a long development (evolutionary pantheism), Christians being mistaken in locating the divinity at the beginning – one is justified in distrusting any equation of Scheler's God with the Christian God.

The principal members of the phenomenological school include *A. Pfänder* (1870–1941), *A. Reinach* (1883–1916), *Edith Stein* (1891–1942), *D. von Hildebrandt* (b. 1889) and *H. Conrad-Martius* (1887–1966).

3. Ontology and Metaphysics

A rekindling of interest in the object is even stronger in present-day ontology and metaphysics than in phenomenology. It is true that the word ontological is somewhat freely bandied about – is there anybody not talking about being these days? – and things are now called ontological which before would have been referred to as transcendental-logical or subjective. Nevertheless, there is no reason to suppose that the renewed interest in being is not genuine and serious, and in fact the philosophy of being has proved one of the most fruitful currents in the history of philosophy. There are several different approaches. One kind of ontology (practised by Nicolai Hartmann) is really a form of phenomenalism; another kind, inductive metaphysics, its proponents prefer to call critical realism; then there is ideal realism; an ontology on the lines of classical metaphysics, drawing particularly on neo-scholasticism; and an existential ontology (Heidegger), which will be dealt with under existentialism.

(a) Phenomenological Ontology

Nicolai Hartmann (1882–1950) was the main representative

of a phenomenalistic anti-positivist ontology. Originally a Marburgian Neo-Kantian, he eventually rejected critical dogmatism in epistemology and in defiance of Kant espoused the eternal conviction of man that knowledge is not a quasi-magical production of an object from some conceptual hat, but a receptive grasp of something that is independent of our knowledge and pre-exists it. All knowledge is a reaching out beyond oneself in gnoseological transcendence. This is a confession of realism. The main argument for this point of view rests on the sense of resistance experienced in our encounter with adamantine reality. When Hartmann acknowledged that we come to know this pre-existent reality, he had in mind not essences on the lines of the ancient doctrine of *nous* or of Hegel's categories and their grasp of being, but only the perceived phenomena, which he called beings, as in positivism and phenomenalism. We gradually wrest our concepts from the realm of beings, but the concepts remain hypothetical, in the sense that, as in the natural sciences, we rely on certain assumptions in our knowledge of being, describing, assessing and predicting being in this or that way, and then waiting to see whether our assumptions or 'knowledge' prove correct. On top of this there is always a considerable residue of the unknown which prevents any identification of being and truth as on the old metaphysics. The 'new' ontology, then (to use its author's own title), was not a metaphysics and provided no knowledge of being *qua* being. There were no inner natures, forms or essences lying behind the phenomena. For Hartmann noumena were unknowable, and his philosophy was therefore, despite his protestations to the contrary, no different from Kant's. The strength of his position generally lay in his analysis of the phenomenal world into levels, modes and categories of being. As for Scheler, the lower levels of being were more powerful than the higher ones which derive from them, although these latter were new and could not be reduced to the lower ones: Hartmann was a forceful advocate for the unique value of life, soul, freedom and spirit, all of which empiricism analyses down to inferior components and reduces to particular forms of causal determination. Hartmann's ethical philosophy was similar to Scheler's. He may be called the other representative of the material ethics of value. Values were a priori, and if they existed in themselves, it was in the sense of being independent of the subject's acceptance or rejection of them, not of a transcendent mode of extra-conceptual existence. Again they were weak and depended on man's realization of them in practice. They constituted ideals which did not place man under any obligation but left him perfectly free and respected his autonomy; they were not permanent goals of human striving, because that would de-tract from man's freedom. For the same reason there could be no God. Man must be his own God in miniature, his own demiurge (a position with the splendid title of postulatory atheism). According to Hartmann, purpose was not a con-stitutive category of nature either; we just acted as if it were.

(b) Critical Realism and Inductive Metaphysics

Critical realism starts from the universal conviction of human common sense which defies the objections of critical philosophy. The realists, however, do not limit themselves to phenomenalistic ontology, like Hartmann, but frequently pronounce on being in itself, from the standpoint of either in-ductive or classical metaphysics. One of the founders of modern critical realism was *Oswald Külpe* (1862–1915). Representatives of the school include *J. Reinke, H. Driesch, E. Becher, B. Bavink, A. Wenzl, H. Conrad-Martius*. They all started from the natural sciences, but preferred a comprehensive view of reality to the partial views afforded by science. The most important con-cepts of their philosophy, apart from reality, were (1) the stratification of being, (2) purpose, which was now a con-stitutive and not merely a regulative principle, (3) entelechy (Driesch), by which was meant a purposeful agent, a deter-mining controller of life's events, (4) wholeness and meaning, ideas closely connected with the notion of entelechy, (5) the individual soul and the world soul, (6) freedom, present at all levels of being (in different ways), and finally, (7) the world-ground.

(c) Ideal Realism

It is a small step from critical realism to the ideal realism of philosophers like *A. N. Whitehead* (1861–1947), *N. Losskij* (1870–1959) and *O. Spann* (1878–1950), if, that is, one does not regard their essences, wholes, structures of meaning and ideas as mere nominalistic entities coinciding with individual beings. Ideal realism, however, accepts the existence of the One in the Many, and in fact attributes to the One, as a universal, more reality than to concepts and thoughts. Whitehead posited 'real essences', similar to Leibniz's monads and all interconnected. He regarded the separation of being into subject and object, and into individuals, as quite perverse. In reality being, as a collectivity, was an organic whole with a community of shared experience. Things were torn apart into 'autonomous' individuals by thought, while feeling continued to know that only the whole existed. The result of Whitehead's philosophy was not a vitalism like Bergson's (although the two were not dissimilar) so much as an idealism. The experience of the world was possible because of the so-called eternal objects, which enabled us to understand the data of sense-experience. These eternal objects (strongly reminiscent of the Platonic ideas) were, admittedly, only possibilities, because they needed the medium of reality if they were to be apparent to man, but on the other hand they made reality possible. Since the real existed only because of the ideal, and the ideal could not exist without the real, the result was ideal realism. The ideal preceded the real and did not come to be only on the occasion of a sense-experience; conversely, the data of sense-experience were only examples or symbols of eternal reality which we could not come to know through abstraction or intuition or in any other way. O. Spann similarly talked about a whole which preceded nature, about a 'secret life of the soul', a 'higher light', a 'suprahistorical' reality on which the temporal depended. Basically, I suppose, all classical metaphysics was ideal-realist, because the idea *qua* idea was regarded as real and effective, even in Aristotle.

199

4. Existentialism

Of all modern philosophical trends, existentialism is the strongest. One cannot say that its achievements have been the greatest, only that it has attracted the most attention. It has popularized a whole gamut of phrases, ideas and attitudes, even more so than vitalism. The historian, however, is hard put to it to pinpoint any specific content common to all the Existentialists. If we wanted to sum existentialism up in a concise phrase, apart from saying that for the philosophers of this persuasion existence is more important than essence, we could describe it, negatively, as a rejection of classical metaphysics and all forms of idealism and absolutism which it regards as objectivist and apersonal, and, positively, as an attempt to articulate a widespread concern in modern Europe, particularly in Germany and France, which we could define as a concern for the uniqueness and inalienable freedom of the human individual.

(a) German Existentialism

The reader of works of German existentialism is immediately struck by a prevailing mood of gloom. He hears of little else but tragedy, failure, doubt, dread, care and the nothingness of life. German existentialism is not an anthropology or an ethic or a critique of culture, but a philosophy of being, and specifically a metaphysics. Jaspers explicitly says: 'What Hegel developed in his metaphysical logic as a theory of categories . . . is the fulfilment of a task appropriated by the present.' And Heidegger begins where Husserl started to elaborate the basics of an absolutely pure first philosophy in the style of Kant's transcendental deduction. But despite the call for a return to things-in-themselves, German existentialism does not proceed much further than the area explored by Kant and German idealism. The content and colouring are different, but the novelty an unwary reader might be expecting is not quite so new as he might hope and believe. The two proponents of German existentialism are Jaspers and Heidegger.

Unlike Heidegger, *Karl Jaspers* (1883–1969) concentrated almost entirely on existence. He took the word to mean an interplay of life and thought. The person who lets life go its own way in an unreasoning existence and, like many Nietzscheans, reckons exclusively with feeling, instinct and desire, is more than likely to resort to violence as a means of furthering his own ambition. On the other hand the person who lets thought go its own way in an existenceless process of reasoning, like many Hegelians, will move in a world of generalities, schematized, impersonal and unhistorical, as Kierkegaard pointed out against Hegel in the last century. Life and thought, then, go hand in hand. If either is lost, both are lost. 'Existence must be illuminated by reason, reason has no content apart from existence.' The 'illumination of existence', which plays such an important part in Jaspers' philosophy, does not mean mere knowledge or a purely intellectual function: that would be a relapse into the type of philosophy of consciousness superseded by Kierkegaard and Nietzsche. It is rather an appeal to one's own possibilities, a fruitful appreciation of the tension between reason and existence in which those possibilities are clarified and strengthened so that the best in one can be disclosed. Jaspers therefore required man never to settle down but always to be on the move, to be open to new possibilities. 'It is vital to break through any form which threatens to atrophy, just as it is vital to appreciate the relativity of any standpoint one could think of.' Even failure can be of positive significance by demonstrating, perhaps more vividly than any other human experience, the fragility and relativity of the world. Everything we encounter is a symbol or 'cipher', nothing is reality and truth itself, everything no sooner acquired must be abandoned again as inadequate and replaced by something else. Transcendence, or 'encompassing', is revealed in this process of continually pressing forward towards new modes of being, not in its totality, rather as the possibility of possibilities, or as the 'movement of a philosophical logic'. This is pure Hegel. And like Hegel, Jaspers introduces the divine as the goal of an infinite movement not of mind and thought, but of 'existence'. Human knowledge is an 'endless play of ciphers in which we can never reach God; things would be different if there were a direct and exclusive revelation of God.' Revelation then is included in the illumination of existence, as German idealism had included it in reason. And as in German idealism, faith is a 'philosophical faith', and the 'Christ-myth' is interpreted philosophically, that is, as a reference to the fact that all men can approach God. Far from demythologizing, Jaspers concludes that, since everything is a cipher, we must stay at the level of myth, and indeed have no choice. But then myth too can illuminate existence.

Martin Heidegger (b. 1889) should properly have been mentioned under Ontology, because his chief interest is being, not existence. His concern is to provide the rudiments of a first philosophy more rudimentary than Aristotle's or anyone else's. Conventional metaphysics, he says, has not really dealt with being as such at all: it has never managed to get beyond beings. Descartes, Kant and idealism were as deficient in this respect as the ancients and medievals. Nobody has managed to discern the ontological differential between beings and being. The point of departure for Heidegger's investigation of being is man, as it was for Kant. Man is not simply consciousness, however, as he might have been for Kant, but existence, and by existence Heidegger means being-in-the-world, being-with, being-in, understanding, speech, grasp of one's own possibilities, being-in-front-of-oneself, care, dread, being-to-death, being-held-by-nothingness. Time or historicity gives human existence its wholeness by permitting self-projection or being-in-front-of-oneself and by enabling being to emerge from man's becoming: what is something one minute is nothing the next, and man is moving towards nothing, and as soon as he has grasped that nothing, it vanishes into nothingness. Being is temporality, is being-thrown-into-nothingness – being is appearance, becoming and nothing, Hegel had said – and is not 'existence' (life + thought) as in existentialism, but 'ek-sistence', that is, standing outside oneself – in nothingness. Man is to be understood from being. Sartre had said that today we are in a situation in which only man exists, and he quotes

Heidegger. Heidegger, on the other hand, says that only being exists. Man is not himself identical with being, even as consciousness, mind or ego, but is the guardian or shepherd of being because of his speech and thought. Being discloses itself to him in his thought. And truth emerges. By truth Heidegger means not coincidence of fact and statement, but self-illuminating being. And that is also freedom. To be free is to let being disclose and concentrate itself. Does this mean that for Heidegger being, not man, is free? is the person still a person if he exists in something else and not in himself? Heidegger is keen to guard against that overemphasis on the subject, characteristic of not a few philosophies, which identifies human subjectivity with the world. This is laudable. But has he not gone too far? The person cannot be permanently empty. The main thing the unbiased reader would like to know is what exactly Heidegger means by 'being'. He mentions it more often than any other word, everything is said to live by its favour, we are said to forget it in our immersion in the realm of things: but what is it? Heidegger, who approaches being mainly through time, has also tried to start from being and conclude to time and history, taking being as the historicity of history, the being of becoming, the being in nothingness. In this he has been unsuccessful, and could not of course hope to succeed because although he has given much thought to the nature of being, he has really divorced it so far from the world of beings that it has ceased to be the ground of reality and has become instead an empty nothingness. Theologians make the same mistake when they effectively annihilate God by excessively detaching him from the world as the Wholly Other. Similarly Nietzsche's philosophy boiled down to a form of nihilism because his values were not only beyond good and evil, but also beyond everything else. And in Pre-Socratic philosophy – there is nothing new under the sun – the *physikoi* became the *aphysikoi* (as Aristotle said) when they excised the Many from their notion of being.

(b) French Existentialism

French existentialism is more interesting as a literary than as a philosophical phenomenon. Two basic trends may be distinguished: atheistic (Sartre) and Roman Catholic (Marcel).

Jean-Paul Sartre (b. 1905), novelist, dramatist, essayist and philosopher, has been strongly influenced by Heidegger, although his work has a character all its own. He has also drawn extensively on the Enlightenment. Like Heidegger, Sartre disagrees with the old metaphysics of essences. Applied to man, the notion of essence is inadmissible. Only things can be fitted into some preordained scheme: no scheme or essence can precede man as his life's goal, his duty or a value to be striven for. 'Existence comes before essence': if man is to be free, he must be allowed to create his own essence. Sartre exaggerates this freedom to the extent of excluding from man's composition anything pre-given on which he could base his activity: truths, values, world, God. Surrounded by nothingness, man finds himself in a position of total loneliness and isolation, and his freedom is therefore not a gift so much as a burden. Sartre claims to favour humanism, because for him only man exists, but in fact his philosophy is a form of nihilism which destroys but cannot rebuild.

Gabriel Marcel (b. 1889) puts his first emphasis on metaphysical being. He has, however, accepted from Kierkegaard, as all Existentialists do, that our own existence in some way precedes being, or more accurately our approach to being: we have no access to being except through existence. This is at the root of the problem all Existentialists experience: how not to cut man loose from the sense of responsibility and the purpose of life which only a metaphysics can provide. If there is no God, existence becomes meaningless. The problem is much more acute in Sartre than in Marcel, for whom ancient metaphysics and modern existentialist thought achieve a tolerable balance.

5. Logical Philosophy Today

Logos has been one of the decisive principles of western philosophy from Heraclitus to Hegel, and modern philosophy is no exception. Although it draws on the language of classical metaphysics, transcendental philosophy and idealism, its Logos is not world reason, or God's thought, or God's Son, or Mind, but only a shadow of its former self, on the pretext that the resultant philosophy is more exact than any other philosophy to date.

(a) Formal Logic

Kant was of the opinion that since Aristotle's time logic had made no progress. Formal logic, however, had made vast strides, to the extent of becoming a specialized field on its own. Formal logic is the pure formalism and functionalism of meanings as such. Logic had always been formal, but not exclusively so: material logic had considered the content of concepts and judgements. In formal logic, however, the 'is' of a judgement has no particular reference to being: it expresses the purely syntactical relation of the terms, and has as much significance as the equals-sign of an algebraic equation. While Leibniz, the real founder of formal logic, regarded the *ars combinatoria* as a closed system but with an ultimate reference to reality, modern-day logic is purely formal. It is questionable whether all our statements must be reduced to sentences of the type: a metre is a hundred centimetres, in which the predicate merely explicates the meaning of the subject. In fact it is not only questionable, it is incredible. However, if formal logic refrains from replacing metaphysics and philosophy, if in other words it does not identify its particular art with the whole of knowledge, it can be extremely useful. Apart from Leibniz (and the Spaniard Raymond Lull, *c* 1233–*c* 1315), its most prominent practitioners have been *G. Frege, L. Couturat, L. Wittgenstein, J. Lukasiewicz, A. N. Whitehead, B. Russell, H. Scholz,* etc.

(b) Logical Positivism

Formal logic has played an important part in the recent generation of positivists: *M. Schlick* (d. 1936), *O. Neurath* (d. 1945), *R. Carnap* (b. 1891), *H. Reichenbach* (d. 1953), *A. J. Ayer* (b. 1910), *G. Ryle* (b. 1900) and others. Their purpose is to improve the old positivism with a universal logical functionalism, the idea being to detach positivism more effectively from being. Even the notion of positive data smacks excessively of metaphysics, they say. Their attitude is now completely antiphilosophical. They confine their attentions to a logical analysis of concepts and language in the attempt to give unequivocal and verifiable meaning to scientific statements. For example, a concept has no other function than to stand as a sign for objects; a judgement no other function than to denote the relationship between concepts. This is supposed to be knowledge. That this game of chess is insufficient to characterize what we call knowledge is more than obvious. It does not, however, prevent the Logical Positivists from wanting to interpret the meaning and verifiability of *all* sentences on the same principles. The first rule is that a sentence must be constructed according to the syntactical rules of language. 'The horse eats' is permissible, 'eats eats' is not. It follows that Heidegger's 'Nothing nothings' is meaningless, because 'nothing' has the form of a substantive but is not a substantive. Another rule is that of verifiability: there must be an empirical criterion for any object to which one refers in language. Because there are no empirical data for God and other terms common in metaphysics, these terms are meaningless and the problems of metaphysics are pseudo-problems. However, it escapes the attention of the Neo-Positivists, as it escaped the attention of the old Positivists, that the demand for empirical verification and the talk about language and substantives raises eminently philosophical, indeed metaphysical, problems, that their critique of metaphysics is itself metaphysics (albeit unintentional). Philosophy is not a technique, but open thinking, responsible humanity in converse with the world and men. It needs the whole man. This means not only man living in the present – the person who lives nowhere but in the present lacks roots – but man drawing on history. History being a part of man's essence, man cannot know himself unless he has a sound knowledge of history, just as he does not know himself if he does not see the world as something preceding language and its syntax.

INDEX OF NAMES

208

INDEX OF SUBJECTS

Evolution, 171, 181
Evolutionary pantheism, 196
Executive, 123
Exemplarism, 55, 74
Existence, 62, 71, 74, 81, 86, 137, 172, 186, 200 f.
Existentialism, 172 f., 189, 196, 200 f.
Existential ontology, 196
Experience, 98, 120, 133, 136, 181, 185, 193
Exposure of children, 40

Failure, 200 f.
Faith, 53, 58, 69, 86, 124, 129, 173, 202
Fate, 43, 60, 176
Feeling, 146, 199, 201; *see also* Sentiment
Fetishism, 178
Fides quaerens intellectum, 64
Finalistic idealism, 186
Fire, 5, 6, 36, 43
First heaven, 36
First philosophy, 3, 30, 202
First substance, 30, 80
Five Ways, 37, 81 f.
Force, 84, 112, 115, 170
Form, 2, 3, 8, 31, 34, 39, 74, 80, 106
Formalism, 142, 144, 195
Freedom, 21, 23, 44, 51, 61, 68, 72, 97, 100, 106, 109, 113, 115, 127 f., 130, 132, 138 f., 142, 144, 146, 148, 153, 156, 172, 184, 190, 197, 198, 204
Free will, 35, 71, 109, 123, 160
Friendship, 38
Future life, 144

Generosity, 38
Genius, 162
Germanity, 177
God, 23 f., 33, 39, 43, 45, 46 f., 52 f., 55, 60, 61, 63, 64 f., 71, 73, 81 f., 86 f., 89, 95, 97, 98, 102, 104 f., 107 f., 113, 116, 121, 128 f., 132, 138 f., 144, 148, 149, 150, 151, 154, 157 f., 165, 170, 172 f., 177, 183, 186, 188, 191, 195, 198, 202,
204; *see also* Absolute, *Actus purus*, Divine, *Ens a se*, Unmoved Mover
God's birth in man, 91
Good(ness), 16, 18, 20, 35 f., 38, 55, 57 f., 61, 62, 64, 71, 73, 114, 141
Gospel, 68
Grace, 88, 91
Growth, 161
Guardians of the State, 22

Haecceitas, 87
Happiness, 58, 60, 61, 84, 107, 115, 123, 127, 144, 181; *see also Eudaimonia*
Harmony, 4, 56, 94, 111 f., 115
Hate, 7
Hedonism, 123
Hegelian left, 152, 165 f., 170
Hegelian right, 152
Historical materialism, 167 f.
History, 16, 59, 110, 130, 153, 181, 183, 203, 206
Holiness, 195 f.
Homoiomerien, 8 f.
Humanism, 98, 204
Hylemorphism, 33, 80
Hylozoism, 4
Hypokeimenon, 33

Ideal, the, 117, 199
Idealism, 31, 61, 72, 90, 96, 132 f., 148, 150, 152 f., 164, 181, 189, 199, 200, 202, 205
Ideal realism, 105, 196, 199 f.
Ideas, 15 f., 31, 48, 56, 64, 74, 81, 90, 105, 118, 121, 124, 138, 157
Identity, 18, 48, 108, 152, 170
Illumination, 72, 77
'Illumination of existence', 201
Imagination, 35
Immanence, 46, 121
Immanent philosophy, 103
Immortality, 97, 132, 138 f., 144, 148
Individualism, 123, 186, 192, 200
Individuality, 87, 109, 113, 153, 157
Induction, 180
Inductive metaphysics, 185 f., 196, 198 f.
Inherence, 137